D0876717

DATE DUE

GAYLORD   PRINTED IN U.S.A.

Under the Blue Pennant

Under the Blue Pennant

or

Notes of a Naval Officer

John W. Grattan
Acting Ensign, United States Navy

edited by
Robert J. Schneller, Jr.

Barry University Library
Miami, Fla. 33161

John Wiley & Sons, Inc.
New York • Chichester • Weinheim • Brisbane • Singapore • Toronto

This book is printed on acid-free paper. ∞

Copyright © 1999 by Robert J. Schneller, Jr. All rights reserved.
Published by John Wiley & Sons, Inc.
Published simultaneously in Canada

No part of this publication may be reproduced, stored in a retrieval system or transmitted in any form or by any means, electronic, mechanical, photocopying, recording, scanning or otherwise, except as permitted under Sections 107 or 108 of the 1976 United States Copyright Act, without either the prior written permission of the Publisher, or authorization through payment of the appropriate per-copy fee to the Copyright Clearance Center, 222 Rosewood Drive, Danvers, MA 01923, (978) 750-8400, fax (978) 750-4744. Requests to the Publisher for permission should be addressed to the Permissions Department, John Wiley & Sons, Inc., 605 Third Avenue, New York, NY 10158-0012, (212) 850-6011, fax (212) 850-6008, E-Mail: PERMREQ@WILEY.COM.

This publication is designed to provide accurate and authoritative information in regard to the subject matter covered. It is sold with the understanding that the publisher is not engaged in rendering professional services. If professional advice or other expert assistance is required, the services of a competent professional person should be sought.

Library of Congress Cataloging-in-Publication Data:

Grattan, John W., b. 1843.
    Under the blue pennant, or Notes of a naval officer / by John W.
Grattan ; edited by Robert J. Schneller, Jr.
        p.   cm.
    Includes bibliographical references and index.
    ISBN 0-471-24043-5 (cloth : alk. paper)
    1. Grattan, John W., b. 1843. 2. United States. Navy. North
Atlantic Blockading Squadron (1861–1865) 3. United States—History—
Civil War, 1861–1865—Naval operations. 4. United States—History—
Civil War, 1861–1865—Blockades. 5. United States—History—Civil
War, 1861–1865—Personal narratives. 6. Sailors—United States—
Biography. I. Schneller, Robert J., 1957– . II. Title.
E600.G73   1999
973.7′5—dc21   98-26260
                                                                      CIP

Printed in the United States of America

10 9 8 7 6 5 4 3 2 1

E
600
.G73
1999

To Rebe

Contents

Maps and Illustrations

Acknowledgments

Many people helped me with this book. First of all, I would like to thank the staff of the Library of Congress Manuscript Division. Time and again I pestered them with requests for the John W. Grattan papers and other collections preserved in their excellent facility. Their patience, promptness, and cheerful attitudes have made the Library of Congress one of my favorite places to work. Among the first-rate staff at the National Archives in downtown Washington, special thanks go to Richard Peuser for, among other things, going out of his way to track down obscure and rarely consulted navy records. I would also like to thank the rest of the staffs at the Library of Congress and the National Archives, without whom American naval historians couldn't do their jobs.

Chuck Haberlein, Ed Finney, and Jack Green in the Naval Historical Center's Photographic Section have my gratitude for helping me find obscure naval images from the Civil War. I am grateful to Barbara Auman, David Brown, Davis Elliott, Glenn Helm, Jean Hort, Tonya Montgomery, and Young Park of the Navy Department Library for granting my constant requests for books.

I thank Emilie S. Staisey from the Historical Society of Western Pennsylvania and Mark Adams, a researcher in New York City, for uncovering some of the details of Grattan's life.

Bob Browning, Mark Hayes, and Rick Russell have my special gratitude for suffering through a draft of the entire manuscript and offering valuable suggestions for its improvement. Because of their careful eyes this book is better than it otherwise might have been. Responsibility for its errors and flaws, however, remains with me.

Last and most of all, I would like to thank my wife Rebe and my sons Zachary and Noah for their patience and support during the time I spent with Grattan and not with them.

Robert J. Schneller, Jr.
Lake Ridge, Virginia
April 1998

Under the Blue Pennant

Editor's Introduction

W<small>ALT</small> W<small>HITMAN</small> W<small>ROTE</small> T<small>HAT</small> "the real war will never get in the books." History will take note of the Civil War's battles and leaders, he lamented, but "future years will never know the seething hell and the black infernal background of countless minor scenes and interiors" involving "the actual soldier."[1]

Union naval officer John W. Grattan might have proven Whitman wrong. From the fall of 1863 through the end of the Civil War, Grattan served on the staffs of Rear Admirals Samuel Phillips Lee and David Dixon Porter during their respective commands of the North Atlantic Blockading Squadron, the largest Union naval command by the end of the war. Grattan's berth on board the flagships *Minnesota* and *Malvern* enabled him to observe events as they unfolded in the Chesapeake Bay, along the North Carolina coast, and up the James River.

After the war, Grattan wrote at length about his aquatic peregrinations and entitled the work *Under the Blue Pennant, or Notes of a Naval Officer.* In those days, the ship that carried the squadron commander flew the admiral's blue flag to signal his presence on board. Grattan's title symbolizes both where and whom he served.

Part memoir, part history of the North Atlantic Blockading Squadron, *Under the Blue Pennant* provides Grattan's unique perspective as a junior staff officer on some of the war's most significant naval operations. It includes fresh details on blockade running, underwater warfare, guerrilla warfare, Major General Benjamin F. Butler's ill-fated Bermuda Hundred campaign, the joint expeditions against Fort Fisher, and visits to the front lines by Abraham Lincoln. Grattan included personal observations about key naval and military leaders such as Admiral Lee, Admiral Porter, and General Butler. He also chronicled the exploits of Union naval hero William B. Cushing, and his narrative rescues less celebrated heroes from obscurity.

More importantly, in light of Whitman's lament, Grattan wrote about his own experiences and those of his shipmates. *Under the Blue Pennant* sheds light

1

on how Union naval officers and enlisted men spent their leisure time, dealt with the boredom of blockade duty, reacted to both victory and defeat, behaved under the stress of combat, and coped with death. *Under the Blue Pennant* is a window on some of the "minor scenes and interiors" that constitute the Civil War sailor's experience. Through Grattan's narrative, we catch glimpses of the real war.

Until the appearance of this volume, *Under the Blue Pennant* existed only as an unpublished manuscript of 233 pages, contained within the collection of John W. Grattan papers deposited by the Naval Historical Foundation in the Library of Congress. Grattan penned the work in longhand into a leather-bound volume, which includes a title page, list of illustrations, preface, and, in typical nineteenth-century fashion, a lengthy table of contents, with full descriptions of the topics covered in each chapter. The text is written in clear, finished prose, virtually devoid of cross-outs or insertions, giving every indication that he wrote it from a rough draft. No preliminary versions appear among his papers in the Library of Congress. Grattan dedicated *Under the Blue Pennant* "to the survivors of the Army and Navy who participated in that terrible struggle as well as those who have forgotten or never knew of the incidents here recorded,"[2] but there is no evidence that he ever tried to have it published. Besides the memoir, the Library of Congress also has an account of his service as a private in the New York National Guard in 1862, a diary he kept on board the two flagships, letters he wrote to family members during the war, and captured Confederate documents.

Grattan recorded his experiences not only in words but also in pictures. The Library of Congress collection contains sketches and paintings that Grattan created himself, as well as photographs of him and of people whom he admired. Additional paintings by Grattan are preserved at the Naval Historical Center in Washington, D.C. Grattan was a much better writer than artist, so this book does not include all of his pictures. But like his words, those that do appear provide glimpses of the real war.

JOHN W. GRATTAN HIMSELF remains an elusive figure. His papers in the Library of Congress illuminate his service during the Civil War and provide insights into his character and personality, but they shed no light at all on the years before and after the war. Although he served for three months in the Union army during 1862, his army service record includes almost no information; his naval service record no longer exists. Pension records in the National Archives and records preserved in repositories in Pittsburgh contain only limited information. I have found nothing in the census records pertaining to his family, nor could I find an obituary of him in New York or Pittsburgh newspapers. Thus I can only speculate about the rest of his life.

Grattan was born on 19 April 1843 and raised in Brooklyn. I know nothing about his parents or siblings other than that his mother's name was Mary Ann and that he had brothers and sisters. Grattan's rank of acting volunteer ensign in the navy, his service on the staffs of Admirals Lee and Porter, and *Under the Blue Pennant*'s well-crafted prose indicate that he must have had a solid basic education. This, in turn, suggests that he came from a middle- or upper-class background.[3]

In May 1862, Grattan joined the army. It seems that he was swept up by the wave of patriotism that resulted in the formation of the Forty-seventh Regiment of the New York State National Guard. Unfortunately, Grattan's account of his army service is not more specific about why he enlisted. Historian James McPherson has shown that patriotism and idealistic conceptions of liberty and republicanism motivated many Northerners to enlist. Such soldiers viewed the war as a struggle to preserve the Union, to prevent the Rebels from dismembering the glorious republic set forth on the American continent by the founding fathers. Historian Reid Mitchell declared that while the Civil War was fought in the name of freedom, many soldiers volunteered as a result of "popular pressure or even a mere moment's indiscretion." Bell I. Wiley, who pioneered scholarly studies of Civil War soldiers, argued that "American soldiers of the 1860s appear to have been about as little concerned with ideological issues as were those of the 1940s."[4]

Whether for ideological reasons or because of peer pressure, Grattan signed up for a three-month enlistment as a private in the Forty-seventh Regiment on 27 May 1862. He was nineteen years old. Three days later the regiment departed from the Brooklyn Armory amidst the cheers of thousands of spectators lining the sidewalks.

The next day the Forty-seventh arrived in Baltimore. Here Grattan "first became acquainted with the secession element of the people," as he later recalled. While the regiment marched to its encampment at Druid Hill Park, Grattan and his comrades "were saluted with sneers and insulting remarks by many women who did their utmost to show their hatred of our soldiers." For the next few days, drill occupied the recruits' waking hours.

On 6 June the regiment marched to Fort McHenry for garrison duty. Within a few days "the regular routine of a soldier's life began":

> At sunrise the reveille is sounded by the drum corps, and in fifteen minutes the fatigue is announced. 5.45 Recall: 6 o'clock Breakfast: 6.30 company drill: 7.30 recall: 7.30 Surgeons call: 8 A.M. guard mounting: 9.30 Drill: 11 A.M. Recall: 12.30 1st sergeant's call: 1 P.M. Dinner: 1.30 Fatigue [manual or menial work]: 3.15 Recall: 4.30 drill: 6 P.M. recall: 30 minutes before sunset 1st call for retreat: Sunset dress parade: 8.45 first call for tattoo [a call sounded shortly before taps as notice to go to quarters]: 9 P.M. Tattoo: 9.15 taps when all lights must be extinguished.

Grattan's duties included drilling, walking sentry posts, and marching in funeral escorts for soldiers who died in the hospital attached to Fort McHenry.

Private John W. Grattan, Company B, Forty-seventh Regiment, New York State National Guard (John W. Grattan Papers, Library of Congress)

Sometimes he served as orderly to the officer of the day. On the Fourth of July the men heard a "grand national salute" from Fort McHenry's guns and put on a mock parade with the men dressed as "negroes," "women," and "wild indians." (Sartorial strangeness always fascinated Grattan, who was a bit of a dandy himself and who became a hatter and furrier after the war.) That evening the men witnessed a fireworks display, then marched with paper lanterns in a dress parade. At the end of August the Forty-seventh returned to Brooklyn. Grattan was mustered out on 1 September 1862.[5]

What Grattan did for the next twelve months remains unknown. In filing for a "dependent mother's pension" in 1890, Mary Ann Grattan claimed that her son had contracted pneumonia while in the Forty-seventh Regiment and had been treated for it by the regimental surgeon. War Department officials found no corroborating medical records.[6]

In any case, Grattan re-emerged from the mists of time in October 1863 when he joined the Union navy. His papers contain no clues about why he re-enlisted in the service of his country or why he chose the navy instead of the army.

Grattan did not serve in the regular navy. Wartime volunteers appointed as officers in the Union navy had the term "acting" prefixed to their rank. Acts of Congress passed on 24 July 1861 and 3 March 1863 empowered the secretary of the navy to appoint acting ensigns and other junior officers "until the suppression of the insurrection." These temporary commissions went to merchant mariners and others who passed examinations to demonstrate that they had the necessary qualifications. The navy established officer training schools at navy yards to train those accepted for "temporary service." In all, some 7,500 volunteers received appointments to acting rank during the war.[7]

Grattan entered the navy as a clerk, a steerage officer. On 17 October 1863, he reported to the Gosport Navy Yard at Norfolk, Virginia, where he was given the choice between serving on the blockader *Florida* or the flagship *Minnesota*. Grattan chose the flagship and was appointed clerk to the fleet captain of the North Atlantic Blockading Squadron. On 17 November the officer serving as clerk to Rear Admiral Samuel Phillips Lee, the squadron commander, resigned. The next day Lee assigned the job to Grattan. On 6 December, the admiral wrote to the Navy Department seeking to have Grattan promoted to acting ensign. The promotion came through six days later. On the fourteenth Grattan took his oath and joined the wardroom mess.[8]

As the admiral's clerk, Grattan was responsible for organizing, copying, and maintaining Lee's correspondence and the records of the North Atlantic Blockading Squadron. A constant stream of correspondence flowed between Lee and subordinates in the squadron and superiors in Washington. Orders regularly came down from the Navy Department. Lee submitted weekly reports to the secretary of the navy and, more frequently, issued operational orders to his skippers. Following encounters with the enemy, ship captains sent Lee after-action reports, and Lee, in turn, informed the department. Then there was the endless correspondence involving personnel, maintenance, supplies, and requisitions. The amount of paperwork necessary to run the squadron was comparable to that of a naval bureau.

Grattan adjusted quickly to his new life on board the flagship. On 17 December he wrote his father, asking him to purchase a pair of ensign's straps from "Warnock (as his embroidery is the best in N.Y.)" and some navy gold lace

John W. Grattan in naval clerk's uniform, circa October 1863 (John W. Grattan Papers, Library of Congress)

for his coat from Tiffany's: "the narrow kind & two gold embroidered stars for each sleeve." He added:

> I am now fairly settled in my new position, and never enjoyed myself better in my life. There are twenty-one persons at our table [the wardroom mess on the *Minnesota*] and every thing is first class, with about a dozen nigs jumping around waiting on us ala St. Nicholas. We generally have about a dozen different dishes at every meal. Yesterday we had roast beef, stuffed veal, boiled ham, roast turkey, green *corn*, green peas, tomatoes, roast potatoes, celery, and for dessert sponge cake with wine sauce, black walnuts and apples, &c. &c. The Admiral felt good natured yesterday and gave me a glass of champagne. As it is [a] crime to disobey orders from superior officers, I completely obeyed.[9]

Grattan served on Lee's staff until 20 September 1864, when he went home for a short leave. On the day that Grattan returned to the flagship (12 October), Rear Admiral David Dixon Porter, fresh from command of the Mississippi Squadron, relieved Lee as commander of the North Atlantic Blockading Squadron. Although Porter replaced many of Lee's staff members with officers who had served with him in the Mississippi, Porter's secretary asked Grattan to remain on the flagship. Grattan assented.[10]

On Thanksgiving Day 1864, the wardroom mess enjoyed another meal that inspired Grattan to describe it in a letter. For starters, the officers had vegetable soup and oyster soup. Next came a cornucopia of baked sheepshead (the fish), roast turkey with egg sauce, roast beef, scalloped oysters, oyster pie, stewed kidneys, macaroni, sweet potatoes, mashed potatoes, stewed tomatoes, eggplant, parsnips, turnips, pickles, celery, cranberry sauce, and beets. For dessert they had apple pie, cranberry pie, nuts, raisins, apples, coffee, and chocolate. They washed it all down with claret, burgundy, sherry, raspberry cordial, catawba, and champagne. Officers enjoyed such elaborate fare only on holidays. Grattan's father was so impressed that he had the bill of fare published in a newspaper.[11]

Grattan liked being well dressed as much as he liked being well fed. Several days after Thanksgiving he sent home a box of clothes. "I wish the articles repaired, cleaned, new buttons," he wrote his mother and father, "boots half soled by a french bootmaker, not by a botch dutchman."[12]

Grattan remained on Porter's staff until the end of war. On 20 April 1865, he received an honorable discharge from the U.S. Navy.[13]

Tragedy stalked him for the rest of his life. After the war he returned to New York and married a woman named Albina. Grattan's papers do not reveal who she was, where they met, or when they had become engaged. In the fall of 1863 Grattan recorded in his diary that he had written to and received letters from a "Miss Gaynor." In December 1864 he indicated that he was betrothed.[14] The woman in the diary was probably Albina.

What is certain is that he had an unhappy marriage. In the spring of 1867, John sued Albina for divorce. The New York City Court of Common Pleas dissolved their marriage on 2 May. Divorce was scandalous enough in the Gilded Age, but the Grattans must have been especially juicy to the local gossips, for the judge found Albina guilty of adultery and forbade her from marrying until her ex-husband was dead. John was permitted to remarry without such fetters, but he never did.[15]

Years later Grattan moved to Pittsburgh. The 1881 city directory lists him as a "salesman" with a downtown address at 29 Fifth Avenue. He sold hats and furs.[16]

Grattan apparently carried a dark secret with him to the Iron City. In November 1881 he was admitted to the Homeopathic Hospital, a forerunner to Shadyside Hospital. There he died on 15 November 1881. He was thirty-eight years old. The death certificate lists "mania à potu" as the primary cause of death, with "pulmonary congestion" as the secondary cause. In both contemporary and current medical books, mania à potu is associated with alcoholism and the delirium tremens brought on by withdrawal from alcohol. His remains were buried at Courtlandt Croton Landing (Croton-on-Hudson), a small town in Westchester County upriver from New York City.[17]

Mr. John W. Grattan, hatter and
furrier (John W. Grattan Papers,
Library of Congress)

It was nine years later that Mary Ann Grattan, at the age of sixty-eight,
applied for a "Dependent Mother's Pension," a benefit created by an act of
Congress on 27 June 1890. For a mother to qualify, the son's death had to have
resulted from a wound, injury, or disease acquired in the service, and there
could be no surviving widow or minor children. Mary Ann maintained that John
had died from pneumonia he had contracted in the army. She filed her claim
on 21 August 1890. The case bounced from one bureaucrat to another, dragging
on for at least eight years. Mary Ann never received the pension.[18]

IT SEEMS THAT John W. Grattan's years in the navy during the Civil War were
indeed the best of his life. Fortunately, they are also the best documented years
of his life. He apparently wrote *Under the Blue Pennant* for a popular audience,
seeking to convey what the war was really like and to commemorate the deeds
of fallen shipmates. To help the reader achieve a deeper appreciation for Grattan's work, I will attempt to set *Under the Blue Pennant* within a broader historical context.

In an eloquent letter penned in August 1863, Abraham Lincoln paid tribute to the Union soldiers and sailors who had captured Vicksburg. "The Father of Waters again goes unvexed to the sea," he said of the Mississippi. He thanked the army, then the navy: "Nor must Uncle Sam's Web-feet be forgotten. At all the watery margins they have been present. Not only on the deep sea, the broad bay, and the rapid river, but also up the narrow muddy bayou, and wherever the ground was a little damp, they have been, and made their tracks."[19]

History has neglected "Uncle Sam's Web-feet." In comparison to the mountain of literature on the land side of the Civil War, relatively little has been published on its naval aspects.[20] Of the Union's four major blue-water squadrons, only the North Atlantic and East Gulf Blockading Squadrons have had monographs written about them.[21] You can't swing a saber in a bookstore without hitting a new biography of Sherman or Lee, but you have to be pretty lucky to find the life of any naval figure at all. Until 1995 there was no biography at all of Rear Admiral John A. Dahlgren, the celebrated inventor of the guns that armed Union ships, and the frustrated commander of the South Atlantic Blockading Squadron, who presided over the Union navy's greatest disappointment, the failure to capture Charleston, the "Cradle of the Rebellion." Until recently there was not even a biography of Farragut in print.

This relative dearth of historical literature is partially explained by a perception that the naval war was a sideshow, and by the fact that many fewer men served in the navies than in the armies. Of the 2,200,000 men who wore blue, only 115,000 served in the navy, a figure amounting to 5 percent of Union personnel.[22] Ever since the war, a veritable flood of soldiers' letters, diaries, and memoirs has appeared in print. In contrast, words penned by naval officers and enlisted men have only trickled out of publishing houses.[23] Again, the fact that many fewer men served in the Civil War navies helps explain the disparity. The relative scarcity of firsthand naval accounts enhances the value of *Under the Blue Pennant.*

Grattan framed his narrative around operations. The three prongs of the naval trident that the Union thrust at the Confederacy during the Civil War included a blockade of more than 3,000 miles of Southern coastline, joint operations with the Union army, and the pursuit of Rebel commerce raiders. The amount of ink that historians have spilled over the last prong is totally out of proportion to its significance, particularly with regard to the *Alabama.* The Union navy spent most of its energy in the blockade and in joint operations off the Rebel shore or along the South's inland waterways.

While the Army of the Potomac and the Army of Northern Virginia slugged it out mostly across the same blood-stained patch of land between Richmond and Washington, Yankee ships and sailors planted Federal troops around the Confederate periphery, stabbed inland to threaten Confederate supply lines, and helped Grant slice the Confederacy in two along the Mississippi. The

Union navy caused internal dissension within the Confederacy and bedeviled Robert E. Lee. "Wherever his fleet can be brought no opposition to his landing can be made except within range of our fixed batteries," Lee lamented in January 1862. "We have nothing to oppose its heavy guns, which sweep over the low banks of this country with irresistible force." Each time the navy facilitated the projection of Union power ashore, it strained relations between Jefferson Davis and the state governors, who thought that Richmond was paying insufficient attention to local defense. In an extreme example, the Union navy fomented a civil insurrection among native Floridians against the Confederate government. Although it is has become fashionable in certain circles to malign its performance, the Union navy played an essential part in winning the war.[24]

Historians still argue about the efficacy of the blockade. One side of the debate considers it "one of the outstanding causes of the strangulation and ultimate collapse of the Confederacy." The opposing school portrays the blockade as a sieve through which most blockade runners passed unhindered, and argues that the real cause of the Confederacy's economic collapse was internal problems, including interruptions of transportation, inadequate manpower resources, and ultimately the collapse of the will to win.

Blockade runners indeed constituted "the lifeline of the Confederacy," as historian Stephen Wise put it. It is true that five out of six blockade runners got through and that they supplied the Rebels with more than 60 percent of their small arms, one-third of the lead they used for bullets, and over two-thirds of their supply of saltpeter, an essential component of gunpowder. But if there had been no blockade, how many more ships would have entered Southern ports? The fact is that the blockade reduced the South's seaborne trade to less than a third of its prewar level, at a time when the demand for goods far exceeded the peacetime norm. The blockade also contributed to the ruinous inflation that so eroded the Confederate dollar that, by March 1863, it took ten dollars to purchase what one had bought two years earlier. In short, the blockade seriously undermined the Confederate economy.[25]

In its conduct of joint operations, the Union navy made an equally significant contribution to the Northern victory. Union army commanders led their men against the Confederacy's fortresses, population centers, breadbaskets, important depots, and areas with strong Union sympathy. Because many of these targets lay on or near the coast, close cooperation with the navy proved essential. Joint operations yielded spectacular successes along the western rivers, particularly at New Orleans, Forts Henry and Donelson, and Vicksburg.

Army-navy cooperation did not fare as well in the East. Although the Union established a lodgment in eastern North Carolina early in the war, it failed to exploit that success with any sort of sustained inland thrust. Naval cooperation enabled Major General George Brinton McClellan to push the Army of the Potomac to the gates of Richmond, but could not prevent the ultimate failure of his Peninsula Campaign. The so-called siege of Charleston remains the most salient example of a joint campaign gone awry, for the "Cradle of the Rebellion" held out against combined Union army and naval forces for 587 days, falling only when William Tecumseh Sherman's "bummers" approached from behind and rendered defense of the city untenable. The problems in the East boiled down to poor coordination at the cabinet level and the fact that most of the Union's top-ranking army and naval field commanders each failed to fully understand the capabilities and limitations of the other service.

Nevertheless, naval forces enabled the army to project power ashore and to allow alternative axes of operations in the eastern theater, provided gunfire support to ground troops at critical moments, maintained supply lines, and permitted the establishment of bases deep within Confederate territory. The presence of the Union navy off the Rebel shore forced the Confederates to divide their forces in order to protect widely separated areas of strategic importance. Although the Union high command failed to fully exploit the advantage that naval forces provided, joint operations brought the war to the southeastern seaboard long before the major Union armies could do so, pinned down Confederate troops, diverted scarce resources to building and equipping fortifications, and caused the Rebels a great deal of anxiety.[26]

When John W. Grattan joined the North Atlantic Blockading Squadron in the fall of 1863, its power had not yet peaked. Almost before the guns that had fired on Fort Sumter had cooled down, Abraham Lincoln on 19 April 1861 proclaimed a blockade of the states in rebellion. At first, the Union navy deployed only one squadron to cover the thousand miles of coastline from Alexandria, Virginia, to Key West, Florida. In September 1861, the Navy Department divided this command in two, forming the North Atlantic Blockading Squadron and the South Atlantic Blockading Squadron. The area of responsibility for the North Atlantic Blockading Squadron stretched from the Chesapeake Bay to the North Carolina–South Carolina border and included the coastal and inland waters of Virginia and North Carolina. The northern boundary changed several times, with other commands assuming responsibility for some of Virginia's inland waterways.

At the beginning of the war, the Union navy lacked sufficient numbers of ships to blockade the Southern coast effectively. To augment the few vessels in service when the war began, the North built new warships and leased or purchased merchant vessels to convert into warships. As a result, the North Atlantic Blockading Squadron ballooned from just over one dozen ships at the beginning of the war to fifty-five by the end of 1863, shortly after Grattan joined. Its strength peaked in January 1865 at 120 ships.

Because the government grabbed almost anything that floated to meet the demands of war, the North Atlantic Blockading Squadron consisted of a motley collection of vessels. There were monitors, which represented the height of technological development during the Civil War. There were so-called 90-day gunboats, screw-propelled steamers built quickly during the war of unseasoned timber. There were "double-enders," side-wheel steamers with a rudder at each end built during the war for use in narrow and shallow coastal waters. Double-enders were so named because the bow looked like the stern and they could go forward or backward with equal facility. There were sleek captured Confederate blockade runners, the fastest ships of their day. And there were more mundane vessels, such as tugs, storeships, old sailing vessels, and converted merchant steamers; even New York City ferryboats were pressed into service.[27]

Like the flagship on which he served, Grattan's narrative cruises back and forth among four operational nodes within the North Atlantic Blockading Squadron's area of responsibility: Hampton Roads and the James River in Virginia, the North Carolina sounds, and the waters off Wilmington, North Carolina.

The story begins in Virginia waters. Four major rivers emptied from eastern Virginia into the Chesapeake: the Potomac, the Rappahannock, the York, and the James, each one fed by numerous smaller rivers and creeks. Norfolk and Richmond, Virginia's premier ports, each had good rail connections to the interior. The shallow depth of the James River, however, restricted maritime commerce into Richmond, the Confederacy's political and industrial capital.

Hampton Roads saw a lot of action early in the Civil War, including one of history's most celebrated naval battles. With its strategically vital harbor and deep-water channel, Hampton Roads linked the confluence of the James, Nansemond, and Elizabeth Rivers to the Chesapeake Bay. Canals connected the Nansemond and Elizabeth Rivers to North Carolina, while up the James stood Richmond. Above Hampton Roads lay a peninsula formed by the James and York Rivers. At its tip, a narrow strip of beach connected to 75 acres of Federal property known as Old Point Comfort thrust into Hampton Roads.

Atop this protrusion of land stood Fort Monroe. Dubbed the "Gibraltar of the Chesapeake," Fort Monroe boasted seven 35-foot granite walls. Its heavy guns commanded the channel into the Chesapeake. Conceived in the wake of British depredations during the War of 1812, the fort had emerged in the 1830s as the strongest link in America's chain of coastal fortifications. During the Civil War it became an army stronghold and an important logistical base for the North Atlantic Blockading Squadron. It remained in Union hands throughout the war.

Across Hampton Roads from Fort Monroe, on the north bank of the Elizabeth River, lay the busy port of Norfolk, the major city of the lower Chesapeake. On the opposite bank stood the Gosport (or Norfolk) Navy Yard, the country's premier naval base and the largest shipbuilding and repair facility in the South. On 20 April 1861, the day after President Lincoln announced the blockade, outnumbered Union forces attempted to destroy the Gosport Navy Yard. The drunken, inept naval commander botched the job, allowing 1,200 cannon, a state-of-the-art granite dry dock, machine shops, and immense quan-

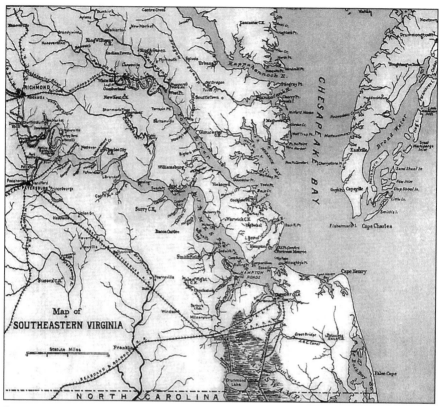

Southeastern Virginia (KH 1865 #7, Record Group 45, National Archives)

tities of small arms, ammunition, provisions, naval stores, and tools to fall into Rebel hands. The Union navy scuttled, burned, or otherwise lost eleven ships worth about $1,980,000 and forfeited close to $8,000,000 in property. The disaster proved a blessing for the Confederacy, for it provided cannon for warships and coastal fortifications and facilities for shipbuilding and repair.[28]

A little over a month after capturing Gosport Navy Yard, the Confederates raised one of the warships that Union forces had lost there. The *Merrimack* had gone to sea in 1856 as one of the U.S. Navy's largest and most powerful warships. Conceptually an updated *Constitution*, the heavy, deep-draft, wooden-hulled frigate was designed to re-fight the War of 1812 with steam power and the world's best ordnance. Her poor engines condemned her to a fiery death and a watery grave when Union forces evacuated Norfolk. Nevertheless, in keeping with their initial naval strategy to beat the Union navy with technologically superior armored warships, the Confederates resurrected the *Merrimack*, converted her into an ironclad warship, and renamed her the *Virginia*, although almost nobody on either side called her anything but *Merrimack*.

On 8 March 1862, the Confederates unleashed the *Virginia* and a handful of smaller vessels from the James River Squadron against the Union ships stationed in Hampton Roads. With Union shells bouncing off her iron armor "like India-rubber balls," the *Virginia* wrought havoc amidst the North Atlantic Blockading Squadron, sinking two wooden sailing warships (the *Congress* and the *Cumberland*), damaging a third (the steam frigate *Minnesota*), and killing some 241 men, at a cost of only two dead. The Rebel ironclad's combat debut sent off shock waves in all directions, causing wild rejoicing in the Confederacy, panic in the Union, and unrealistic expectations everywhere. Northerners feared that she would appear off their ports at any moment. Lincoln worried that she would steam up the Potomac and bombard Washington. Southerners expected the ironclad to take Fort Monroe and drive off the blockaders for good. It was the navy's worst day until December 7, 1941.

The appearance of the *Monitor* changed all that. A far more radical design than the Rebel ironclad, the *Monitor* featured a low iron hull topped by a revolving turret that mounted two guns. She arrived in Hampton Roads on the night of 8 March, her way lit by the still-burning *Congress*. When the *Virginia* reappeared on 9 March to finish off the wooden blockaders, the *Monitor* stood out to meet her. The two ironclads hammered away at each other at point-blank range for nearly four hours, but neither ship critically damaged the other. After the historic slugfest the two ships parted company, never to meet in combat again. Although tactically a draw, both sides declared victory.[29]

The *Virginia*'s success worried Major General George B. McClellan, commanding general of the Army of the Potomac, then in the midst of planning a campaign against Richmond. McClellan proposed to land his army at Fort Monroe and march up the peninsula between the James and York Rivers toward the Confederate capital. The presence of the Rebel ironclad in Hampton Roads threatened his intended supply line. Buoyed by the success of the *Monitor*, naval officials assured McClellan that the North Atlantic Blockading Squadron could "take" the *Virginia* if she ventured above Fort Monroe. The general decided to launch his grand campaign against Richmond.[30]

McClellan began his advance on 4 April 1862. As the Army of the Potomac slogged up the peninsula, Rebel forces fell back, abandoning Norfolk and torching the Gosport Navy Yard. The tiny, ersatz fleet that had accompanied the *Virginia* into Hampton Roads retired up the James to Richmond. The Confederate naval commander realized that the *Virginia* would be unable to retreat in fighting trim, so on 11 May, he ordered her run aground off Craney Island and set on fire. When the flames reached her magazine, the resulting explosion destroyed the threat to McClellan's supply line and laid the James River open to a Union naval advance. Flag Officer Louis Goldsborough, then in command of the North Atlantic Blockading Squadron, ordered the *Monitor* and four other warships to steam upstream to Richmond and to shell the Rebel capital until it surrendered. On 15 May, the flotilla reached the Confederate fortifications at

Monitor vs. *Virginia*, 9 March 1862 (Naval Historical Center NH 45973)

Drewry's Bluff, about eight miles below Richmond. For almost three hours the Yankee sailors traded shots with the Rebel gunners on the bluff, which rose some 100 feet above the water. The *Monitor* could not raise her guns sufficiently to bring them to bear on the Confederate batteries, and the other ships proved too vulnerable to remain within their range. Unable to reduce the fortifications, the ships withdrew. The North Atlantic Blockading Squadron would not steam that far up the James again until 1865.

After the repulse at Drewry's Bluff the squadron focused on supporting the Army of the Potomac, but not nearly to the extent that McClellan had envisioned. The general asked for naval support in the reduction of the Confederate batteries at Yorktown. Flag Officer Goldsborough dispatched seven gunboats under Commander John S. Missroon to do the job. Deterred by Confederate batteries at Yorktown and Gloucester Point, Missroon failed to take any initiative, neither attacking nor attempting to pass the batteries, as Farragut had done at New Orleans. Nevertheless, navy ships convoyed and protected army supply vessels bound to and from McClellan's base at White House on the York River and provided gunfire support to the troops. In seven days beginning at the end of June, the Army of Northern Virginia turned the tide on the Army of the Potomac. On 1 July, the Union general made a defensive stand at Malvern Hill. The Army of Northern Virginia tried to drive the Army of the

Potomac into the James, but fire from the heavy naval cannon on the gunboats ripped into their ranks and helped to drive them back. The North Atlantic Blockading Squadron then covered McClellan's final retreat.

The Peninsula Campaign was not a total disaster for Union forces, however, for they had recaptured Norfolk and the Gosport Navy Yard on 10 May, and held on to them for the rest of the war. Although the Yankees effected sufficient repairs to make the navy yard a usable base for the North Atlantic Blockading Squadron by the time Grattan arrived there in October 1863, the ruins and devastation in Norfolk, the Gosport Navy Yard, and the surrounding countryside moved him to comment on the destructiveness of war in his opening chapter.

In command of the North Atlantic Blockading Squadron when Grattan came on board was Rear Admiral Samuel Phillips Lee. Nothing unusual marked Lee's naval career before the Civil War. A Virginian by birth, he remained loyal to the Union when the war broke out. He distinguished himself under Farragut at New Orleans before taking command of the North Atlantic Blockading Squadron on 4 September 1862, at the relatively young age of fifty. What really set Lee apart from his brother officers were his family connections. He was related by marriage to Montgomery Blair, Lincoln's postmaster general, and to Assistant Secretary of the Navy Gustavus Vasa Fox, and he had blood ties to the most famous Lee of all, his cousin Robert E. Lee.

Average in height with a sparse frame and handsome appearance, Samuel Phillips Lee had a mixed reputation among his brother officers. Some considered him one of the navy's most conscientious and efficient leaders. Others thought him timid and felt he owed his command to influence. His nickname, "Old Triplicate," stemmed from perhaps excessive attention to routine details. His fleet captain and second in command, John Sanford Barnes, characterized him as "too modest and retiring, careful and conservative in his views of duty, never expressing himself, or giving his opinions, impulsively or emphatically." Barnes found Lee sensitive to criticism but endowed with tremendous personal courage. Grattan respected and admired Lee and penned only kind words about him.[31]

Grattan first served under the blue pennant on Lee's flagship, the USS *Minnesota*. Like her sister ship the *Merrimack*, the steam frigate *Minnesota* represented the cream of the antebellum navy. Also one of the navy's largest ships, she measured almost 265 feet at the waterline, displaced 4,833 tons, could make 12.5 knots, and carried 52 guns and more than 500 officers and men.[32]

Grattan came on board the *Minnesota* during a relatively quiet period in Hampton Roads. For six months after his arrival in October 1863, Union army commanders failed to exploit the advantage conferred by the North Atlantic Blockading Squadron's command of the water in that vicinity. Nevertheless, the squadron prevented the Confederates from building earthworks along the York and lower James Rivers, helped the army maintain its positions, and constantly patrolled the tidewater area, interdicting contraband trafficking, regulating legal trade and fishing, removing torpedoes, and fighting guerrillas. Grattan's account of the raid on "Lieutenant Roy's guerrillas" describes a type of small-scale brown-water operation that the Union navy conducted throughout the war, a type that historians have largely overlooked. But in terms of large-scale operations, between McClellan's flight from the peninsula in the summer of 1862 and the opening of Grant's campaign in Virginia the spring of 1864, Union naval forces did little more than maintain the status quo in the East.[33]

Meanwhile, the Confederate navy beefed up its defenses in the James River. Richmond became a naval-industrial complex, churning out three ironclads, four specialized torpedo boats, and an unarmed all-purpose vessel to join the James River Squadron. Commissioned by the end of 1863, the ironclads *Richmond, Fredericksburg,* and *Virginia II,* all of which resembled the original *Virginia,* were a remarkable achievement for a country so poorly endowed with industrial resources and facilities, relative to its antagonist. Nevertheless, these vessels proved slow, difficult to maneuver, mechanically unreliable, and too thinly armored to stand up to the Union navy's newest heavy ordnance, fielded in the wake of the *Monitor-Virginia* duel. Although Admiral Lee was apprehensive about the Rebel ironclads at first, he soon lost much of his fear. Grattan felt sanguine that Union monitors could "conquer and destroy" them. The James River Squadron remained largely a fleet in being until the end of the war, rarely going into action. Even when the Confederate ironclads did sortie down the James, Grattan had little to say about them. Incidentally, because the Confederates equipped several of their ironclads with rams, the ships were often referred to as "rams."[34]

Grattan had a lot more to say about the Rebels' "damned torpedoes," as mines were called in those days. The Confederates achieved far more success at waging underwater warfare than they did with their ironclads. Using Richmond's industrial resources and the best scientific minds in the South, the Confederate navy embraced torpedoes and ironclads to compensate for its severe disadvantage in ships. The Rebels began experimenting with torpedoes shortly after the bombardment of Fort Sumter in April 1861. By the end of the war, Confederate torpedo experts Matthew Fontaine Maury, Hunter Davidson, Gabriel J. Rains, and others had developed a sophisticated array of underwater weapons, including contact torpedoes designed to explode when struck by a ship, and electric or "galvanic" torpedoes designed to be detonated by a battery from shore when a ship steamed over them. The most common Confederate torpedo consisted of a water-tight wooden keg with conical metal ends, filled with about forty pounds of gunpowder, equipped with contact fuses, and anchored just below the surface. The largest electrically detonated torpedoes contained up to 2,000 pounds of powder. The Confederates also employed free-floating contact torpedoes designed to drift with the current into their targets, and "spar torpedoes" mounted on the end of a pole attached to small steam vessels. The most famous Confederate spar torpedo, mounted on the human-powered submersible *Hunley*, sank the USS *Housatonic* on 17 February 1864. The Union navy lost some fifty ships to torpedoes, more than to all other Confederate weapons combined. Maury himself privately fretted that there was something vaguely dishonorable in blowing up ships with unseen weapons. The Confederate sailors who served in what came to be known as the "Submarine Battery Service" were issued letters signed by Jefferson Davis declaring their bearers to be legitimate members of the Confederate States Navy, in case Union authorities saw fit to treat them as spies or guerrillas. Union naval officers indeed derided torpedoes as barbaric, dubbed them "infernal machines," and sometimes carried out reprisals against those who operated them.

The Confederates began laying torpedoes in the James River in the summer of 1862. They planted a minefield at Chapin's Bluff, just below Drewry's Bluff, and established smaller "torpedo stations" at various other points along the river.

The typical station consisted of a pair of 1,000-pound electric torpedoes submerged in 12 feet of water and connected by wire to a galvanic battery stowed in a small hut on shore, itself wired to an observation post on higher ground. The lookouts sighted the torpedoes using posts set in the water and aligned on shore as reference points. Piles, chains, spars, sunken vessels, and other underwater obstructions complemented the torpedoes at various points on the James.[35]

Grattan's experience with infernal machines dated almost from the beginning of his naval service. His first encounter occurred in November 1863, when lookouts on the *Minnesota* spotted floating torpedoes in the James. Grattan seemed nonplussed by this event.

His next encounter was far more frightening. On 9 April 1864, the tiny Confederate torpedo boat *Squib* attacked the huge *Minnesota* near Newport News. The *Squib*, one of the James River Squadron's four torpedo boats, measured 46 feet long by 6 feet wide, steamed as fast as 10 miles per hour, and carried a single torpedo mounted on a 16-foot-long oak boom. The *Squib* launched her attack in the black of night, successfully detonating a 53-pound torpedo against the flagship's side. Grattan's account of the incident shows how close the little vessel came to sinking the huge ship. This proved a mere foretaste of what was to come from torpedoes in the James.[36]

The appointment of Lieutenant General Ulysses S. Grant as general-in-chief of all Union armies in March 1864 spurred the North Atlantic Blockading Squadron back into action in Virginia. Union grand strategy that spring envisioned a vast turning movement by Sherman through the heartland of the South and a campaign by Grant, in *de facto* command of the Army of the Potomac, to destroy the Army of Northern Virginia. In support of Grant, the Army of the James was to land at Bermuda Hundred, establish a fortified base on the peninsula between the James and Appomattox Rivers, and from there attack

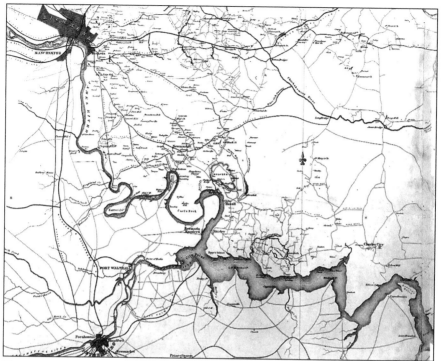

The James River from Richmond to Kennan's Marsh (drawer 150, sheet 13, Record Group 77, National Archives)

Richmond from the south. Butler, commander of the army's Department of Virginia and North Carolina, would lead the Army of the James. The North Atlantic Blockading Squadron was to support Butler.

A lawyer, political general, and radical reformer, Benjamin F. Butler was one of the most colorful figures of the Civil War and Gilded Age. He was downright ugly, with a pudgy body, spindly legs, puffy eyes (one of which wandered), and drooping mustache. Rutherford B. Hayes described him as "unscrupulous, able, untiring . . . the most wicked demagogue we have ever had." Lincoln said that Butler was "as full of poison gas as a dead dog." Yet Butler could be generous, had many friends, and sometimes fought for the underdog. Born in 1818 on the wrong side of the tracks in Lowell, Massachusetts, the first American factory town, he became one of New England's best lawyers and wiliest politicians. He championed the rights of Lowell factory girls against the textile tycoons, was elected brigadier general in the Massachusetts Militia, and by 1860 was earning the astonishing sum of $18,000 a year. When the Civil War came, Butler doffed his lawyer's garb for his general's uniform, seized secessionist-ridden Baltimore, hastened Lincoln toward emancipation with his "fugitive

B-398

USS *Saugus* with antitorpedo net mounted on the bow, James River, late 1864. This photograph symbolizes the most advanced naval technology employed during the Civil War. Equipped with XV-inch Dahlgren guns, the most powerful cannon of their day, the steam-powered, thickly armored, turreted, monitor-type ironclad was impregnable to enemy gunfire, but vulnerable to torpedoes. The only monitors lost to Confederate action during the Civil War, the *Tecumseh* and the *Patapsco*, struck torpedoes and sank like stones, carrying most of their crews with them. (Courtesy of Robert M. Browning, Jr.)

slave law," and, as commander of Union troops occupying New Orleans, enraged its citizens with his notorious order to treat any female who insulted a Union soldier as a "woman of the town." For the last, Southerners dubbed him "the Beast." Butler expressed contempt for army regulations but loved the pomp and circumstance of command and, like Grattan, the uniforms. David D. Porter hissed that Butler "was all jingle and feathers and [had a] staff as large as all outdoors." After the war Butler became one of Grant's "backstairs cabinet" advisers, chairman of the House Committee on Reconstruction, and governor of Massachusetts. As a politician Butler was the ultimate cat, always able to land on his feet even though his name was frequently associated with financial scandals. As a general, Butler was a disaster. One of his worst blunders occurred on the James.[37]

The prospect of action in the James excited Rear Admiral Lee. According to Butler's plan, the army would land at City Point, at the confluence of the James and Appomattox Rivers, then advance on Richmond along the south bank of the James. The North Atlantic Blockading Squadron was to clear the

James of obstructions and cover Butler's flanks and supply line. Lee envisioned a naval dogfight with the Rebel ironclads between Drewry's Bluff and Richmond. Assistant Secretary of the Navy Gustavus V. Fox noted that Lee was eager "to do this big thing," for "the upper James is the point of naval cooperation and now is the time."[38]

Because the *Minnesota* drew too much water to operate in the James, Lee transferred his flag to the sidewheeler USS *Malvern* on 4 May 1864. Built in 1860 as the *William G. Hewes*, the ship had made regular runs between New Orleans and New York City until the Confederates seized her in April 1861 and put her into service as a blockade runner. A blockader recaptured the ship off Wilmington on 8 November 1863. The Union navy armed her and renamed her the *Malvern*. Measuring 234 feet at the waterline, displacing 1,477 tons, and drawing only 10 feet of water, Lee's fast and maneuverable new flagship was well suited for operations upriver.[39]

On the day that Rear Admiral Lee transferred to the *Malvern*, the Army of the Potomac crossed the Rapidan River and began its bloody odyssey to the Wilderness, Spotsylvania, Cold Harbor, Petersburg, and Appomattox Court House. The North Atlantic Blockading Squadron started its ascent of the James on 5 May. In the van, seven wooden gunboats dragged for torpedoes as they steamed upstream. Next came four monitors and the captured Confederate ironclad *Atlanta*, each towed by two smaller vessels. Army transports and supply vessels brought up the rear. "It was a motley array of vessels," wrote one of Butler's subordinates. "Coasters and river steamers, ferry-boats and tugs, screw and side-wheel steamers, sloops, schooners, barges and canal-boats raced or crawled up the stream . . . in what seemed to be some grand national pageant."

Like their descendants at Anzio eighty years later, Union commanders had hoped to hurl a wildcat ashore at Bermuda Hundred, but instead they wound up with a beached whale. Butler landed 30,000 troops. Only 5,000 Confederate soldiers plus some hastily mobilized government clerks serving as militia were on hand to defend Richmond and Petersburg. If Butler had moved quickly, he might have cut the railroad between the two cities and smashed into the capital from the south. But instead of advancing, Butler spent the first week fortifying his advance base at Bermuda Hundred. By the time he finally moved forward on 12 May, Confederate reinforcements had arrived. A Rebel attack near Drewry's Bluff four days later drove Butler's men back into their trenches across the neck between the James and Appomattox Rivers. There the Confederates dug a line of trenches opposite Butler's, sealing off his army "as if it had been in a bottle strongly corked," as Grant put it. There Butler sat, content not to risk trying to pop the cork.

Likewise, Rear Admiral Lee threw boldness to the wind. Below the complex of obstructions at Drewry's Bluff, the cornerstone of the Confederate defense of the James remained torpedoes. Lee knew what infernal machines could do, and after local slaves apprised him of the general location of the torpedo stations, he moved cautiously. As the first of Butler's men debarked at City Point on 5 May, Lee began probing upstream to locate and clear the torpedoes, in anticipation of the army's intended advance. While smaller ships dragged the channel, larger ships bombarded the shore and marines combed the riverbank looking for torpedo stations.

Despite Lee's careful preparations, the Confederates exacted a toll. On 6 May, the Rebels detonated a 2,000-pound torpedo under the ex-ferryboat *Commodore Jones* in the vicinity of Four Mile Creek. The blast lifted the ship into the air with her paddle wheels still spinning, then blew her to splinters. The explosion killed sixty-nine men. The next day, near Turkey Bend, the little sidewheeler *Shawsheen* unknowingly drew within range of six Confederate cannon concealed on a bluff. The Rebel gunners opened fire, disabled the ship, captured her, and set her on fire. Twenty-seven of the *Shawsheen*'s crew fell into enemy hands; the rest fell dead. Torpedo-clearing operations continued without further loss of ships. By 13 May, Rear Admiral Lee's ascent of the James had ground to halt at Trent's Reach.

Meanwhile, Grant's staggering losses in the Wilderness, at Spotsylvania, and at Cold Harbor led him to revise his campaign plan. On 12 June 1864, he began to shift his army south of the James across a pontoon bridge. Before making the move, Grant ordered obstructions placed in Trent's Reach to prevent Confederate vessels, fire rafts, or floating torpedoes from interfering with the crossing. Lee disliked the idea of obstructing the river but cooperated anyway. Grant intended to capture Petersburg, then attack Richmond from the south, but Robert E. Lee shifted his own troops to Petersburg before Grant could take it. The opposing armies dug in for a ten-month siege, featuring trench warfare that anticipated the Western Front of World War I. To supply the army, Grant established the war's largest logistical base at City Point, located at the confluence of the James and Appomattox Rivers.

Meanwhile, stalemate returned to the James. Writing to a friend about the Union obstructions in Trent's Reach, Confederate naval officer Robert D. Minor lamented: "There is but a slim prospect of an action here, for the Yankees have penned us in and themselves out." On 19 June, Confederate ironclads dropped down the James to Trent's Reach, but a few near misses by 15-inch shells fired from Union monitors sent them skedaddling back upriver. Earlier that month, the Confederates had emplaced a line of gun batteries covering Trent's Reach at Howlett's Farm, anchored by a formidable earthwork named Battery Danzler. On 21 June, the James River Squadron steamed back downstream and, together with the new batteries, opened fire on the Union monitors in Trent's Reach. For some six and a half hours, Confederate ironclads banged away at their Union counterparts at extreme range across the wooded neck of Farrar's Island. The Rebel ships sustained more damage from mechanical problems than they inflicted on the monitors. The Union vessels concentrated their fire on the Confederate shore batteries, which posed a greater threat to them than the James River Squadron. Nothing was decided. For the next seven months, Union and Confederate shore batteries in the vicinity of Trent's Reach periodically traded shots with one another. Union and Confederate ships supported their own troops during this period, but the naval dogfight that Lee had hoped for never materialized.

In July, Butler conceived the idea of digging a 174-yard-long canal through Farrar's Island at Dutch Gap so that Union ironclads could bypass the Confederate shore batteries overlooking Trent's Reach. Many observers in the Navy Department scoffed at the idea. Butler's troops began digging the Dutch Gap Canal in August, but the war ended before they finished. The project served no purpose other than keeping Butler's men busy and allowing the Confederate ironclads to get in a little target practice by firing at the laborers.

In January 1865, the Rebel ironclads made one last descent of the James, this time on a mission to attack Grant's base at City Point. Eleven Confederate vessels started downstream on the twenty-third. Early the next morning the operation degenerated into a comedy of errors when the *Virginia II* and the *Richmond* ran aground while attempting to pass the obstructions at Trent's Reach. Union shore batteries opened a heavy fire on the armored sitting ducks. The double-turreted monitor *Onondaga* came up just as the Rebel ironclads floated free and began to retire. Parting shots from the *Onondaga*'s 15-inch guns smashed into the *Virginia II*. The Confederate ironclads got away before the monitor could finish them off. Thus ended the battle of Trent's Reach and the last offensive undertaken by the James River Squadron. In keeping with his general disregard for the Rebel ironclads, Grattan had nothing at all to say about this battle.[40]

Curiously, Grattan had nothing to say about Butler's abortive drive on Richmond, either. Perhaps Grattan was unwilling to criticize any aspect of the James operations because the navy under Admiral Lee had faltered, too, and he was loathe to criticize either Lee or his own service. Grattan preferred to focus on operations in North Carolina, which had a much happier ending for the North Atlantic Blockading Squadron.

As in Virginia, the North Atlantic Blockading Squadron alternated between action and stagnation in North Carolina waters. North Carolina had a more rugged and extensive coast, as well as a much larger inland waterway system. North Carolina's border with the Atlantic featured a long stretch of narrow barrier islands that protruded into the ocean at Cape Hatteras, Cape Lookout, and Cape Fear. The barrier islands were separated by several inlets, which opened into two big sounds, Albemarle in the north and Pamlico in the south. Several large rivers emptied from eastern North Carolina into these sounds. Numerous small ports dotted North Carolina's extensive inland waterways, but their shallow depth prevented large vessels from reaching them.

On 29 August 1861, a joint Union amphibious expedition captured Forts Hatteras and Clark, just below Cape Hatteras on the Outer Banks, thereby

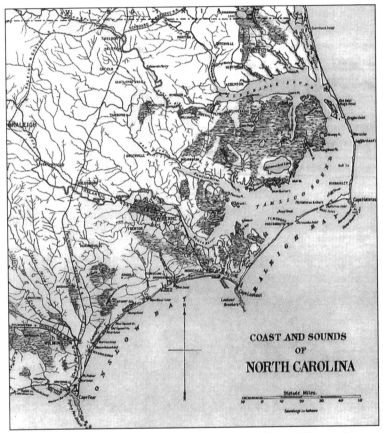

Coasts and sounds of North Carolina (KH 1865 #9, Record Group 45, National Archives)

sealing off Pamlico Sound. On 8 February 1862, another joint Union amphibious expedition secured Roanoke Island. The North Atlantic Blockading Squadron's destruction of the so-called mosquito fleet below Elizabeth City two days later denied Albemarle Sound to the Confederates. Subsequent Union operations yielded New Bern, Washington, Beaufort, and Plymouth. By the end of 1862, all of eastern North Carolina had fallen under Union control. With no Confederate naval threat to oppose them, the Union army garrisoned the major towns and probed inland while the navy maintained control of the waters. Wilmington, located 150 miles south of Cape Hatteras, remained the only North Carolina port open to blockade runners.

But the strategic picture in North Carolina for the Union was not all that rosy. The army had divided itself into several small forces, each isolated from the others and reliably connected only by water. This provided the Confederates with the opportunity of exploiting their interior lines to attack and defeat each garrison in detail. The Confederates tried to do exactly that with thrusts against Washington in September and Plymouth in December, but Union forces turned them back.

Stalemate descended upon eastern North Carolina in 1863. Union troops and ships repulsed Confederate attacks against New Bern and Washington in the spring, but made no further inroads into the state. The Union navy's presence prevented yet another attack on New Bern, planned for February, from ever materializing. Part of the Rebel scheme involved an attempt to capture the Union gunboat *Underwriter*. When the attempt floundered, the Confederate commander, Major General George E. Pickett, whose name became forever linked to the epic Confederate charge on the third day at Gettysburg, called the whole thing off.

Union forces would not be so lucky the next time. While the Confederate army launched its ill-fated attacks against Union garrisons, the Confederate navy built an ironclad in a cornfield on the Roanoke River above Plymouth. Begun in the spring of 1863, the CSS *Albemarle* measured 152 feet long, drew 8 feet of water, and bore the usual Rebel ironclad appearance. Armed with an iron-tipped ram and two rifled cannon, she could beat any available Union ship with a shallow enough draft to operate in the sounds. Rear Admiral Lee had repeatedly urged General Butler, as commander of the Department of Virginia and North Carolina, to attack the building site. Although Butler had the men to do it, army forces in North Carolina refused to budge unless escorted by the navy. Since the site lay too far upstream in shallow water for Union ships to operate safely, the *Albemarle* had remained unmolested.

In the spring of 1864, the Confederates unleashed the ironclad and 7,000 men against Plymouth. Against this onslaught the Union mustered 3,000 troops and the gunboats *Miami, Southfield, Ceres,* and *Whitehead* under Commander Charles W. Flusser, whom many brother officers considered courageous to the point of foolhardiness. Flusser longed to fight against a Rebel ironclad.

He got his chance on 19 April. At 3:30 that morning, the *Albemarle* attacked his flotilla. Flusser had the wooden double-enders *Miami* and *Southfield* lashed together with a hawser in hopes that he could handle them as one ship. He stood to meet the Rebel ironclad with guns blazing. While Union shells caromed harmlessly off the *Albemarle*'s armor, the ironclad rammed and sank the *Southfield* and drove off the other ships. A fragment of a projectile Flusser fired at the ironclad ricocheted and killed him instantly. With support from the *Albemarle*, Rebel soldiers took Plymouth later that day.

Union forces subsequently withdrew from Washington and the Confederates planned another attack on New Bern. On 5 May, the Rebel ram moved out, steaming into Albemarle Sound. This time she faced four double-enders and four smaller wooden gunboats. A fierce fight ensued. Some 280 Union projectiles struck the *Albemarle*, killing one man. The ironclad's gunfire killed eight

Union sailors, wounded twenty-one, and disabled the double-ender *Sassacus*, but the Union flotilla drove her off. The ram steamed back up the Roanoke River. Although the naval battle ended in a draw, the Confederate thrust against New Bern failed without support from the *Albemarle*. Stalemate once again descended onto eastern North Carolina. For the next several months, the Confederate ironclad remained in the Roanoke River, defending Plymouth and posing a threat to Union naval forces in eastern North Carolina, while a flotilla from the North Atlantic Blockading Squadron remained on station at the river's mouth in case she reappeared. The Yankees could not recapture Plymouth without first destroying the *Albemarle*. Grattan described an attempt by five men from the *Wyalusing* to sink the ironclad with torpedoes that came to naught.[41]

Enter Lieutenant Commander William Barker Cushing, one of the most daring men in American naval history. Born on 4 November 1842, Will came of brave stock. His brother Alonzo Hersford Cushing won immortal fame during the Civil War when he stood with his Battery A of the Fourth U.S. Artillery at the "angle" at Gettysburg and died at his guns as the gray tide reached its high-water mark around him.

Will's career at arms got off to a rockier start. He entered the Naval Academy with the class of 1861 at the tender age of fourteen. One of his instructors described him as "a delicate-looking youth; fair, with regular, clear-cut features, and a clear, greyish-blue eye." Cushing held the dubious distinction of being "anchor man" of his class, the midshipman with the lowest grades. Although amazingly strong and energetic, he seemed to catch a cold each winter that lasted the season long. When he left the academy he stood 6 feet tall but weighed only 150 pounds. Always the youngest midshipman in his class and ever the prankster, Cushing amassed large numbers of demerits and was forced to resign in the spring of his "first class" or senior year. When Rebels fired on Fort Sumter less than a month later, Cushing begged Secretary of the Navy Gideon Welles for another chance. An astute judge of character, Welles was impressed by Cushing's perseverance, enthusiasm, and zeal. He appointed him an acting volunteer master's mate and assigned him to the *Minnesota*.

Welles was not disappointed. During an engagement with Confederate batteries near Suffolk, Virginia, Cushing struck a note that reverberated throughout his Civil War service: "We will beat the enemy or sink at our post." Before it was all over, the Navy Department would commend Cushing a total of four times, and Lincoln and Congress would thank him for his service. His biographers dubbed him "Lincoln's commando."

Late in the spring of 1864, Rear Admiral Lee approached Cushing with the idea of attacking the *Albemarle* with a spar torpedo fitted on a steam launch. Cushing leapt at the chance and immediately went to New York to supervise the fitting out of two torpedo boats. Each measured over 40 feet in length, drew less than 3 feet of water, and carried a 12-pound howitzer and a torpedo mounted on the end of a 14-foot boom. Cushing lost one of the launches on the way to North Carolina "owing to stupidity or drink," as Rear Admiral Porter put it after the war, but decided to continue with the mission.

On 27 October 1864, Cushing and thirteen officers and men entered the Roanoke, steamed 8 miles upstream, and pressed their attack. Although Cushing lost the launch and all but two of his men, he succeeded in detonating his torpedo under the *Albemarle*, blowing open a hole "big enough to drive a wagon in" and sending the ironclad to the bottom. Cushing, of course, was one of the two that got away. He became an international hero, and for the rest of his life, he had to live with the nickname "Albemarle" Cushing.[42]

Four days later, a flotilla from the North Atlantic Blockading Squadron recaptured Plymouth. Quiet returned to the sounds of North Carolina as the Union navy turned its attention to the capture of Wilmington.

Although Grattan never sailed into North Carolina's sounds during the war, *Under the Blue Pennant* covers Union naval operations there, particularly Cushing's fateful rendezvous with the *Albemarle*. Because Grattan was not present, his narrative of those events is more history than memoir, resting upon documents and conversations with participants rather than on personal experience. He wrote at length about the operations in the sounds because they involved people he knew, and because they were significant to the history of the North Atlantic Blockading Squadron.

Like the situations in Hampton Roads and eastern North Carolina, the blockade of Wilmington had also remained somewhat of a standoff for most of the period that Grattan served under the blue pennant. However, Grattan could draw from personal experience in writing about the Wilmington blockade.

At this point in the war, Wilmington was North Carolina's largest port and the Confederacy's most important city after Richmond. Geography made the port strategically valuable and the hardest to blockade. Wilmington stood along the east side of the Cape Fear River, which had two navigable ocean entrances. New Inlet lay some 18 miles below the city, with Old Inlet, or Western Bar Channel, lying another 7 miles downstream. Separating the two were a cluster of islands, the largest of which was an inverted triangle called Smith's or Bald Head Island, whose southern tip was Cape Fear. Frying Pan Shoals, one of the biggest hazards to shipping along the entire East Coast, was a series of reefs that streamed south from Smith's Island for 20 miles into the Atlantic, extending the navigable distance by sea between the two inlets to some 40 miles.

During the antebellum era, improvements in the Cape Fear's navigability, North Carolina's adoption of the plank road system, and the construction of railroad lines connecting Wilmington to Richmond and elsewhere in the South had stimulated Wilmington's rise. At the beginning of the war, when all of the South's ports still lay in Confederate hands and the Union navy was too numerically weak to guard them all effectively, almost any kind of sailing vessel or steam-powered craft could slip into Wilmington. But as Union forces sealed off

Approaches to Wilmington, North Carolina (KH 1865 #5, Record Group
45, National Archives)

or captured other Confederate ports and more and more Union ships appeared
off Wilmington, running the blockade became a risky business. By the time
Grattan joined the squadron in October 1863, Wilmington remained the only
major port through which the Rebel war effort received supplies from overseas.

Under Rear Admiral Lee, the Wilmington blockade reached its highest
state of development. The distance between Old Inlet and New Inlet prevented ships stationed off one to communicate with or support ships off the
other, so Lee assigned a separate flotilla to blockade each inlet. The First Division stood off the bar at New Inlet. The Third Division kept watch at the Western Bar and adjacent smaller inlets. Lee arranged the ships in each division to
form two concentric rings, so that inbound or outbound ships would have to run
two gauntlets. Lighter-draft blockaders moved in as close as the weather, time
of day, and range of Confederate guns permitted, while faster or deeper-draft
vessels patrolled farther out to sea. Lee periodically updated his tactics as conditions warranted.

You might think that the North Atlantic Blockading Squadron would have
shut Wilmington down in short order, but blockade runners made nearly 300

runs into the city during the war. After Union operations on Morris Island effectively closed off Charleston in the summer of 1863, the steamers running into Wilmington became the most important element in the Confederate supply system. It is true that fewer blockade runners succeeded as increasing numbers of Union warships appeared offshore, but even toward the end of the war, from 26 October 1864 to 13 January 1865, thirty-one runners unloaded 4,000 tons of meat, 750 tons of lead, 950 tons of saltpeter, 43 artillery pieces, 69,000 Enfield rifles, and tens of thousands of blankets and pairs of shoes onto Wilmington's wharves. Much of this stuff went right up the railroad to Richmond and the Army of Northern Virginia. During the same period, the North Atlantic Blockading Squadron captured or destroyed only ten blockade runners.

The Confederates pulled this off because of strong defenses and fast ships. Wilmington's inland location and narrow river approach limited options for a naval assault. To augment these natural advantages, the Confederates planted batteries along the banks of the Cape Fear, sank obstructions and torpedoes in its waters, and built large forts to guard the entrances to the inlets. Fort Fisher, which defended New Inlet, eventually became the Confederacy's largest earthwork. The guns of the forts kept the blockaders out of the Cape Fear River and provided a sanctuary for blockade runners.

The technological evolution of blockade runners outpaced the tactical evolution of the blockade. Improvements in steam engineering, hull design, and camouflage gave blockade runners an edge in speed, maneuverability, and stealth over their pursuers. By the time Grattan had joined the chase, the quarry were sleek and rakish stilettolike vessels built for speed. The typical blockade runner was constructed in Britain of iron or steel, displaced between 400 and 600 tons, and was painted a dull gray to blend into the background. While twin-screw runners were less noisy, more maneuverable, and less vulnerable to gunfire, paddlewheelers were faster and easier to extract from shoals. Blockade runners burned anthracite coal whenever possible because it made little or no smoke. Some had telescoping smokestacks to reduce their profile. Under certain weather conditions and stages of the moon, blockade runners blended so perfectly with their surroundings that they remained invisible to blockaders as close as one hundred yards away. On dark nights, only their wakes could be seen as they slipped by. The famous blockade running skipper John Wilkinson boasted that the ships seemed "almost as invisible as Harlequin in the pantomime." Well-handled steamers could average one trip a month between Wilmington and Nassau or Bermuda, the principal transshipment points for European goods bound for the Confederacy. Captains and crews of successful blockade runners grew rich.

Their antagonists also had the opportunity to become rich. Steamers carrying contraband for the Confederacy that fell into Union hands became legal prizes of war. Picked crews sailed captured blockade runners to Northern ports where prize courts condemned and sold the vessels and their contents, and

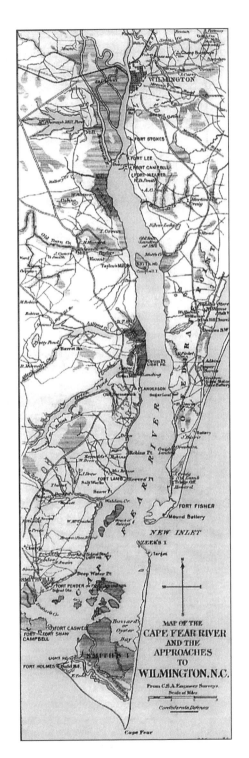

The Cape Fear River from Wilmington to the Atlantic (KH 1865 #8, Record Group 45, National Archives)

after withholding adjudication costs, divided up the proceeds between the blockaders involved in the capture, with one half going to the navy pension fund and the other to the captors in amounts proportional to their regular pay. Since a valuable prize could yield the equivalent of several years pay in one fell swoop, blockaders took extraordinary risks to capture blockade runners intact.[43]

Because most blockade runners were built in British shipyards, particularly along the Clyde River, Grattan harbored bitter feelings toward the British. He expressed these feelings by deriding blockade runners as "anglo-rebel steamers." Like most of his contemporaries, watching for blockade runners bored him but chasing them thrilled him. His account reflects the fact that storms, shoals, and Confederate weapons made blockade duty hazardous. Although Grattan tried to put the best possible face on it, his frustration at the government's inability to provide the North Atlantic Blockading Squadron with sufficient numbers of steamers fast enough to catch their prey also comes through in the narrative.

Samuel Phillips Lee pressed for a joint expedition against Wilmington throughout his command of the North Atlantic Blockading Squadron, but with the Navy Department focusing on the Mississippi River, Charleston, and Mobile, his pleas fell on deaf ears. But by the fall of 1864, Union forces had taken the Mississippi River and Mobile. The Charleston campaign, like the James River operations, had bogged down. Now, with Wilmington being the only major Southern seaport open to blockade running, Gideon Welles lobbied Lincoln for a joint campaign to capture it. The president liked the idea, but left the final decision up to his general-in-chief. Grant approved the operation, but on the condition that Welles replace Admiral Lee.

Why Grant wanted Lee sacked is unclear, and although Welles did not relish the idea, he agreed with it. The secretary thought Lee had served faithfully and intelligently, but considered him overcautious. Welles offered command of the North Atlantic Blockading Squadron to Rear Admiral David Glasgow Farragut, whom he considered the navy's best officer. Worn out from the Mississippi and Mobile campaigns, Farragut turned him down. Welles then offered the job to David Dixon Porter. Porter accepted it. Welles gave Lee command of the Mississippi Squadron.[44]

In *Under the Blue Pennant*, Grattan bids Samuel Phillips Lee adieu without much ado. He announces Lee's relief, praises him, and summarizes his service as squadron commander in just two sentences. None of the political intrigue that surrounds the decision to replace Lee with Porter appears. Grattan never said whether he objected to Lee's sacking or welcomed it. His introduction of Lee in *Under the Blue Pennant* exudes a warmth and fondness akin to the feelings one might express about a crusty but beloved uncle. In contrast, the ink that Grattan spent on Porter focuses on the admiral's professional qualities rather than personal attributes. It is safe to say that while Grattan respected both admirals, he liked Lee better.

However Grattan felt about the decision to put Porter in command, it pleased General Grant, for he believed Porter to be as great an admiral as Lord Nelson. Born the son of a naval hero of the War of 1812, Porter had gone to sea, served in the Mexican navy, fought a battle against a Spanish warship, and suffered through six months in a Cuban prison before joining the U.S. Navy at the age of sixteen. Porter spent much of the next thirty years engaged in coastal and harbor surveys. Early in the Civil War he masterminded a scheme that saved Fort Pickens near Pensacola, Florida, and devised the plan by which he and his foster brother Farragut captured New Orleans. Sixteen months after entering the war as a lieutenant, Porter assumed command of the Mississippi Squadron as an acting rear admiral. Porter's crowning achievement in the Mississippi was the naval support he provided to Grant during the campaign that brought down Vicksburg on 4 July 1863. Porter and Grant deeply respected one another, and as partners in command they had formed one of the Civil War's most effective joint teams. Porter's final campaign in the West, the Red River fiasco of spring 1864, did not sour the Navy Department on him. Witty, energetic, audacious, acerbic, ambitious, prone to exaggeration and braggadocio, blunt to the point of imprudence, and blessed with a photographic memory and a keenly analytical mind, Porter stands behind only Farragut in the pantheon of Civil War naval heroes. Porter's biographer wrote that he "obtained more difficult assignments, commanded more ships and men, won a greater number of victories, and was more often awarded the Congressional vote of thanks than any other officer who ever served in the United States Navy." People either despised or loved Porter.[45]

On 12 October 1864, Porter hoisted his flag on board the *Malvern*. Much to his dismay, the admiral found that Butler would be leading the army forces assigned to the Wilmington expedition. Grant had selected Major General Godfrey Weitzel for the job, but since Weitzel was Butler's subordinate, and the operation would take place within the geographic area of the Department of Virginia and North Carolina, Butler exercised the right to lead it himself. Porter and Butler had become bitter enemies during the New Orleans campaign when Butler took what Porter considered undue credit for the capture of the Crescent City. As a result of their enmity, the admiral and general never met during the planning of the operations against Wilmington.

The key to Wilmington was Fort Fisher, situated on the north side of the more easily accessible and more frequently used New Inlet. Sited at the tip of Federal Point, the long peninsula that formed the east bank of the Cape Fear River, Fort Fisher resembled the number 7, with its elbow pointing northeast. The short bar faced north to defend against an attack by land from up the peninsula. It measured 480 yards and contained nineteen heavy guns and two mortars behind log-and-sand breastworks overlooking a minefield and a 9-foot-high palisade. The elbow towered 32 feet above the beach. The long arm of the 7 faced the sea and stretched 1,300 yards. It consisted of a series of sand, turf, and log batteries, which resembled a row of haystacks connected by walls when viewed from the Atlantic. Including those in the elbow or "Northeast Bastion," twenty-four heavy cannon in the long-arm batteries faced the sea. The Mound Battery, rising 43 feet above the beach, tipped the southern end. West of the Mound Battery on the river side of Federal Point lay Battery Buchanan, mounting four heavy cannon. The garrison numbered between 800 and 1,500 men, with varying numbers of additional troops available from Wilmington. By this point in the war, Fort Fisher was the Confederacy's most intensely fortified piece of coastline. Reflecting the hubris that often accompanies great achievements, Confederate authorities considered Fort Fisher impregnable.

Welles and Grant approved a campaign plan developed by Major General Quincy A. Gillmore for what came to be called the first Fort Fisher expedition, or Butler's expedition. The plan was simple. While the fleet bombarded Fort Fisher from the Atlantic and ran light-draft vessels into the Cape Fear River, troops would land on Federal Point above the fort, then move south to carry Fort Fisher in a frontal assault. If the assault failed, they were to dig in for a siege, cutting off the fort with a line of entrenchments across the peninsula.

Butler added his own twist to the plan. He proposed to blow up Fort Fisher with a gigantic floating bomb before landing his men. The idea was to run the steamer *Louisiana*, loaded with 215 tons of gunpowder, as close to the fort as possible, then detonate the powder. Porter believed that the blast would kill everything within three miles.

Stormy weather delayed the first Fort Fisher expedition until the end of 1864. On the night of 23–24 December, Porter tried Butler's experiment. It failed miserably. The *Louisiana* exploded half a mile or more away from the fort. The elaborate system designed to detonate all of the gunpowder simultaneously didn't work. Only a portion of the powder went off. The balance was either blown overboard or sank with the burning wreck. Intended to knock Fort Fisher's defenders senseless, the *Louisiana* did not even wake them all up. Many of those who saw the explosion figured a blockader's boiler had blown up. An enraged Butler blamed Porter for detonating the ship before his men were ready to land, and for botching the job to boot.

The failure of the powder ship foretold the outcome of the expedition. The North Atlantic Blockading Squadron opened fire early in the afternoon of Christmas Eve, 1864. By nightfall, the fleet had poured some 10,000 rounds into the defenses. Nevertheless, the navy cannonade inflicted only minor damage on Fort Fisher and only twenty-three casualties among its defenders. Many Union gunners concentrated their fire on the fort's flags. Numerous shots sailed right over the defenses. Confederate return fire inflicted fewer casualties on the fleet than the explosions of defective heavy 100-pounder Parrott rifles on some of the ships. Meanwhile, Butler's men had arrived and began landing on Federal Point above the fort. On Christmas Day the fleet resumed the bombardment while Weitzel reconnoitered the fort. The general determined

Barry University Library
Miami, Fla. 33161

that the naval bombardment had inflicted almost no damage on Fort Fisher. He reported to Butler that "it would be butchery to order an assault on that work under the circumstances." Butler concurred. After receiving word of the approach of a Confederate division from Wilmington, Butler decided to withdraw his men.

Porter exploded when he realized Butler was going for good. "We attacked Fort Fisher, silenced it, blew it up, burned it out, and knocked it to pieces," he wrote his friend William T. Sherman. "Notwithstanding all this, General Butler decided not to attack Fort Fisher, 'as the navy fire has not injured it as a defensive work.' Great heavens! what are we coming to? . . . let our people see the folly of employing such generals as Butler." Worse, Butler departed early on 26 December while many of his men remained stranded on the beach, leaving Porter to finish re-embarking them.[46]

Grattan railed at Butler for his actions at Fort Fisher. "Had the general attempted the assault and been defeated there would have been some excuse for his retreat," he hissed, "but to run away without firing a shot or making the slightest effort to capture the fort . . . [was] a most cowardly, humiliating and dishonorable proceeding. All our hard fighting and the loss of many valuable lives were thrown away."[47]

Grant called Butler's withdrawal a "fearful mistake." Before the expedition had set sail, Grant had left explicit instructions that if the troops failed to carry the fort by storm, they were to besiege it. Grant told Lincoln that the expedition proved a "gross and culpable failure." At the general's request the president relieved Butler of command of the Department of Virginia and North Carolina on 7 January 1865.

Porter sent dispatches to the Navy Department begging that the troops be sent back to Fort Fisher under a new commander. Welles and Fox lobbied Lincoln for a second expedition. Sherman, whose army had recently reached the sea at Savannah, proposed attacking Wilmington in the course of marching his army through the Carolinas toward Virginia. Grant figured that Wilmington would make a good point for supplying Sherman, so he approved a second expedition, with Major General Alfred Howe Terry leading the troops.

The second expedition departed on 6 January 1865. Terry commanded some 9,600 men; Porter's fleet numbered fifty-eight ships with 396 guns. Storms delayed their arrival off Fort Fisher until late in the afternoon of the twelfth. Some 1,500 Confederates manned Fort Fisher, while a division of some 6,424 infantry and cavalry occupied the peninsula north of the fort.

After dawn on 13 January, the guns of a division of wooden vessels sent to cover the landing opened up on Federal Point. Soon, the assault troops began stepping ashore. By three o'clock that afternoon, the infantry had landed and dug in opposite the Confederate division above them. Meanwhile, Union ironclads closed on Fort Fisher. A spirited engagement ensued, with the Rebels scoring many hits on the ironclads but inflicting no serious damage. The entire fleet reopened on the fort mid-morning on the fourteenth. This time, the naval bombardment proved much more accurate and effective, with the ships concentrating their fire on the enemy's guns. By the end of the day, the Rebels had lost all but three or four of their land-face-cannon and at least 200 killed and wounded, some 13 percent of the garrison.

This time, the army and navy commanders devised a joint plan for an assault. On the evening of the fourteenth, General Terry rowed out to meet with Admiral Porter on the *Malvern*. They hammered out a plan calling for Union forces to bombard Fort Fisher until 3:00 in the afternoon of 15 January. Then Terry would signal Porter to shift the fleet's fire from the fort's land face to its sea face. At that moment, a column of about 3,200 troops would assault the land face from the west along the road from Wilmington. To the east, a volunteer force of 2,261 sailors and marines under Captain K. Randolph Breese, Porter's fleet captain, would attack the northeast bastion at the angle of the 7.

At 8:00 A.M. on the appointed day, the fleet opened up at point-blank range. The ships directed their fire against the front, flank, and rear of the land face until approximately 3:00 P.M., when they blew their steam whistles to signal the shifting of their fire and the beginning of the assault. The "Naval Brigade" sprang forward through a hail of canister and bullets. Some 150 to 200 sailors made it to the palisade and perhaps two dozen reached the foot of the bastion. Despite their magnificent but ill-advised effort to "board" Fort Fisher with pistols and cutlasses, the sailors were repulsed, losing about 300 killed and wounded.

But the naval brigade contributed decisively to the outcome, for it diverted the defenders' attention from the troops moving in to the west. The Confederates thought that the naval brigade was making the main attack. While nearly the whole Rebel garrison joined to fight off the sailors, General Terry's men secured a lodgment in the other side of the fort. By the time the Confederates realized that another attack was materializing, it was too late. After a vicious fight with bullets, bayonets, and grenades, the defenders surrendered. When the Union ships received word of the victory, they filled the sky with fireworks.[48]

Fort Fisher had fallen, but Wilmington remained in Rebel hands. With General Sherman about to commence his march through the Carolinas, General Grant remained strongly interested in supplying Sherman through Wilmington. On the night of 28 January, Grant, Assistant Secretary Fox, and Major General John McAllister Schofield, commander of the XXIII Corps, Army of the Ohio, and General Terry arrived on board Porter's flagship to plan the capture of the city. After poring over maps and charts for almost four hours, Grant decided to transfer Schofield's corps to the Cape Fear, reconstitute the army's Department of North Carolina, and put Schofield in command of it. Although the decision hurt General Terry and angered Admiral Porter, Schofield was a good commander.

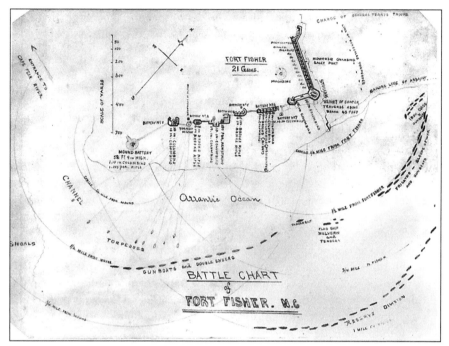

"Battle Chart of Fort Fisher, N.C.," by John W. Grattan, 15 January 1865 (John W. Grattan Papers, Library of Congress)

Early in February, Union troops began advancing along both banks of the Cape Fear, with Terry on the east and Major General Jacob Dolson Cox on the west. A flotilla numbering twenty to thirty ships from the North Atlantic Blockading Squadron advanced up the middle, covering both columns of troops. On the seventeenth, Porter's flotilla opened a two-day bombardment of Fort Anderson, a miniature version of Fort Fisher and the largest earthwork on the Cape Fear, located 9 miles above Smithville. Meanwhile, Union troops took positions near the fort. On the night of 18–19 February, Porter sent a dummy monitor up the Cape Fear on the flood tide past Fort Anderson. It was Cushing's idea. He believed that the Confederates would detonate the torpedoes covering the fort to try to sink the dummy, enabling the real ships to close in with greater safety. The Confederates, however, proved more concerned about the advancing troops and abandoned Fort Anderson that same night.

After the Rebels skedaddled, Porter had some fifty boats rigged to drag the Cape Fear for torpedoes. Both the army and navy resumed the advance. The next obstacles standing in Terry's path were Batteries Lee, Meares, and Campbell, collectively called Fort Strong by Union troops. On 20 February, the flotilla opened a terrific bombardment on Fort Strong, but inflicted little damage owing to its high elevation. That night, the Confederates unleashed 200

The Naval Brigade assault on Fort Fisher, 15 January 1865, the climactic moment of *Under the Blue Pennant*, by John W. Grattan. The second paddlewheeler from the left is the *Malvern*, with the signal flags flying from the foremast and the blue pennant from the mainmast. To her right are four monitors and the ironclad USS *New Ironsides*. (John W. Grattan Papers, Library of Congress)

torpedoes, each filled with 100 pounds of gunpowder, to drift with the current of the Cape Fear into Porter's flotilla. Sailors manned the boats and stopped most of them, but one blew up a warship's wheelhouse and another destroyed one of the boats. The torpedo attack had been a last-ditch effort, for the Confederates abandoned Fort Strong on the twenty-first and Wilmington on the twenty-second. That day, the Yankees entered the city.[49]

The capture of Wilmington essentially ended the North Atlantic Blockading Squadron's mission in North Carolina waters. With the Civil War approaching its climax in Virginia, Porter took the *Malvern* back to Hampton Roads. After getting a few badly needed repairs, the *Malvern* steamed up the James on 19 March. Over the next few days Porter received several distinguished visitors on board the flagship, including General Grant, Major General George G. Meade, and President Lincoln. Grant had invited the president down to City Point for a few days, suggesting that the rest would do him some good. Lincoln had left Washington on board the *River Queen* on 23 March and spent two weeks at the front. The Army of the Potomac's odyssey in Virginia was nearing its climax as the remnants of Robert E. Lee's shattered army strove in vain to stave off the Union juggernaut in the blood-soaked trenches around Petersburg. For

Grattan and the rest of the officers and men of the North Atlantic Blockading Squadron, there was little else to do but to watch the curtain come down on the Confederacy.

On 28 March, Lincoln brought Grant, Sherman, and Porter together for a conference on board the *River Queen*. The president discussed the approaching end of the war and talked of offering generous terms to "get the deluded men of the rebel armies disarmed and back to their homes."[50]

On 29 March, Union forces launched the final major campaign of the Civil War. General Grant sent newly arrived cavalry under Sheridan, together with some infantry, to envelop the Confederate right flank to the southwest of Petersburg. Heavy rain stalled the Union drive for two days. On the thirty-first, outnumbered Confederate soldiers under Pickett retreated to Five Forks, where Sheridan crushed them the next day. On 2 April, Grant ordered a full-scale assault all along the lines at Petersburg. Union troops broke through at several points. Grattan witnessed the grand charge from Fort Stedman near the extreme right of the Union lines. That night, Robert E. Lee withdrew his men toward Amelia Court House. On 3 April, Union troops entered Petersburg and Richmond.

The next day, Admiral Porter took President Lincoln to the fallen Rebel capital. Grattan numbered among the officers accompanying them. Lincoln stepped ashore in Richmond without fanfare, but word of his arrival spread quickly. Throngs of African Americans surrounded him, expressing gratitude and joy. Lincoln visited the Confederate executive mansion and sat in a chair in what had been Jefferson Davis's office. After a simple lunch, the president toured Richmond in a carriage. He returned to the *Malvern* that evening. Grattan related a number of anecdotes about Lincoln's visit. On 8 April, Lincoln departed for Washington on the *River Queen*.[51]

Grattan's narrative ends on 10 April with the celebration of Lee's surrender to Grant. It is possible that he deliberately chose not to spoil his marvelous account of Lincoln's visit to Richmond by following it with an account of the president's assassination.

GRATTAN SPICED HIS NARRATIVE of the North Atlantic Blockading Squadron's operations with incidents and anecdotes from his own and his shipmates' personal experiences. These recollections provide the best glimpses of Grattan's real war.

Like American sailors throughout history, Grattan spun yarns about being a greenhorn, shipboard routine, entertainment at sea, and what it was like to weather storms. He also focused on themes unique to his own era.

During the Civil War, although blacks were not permitted to enlist in the Union army until the latter part of 1862, they could always join the navy. From the very start of hostilities, southern blacks flocked to the vessels patrolling Rebel waters. Dubbed "contrabands" because they had been Confederate "property" and were therefore liable to "confiscation" as an act of war, they came in such numbers that Union naval commanders could not resist putting them to work. On 20 September 1861, Secretary of the Navy Gideon Welles declared that escaped slaves could be enlisted, but at "no higher rating than 'boys.'" The Union navy subsequently enlisted a greater proportion of blacks into its ranks than did the army.

Nevertheless, the Union navy treated African Americans as second-class sailors. Rear Admiral Porter's correspondence provides a window on how black sailors fared. Like many of his peers, Porter harbored racial prejudice, and often used the word "nigger." In the fall of 1862, Porter began "substituting contra-bands for [white] firemen and coal heavers," the dirtiest jobs on a steamer, not-ing that the blacks' lower pay reduced expenses. In July 1863, because of "increasing sickness in the squadron, and the scarcity of men," the admiral began recruiting large numbers of blacks for service in the Mississippi Squadron. "White men cannot stand the Southern sun," Porter reasoned, "an exposure to which inevitably brings on the disease of this climate, remittent fever. . . . The blacks must therefore be used altogether as boats' crews, or for duty requiring exposure to the sun." The admiral warned that blacks were not "naturally clean in their persons" and insisted that they be "exercised separately at great guns and small arms" and "kept distinct from the rest of the crew." In November 1864, he issued an order prohibiting his skippers from posting black sailors as lookouts, "as they are not fit to [be] intrusted with such important duty."

Despite such prejudice, even though the majority of black sailors occupied the lowest enlisted ratings of boy and landsman, some became petty officers. While most black petty officers served as cooks and stewards, a few became captains of the hold, captains of the foretop, carpenter's mates, coxswains, and even gunner's mates and quartermasters. Black sailors accounted for between 10 and 24 percent of the crew of warships, depending on time and place. The proportion rose even higher on service craft and sailing vessels. Many black sailors distinguished themselves in combat; eight received the Medal of Honor. All told, African Americans contributed decisively to winning their own free-dom.[52]

White Northerners displayed a broad range of attitudes toward black sol-diers, sailors, and slaves during the Civil War. Many a Yankee attributed the South's economic backwardness to the slave system, or commented on its moral depravity. Whether they saw slavery as an injustice that oppressed their fellow human beings or as a system that fostered bad economics, the majority of Northerners came to hate the South's peculiar institution.

By and large, white Northerners cared little about the plight of the slaves when they went to war. For some, firsthand experience with black soldiers, sailors, and slaves, particularly in combat, brought about a change of heart, precipitating greater respect for blacks. A few even came to admire African Americans.

This was not the norm. Despite their hatred for the institution of slavery, many Northerners continued to regard the blacks themselves as inferior human beings. Although the Emancipation Proclamation convinced the majority of Northern white soldiers and sailors that the war for the Union must be a war against slavery, many chafed at the idea of fighting to free the slaves. The common Union fighting man viewed Southern blacks with a mixture of pity, affection, disgust, and hatred. Northern soldiers and sailors often poked fun at the appearance, dress, or bearing of slaves and contrabands. Although escaped slaves tended to welcome Yankees, some observed that their former masters treated them far better than Union officers did. While firsthand experience with blacks diminished the racism of a few Northerners, most emerged from the war with their prejudices intact. In fact, the experience of the Civil War sometimes increased their racism.[53]

The only black sailors that Grattan wrote about were former slaves employed as servants on board the *Minnesota* and *Malvern*. They had names like Robert E. Lee and Moses and were regarded as comical figures. At best, the officers evinced paternal attitudes toward their black servants, whom they considered inferior beings. In stark contrast to his respect, even reverence, for his white shipmates, Grattan did not take black sailors seriously. He referred to them as "contrabands" or "darkeys," and noted that other officers called them "boy," "black rascal," and "black lump of India rubber." Racial stereotypes pepper his anecdotes involving black sailors, particularly their supposed penchant for music and dancing. Curiously, in terms of language and nuance, Grattan treated Southern blacks who remained in bondage and African American soldiers in the Union army with more respect than he did his black shipmates.

In contrast to the writings of many of his contemporaries, Grattan's memoir never denounces the South's peculiar institution. The words "slave" and "slavery" are absent from *Under the Blue Pennant*. Wartime service in close proximity to escaped slaves seems to have exacerbated rather than ameliorated the racial prejudice that Grattan brought to the war. The reality for Grattan, and for too many other white Northerners of his generation, was that the Civil War, fought to preserve the Union and to destroy slavery, did nothing to prevent the birth of Jim Crow in the United States and the return of Southern blacks to a condition approximating slavery after Reconstruction.

Reality also emerges in Grattan's anecdotes about the social interaction between Union naval officers and Norfolk's social aristocracy. The movie *Gone With the Wind* helped perpetuate the "moonlight and magnolias" view of antebellum plantation life, as well as the mythology of the "lost cause." Noble Southern aristocrats, loyal but ignorant slaves, rapacious carpetbaggers, lawless freedpeople, and Union soldiers out to loot and rape populate this racist fantasy. No Southern lady or gentleman would willingly seek the company of a damned Yankee in the world it portrays.

Under the Blue Pennant debunks part of this myth. According to Grattan, "the ladies of Norfolk possessing Union proclivities" frequently hosted gala affairs to which they invited Union naval officers.[54] Although it might seem surprising, the phenomenon of upper-class Southerners socializing with Union officers was not uncommon, even in Charleston. For example, Cornelius Marius Schoonmaker, serving on board the monitor *Catskill* in the spring of 1865, wrote his mother that Union naval officers were popular in that city. A frequent guest at dinners and balls hosted by Charleston's elite social circle, Schoonmaker made many friends among them.[55] The point is not that every Southern aristocrat welcomed Union naval officers with open arms, but that not every Southern aristocrat was a Scarlett O'Hara.

Northern women also appear in *Under the Blue Pennant* in social settings. For example, early in 1865, several women accompanied Major General George G. Meade and his staff on a visit to the *Malvern*. Admiral Porter entertained them in his "luxurious cabin," then took them on a tour of a nearby monitor. When the party entered the wardroom, one of the naval officers mentioned that because of the vessel's low-lying hull, they were actually several feet under the level of the water. Upon hearing this "the ladies scampered on deck like so many scared deer," noted Grattan, "which of course they were with a slight exception."[56] This sexist comment reflects the Victorian view that women belonged in the private, domestic world of wives and mothers.

The Civil War challenged this perception. Two weeks after the war began, women formed thousands of aid societies in the North and South to provide the armies with clothing, food, medical supplies, and money. Women volunteered as nurses in droves. The demand for their services quickly overwhelmed the reluctance of those who recoiled at the image of "refined, modest ladies . . . caring for strange men and crude soldiers from all walks of life." During the war women also worked as teachers, writers, factory hands, and spies. A few even donned uniforms, assumed male identities, and served in combat units. Despite his sexism, Grattan acknowledged women's participation in the public sphere by paying tribute to those "young ladies who had voluntarily abandoned the comforts of home in order to attend to the wounded and dying soldier whose recovery or peaceful exit from the world could only be soothed by a woman's tender and gentle ministrations."[57]

Victorian propriety prevented Grattan from writing explicitly about sex. Yet sex, or at least the desire for female companionship, appears implicitly in *Under the Blue Pennant* in a pair of very peculiar anecdotes. "Amusements upon a man-of-war," as Grattan put it, is a recurrent theme in his memoir. Popular off-duty pastimes included letter writing, spinning yarns, and music. Along with music went dancing. "In the absence of ladies for partners we would be compelled to select the most light and airy to fill their place," noted Grattan. One interesting exception was the rotund Acting Ensign John M. Cowan, who "always insisted upon being a lady" and whose "waist and other general dimensions

[were] about the size of the butt of a XV-inch gun." On one occasion, Lieutenant Joseph P. Fyffe demonstrated some dance steps he had learned in Spain, leading the other officers' "imaginations to wander to the beautiful ladies whose waists he had encircled in that far off clime." On another occasion, the officers of the flagship entertained themselves by putting on a "grand ballet divertissement with the graceful Mr. Cowan as premier" and some of the younger officers attired in a "scanty feminine wardrobe."

Grattan characterized the "ballet" as a comical event, but the image of officers dressed in drag and dancing with one another might lead modern readers to speculate about homosexuality on board the flagship. Victorians considered homosexuality indecent, immoral, a violation of nature. Although written references to homosexual behavior during the Civil War very rarely surface, it certainly occurred. But just because the officers on board the flagship dressed as women and danced with each other, it doesn't mean that they were having sex with each other. Heterosexual men dancing together or dressing in drag are phenomena that cross temporal and cultural boundaries. The morality and sense of honor that Grattan projected in *Under the Blue Pennant* mark him as a Victorian gentleman, and virtually no gentleman of that era would write about what he considered immoral behavior without condemning it. Although there might have been an exception that Grattan remained unaware of, he and his shipmates dressed in drag and danced with one another simply because they missed the company of women.[58]

Officers almost never associated with sailors, for they regarded "the men" as belonging to a lower and inferior social class. In fact, during the age of sail officers considered enlisted men as the scum of the earth. Officers tended to adopt a condescending or patronizing attitude toward sailors instead of respecting them as fellow shipmates, a condition which persists to some degree today. In Grattan's time, it was considered an insult to refer to an officer as a "sailor." As a result, officers accorded themselves better quarters, better food, better uniforms, and more privileges than they granted the enlisted men, often to the embitterment of the sailors. Herman Melville, who served in the navy during the age of sail, bristled with indignity at how the officers treated the enlisted men. In contrast, officers regarded the officer corps as a brotherhood. Relationships between seniors and juniors were far less constrained than those between officers and men.[59]

The flagship's constant travels around the squadron's area of responsibility, the squadron's involvement in joint operations, and the fact that officers from other vessels reported to the admiral almost daily brought Grattan into contact with a wide variety of Union soldiers and sailors. After conducting business with the admiral, many officers often remained on board the flagship to rest, eat, drink, and regale Grattan and his shipmates with tales of their adventures.

This included foreigners. One group deserves special mention. Beginning in the fall of 1863, ten warships and some forty-five hundred men of the Imperial Russian Navy visited New York, Annapolis, Washington, San Francisco,

Hampton Roads, and other American cities. Whether to improve their strategic position vis-à-vis Britain and France, to show off their new war steamers, or to put on a show of strength on behalf of the Union out of friendship and an interest in a strong United States, the Russian naval visit was one of the great diplomatic and social moments of the Civil War. The Russians invaded New York City first. New Yorkers turned out in droves to greet the Tsar's sailors as they paraded from Pier 1 along Twenty-Third Street, down Broadway, past a huge Russian flag displayed at Tiffany's (then at 550 Broadway), and on to City Hall. Prominent Yankees hosted numerous receptions and dinners for Russian officers at fancy New York hotels. A lavish dinner and ball, catered by Delmonico's and featuring two fifty-piece bands and a giant model of a Russian ship suspended from the ceiling, capped the visit to New York. Russian naval officers and enlisted men received similar grand welcomes at other American cities. Their appearance bolstered Union morale and helped prevent Britain and France from taking more action than they did on behalf of the Confederacy.[60]

Grattan saw the Russian ships when they dropped anchor in Hampton Roads on Christmas Day 1863. Fort Monroe greeted them with a gunfire salute. Union naval officers hosted dinners and receptions for their Russian counterparts. Grattan rubbed elbows with Russian officers at one or more of these affairs. He liked the Russians, referring to them as "foreign brothers in arms." He said that visiting with them enabled him and his shipmates to forget about the war for awhile.

Grattan made a broad range of acquaintances and friends during the war. Those whom he admired most appear in *Under the Blue Pennant*. The only individual whom he openly criticized was Ben Butler. Otherwise, Grattan's portraits of individuals are paeans akin to those he painted of Admirals Lee and Porter. William Bunker, the boatswain of the *Minnesota*, was a "perfect specimen of an American man-of-war's man" and a "master of his profession." Lieutenant Commander John H. Upshur was "a favorite of the officers and men, and it was [their] unanimous opinion [that] a more affable gentleman or better officer never graced the quarter deck."[61]

Grattan's greatest praise fell upon the legendary Will Cushing. He wrote at length about the destruction of the *Albemarle*. The ubiquitous Cushing also distinguished himself at Fort Fisher, sounding the channel in an open boat directly under the guns of the fort during the fleet's Christmas day 1864 bombardment and serving ashore with the Naval Brigade in the climactic attack on 15 January 1865.

Even though Grattan did not accompany Cushing on any of these exploits, he devoted a significant portion of *Under the Blue Pennant* to Cushing because Cushing ranked among the greatest heroes of the Civil War and because Grattan knew him personally. The two probably met early in 1864 and crossed paths time and again for the rest of the war. They served together on the *Malvern* in December 1864, when Cushing was in temporary command of that vessel.

It is obvious that Grattan liked and admired Cushing. In fact, he stood in awe of him. Consequently his portrayal of Cushing is nothing but unabashed hero worship. "If there was one officer in the squadron whose name should be handed down to posterity and take equal rank with all those naval heroes whose lives are perpetuated in the pages of history," Grattan gushed when he introduced his idol, "that gallant officer should be Lieutenant Commander William B. Cushing." Grattan described him as a brave, cool, competent, modest, and self-possessed man who was strict with the enlisted men and who often laughed and joked with his brother officers.[62]

Nevertheless, Cushing had his faults. Following the war one newspaper editor described him as the "most ineffable, idiotic young snob that ever trod leather" and an "egotistical ass" who had "blundered into notoriety." After reading this account Cushing strode into the editor's office and lashed him with a rawhide whip. Cushing's biographers balanced their generally positive evaluation of him by pointing out that he was hot-blooded and quick to see an insult. If Grattan perceived similar flaws in Cushing's character, he never acknowledged them in writing. Instead, he focused exclusively on Cushing's deeds and chivalrous bearing.[63]

Grattan's sketches of fallen shipmates were equally romantic. He felt compelled to commemorate those who had been "killed in action" or who had "rendered invaluable aid to the service." One such comrade was Acting Master Charles B. Wilder, who served for a time as the *Minnesota*'s executive officer. Grattan described Wilder as "a very modest pleasant man and a thorough sailor," who "by his own merits had risen step by step in the service." While leading a picked crew of sailors on a raid against Confederate forces near Smithfield, Virginia, Wilder died when a bullet pierced his skull.[64]

Two other fallen shipmates whom Grattan memorialized were Lieutenants Samuel W. Preston of Illinois and Benjamin H. Porter of New York. Preston, Porter, and Cushing had been friends since their days together at the Naval Academy. Preston and Porter were captured by the Confederates during the disastrous Union boat attack on Fort Sumter on 9 September 1863 and released a year later in a prisoner exchange. Both men volunteered for duty with the Naval Brigade and were killed on 15 January 1865 near the palisade of Fort Fisher. Grattan described them as gallant and brave officers. Although "quite broken down in health" by their confinement in Confederate prisons, when they heard "of the contemplated movement against Wilmington, they sacrificed all the comforts and pleasures of home in which they stood in so much need, and reported to the Secretary of the Navy for active service."[65]

Grattan commemorated the deeds not only of fallen shipmates, but also of other North Atlantic Blockading officers whom he considered outstanding. One such man was the "generous, good, and gallant" Lieutenant Commander Charles W. Flusser, whose "untimely death was a real and great loss to the public service." Flusser died in battle against the *Albemarle*.[66]

Grattan wrote about such men because he admired their courage. Civil War sailors and soldiers valued courage above all other attributes of a man's character. They defined courage as taking heroic action without showing fear. Men especially esteemed those who remained cool even though they recognized the dangers and terrors of battle. Courage was never taken for granted; it had to be demonstrated in battle. The best ways to do so were by aggressive offensive action or by remaining cool and controlled under fire. Wounds acquired in courageous action were prized as badges of honor; to be killed in courageous action was the ultimate expression of honor. In commemorating the heroic deaths of brave comrades, Grattan paid them the ultimate compliment.[67]

Grattan had several opportunities to test his own courage. The flagship came under fire or otherwise operated in harm's way much of the time, particularly in the James, where the threat from Confederate torpedoes or snipers remained almost constant. Grattan and his shipmates shared the danger whenever the Confederates targeted the flagship. He was on board the *Minnesota* when the *Squib* attacked her on 9 April 1864; on board the *Malvern* when she came under fire from Confederate shore batteries and ironclads in the James on 21 June; and again on the *Malvern* when she came under fire during the bombardment of Fort Fisher on 24 December. Grattan at least twice experienced being the target himself. On 9 May 1864, he and several brother officers came under fire from Confederate snipers hiding along the bank of the James. The Union officers returned fire with muskets. In his diary, Grattan proudly claimed to have killed one of the Rebels. He omitted mention of the killing from *Under the Blue Pennant*. Perhaps the pride had worn off by the time he sat down to write the memoir. Later in May or early in June, he volunteered to go ashore for a raid. Upon returning to the ship Grattan and the others in the raiding party withstood an attack by Rebel cavalry.

Grattan never admitted to experiencing fear in *Under the Blue Pennant*. Instead of expressing how he felt under fire, he focused on how his comrades behaved. "Well knowing that one shot well aimed would completely destroy the flagship," he wrote of the 21 June 1864 engagement with Rebel shore batteries and ironclads, "it is with great satisfaction I can testify as to the bravery, fearlessness, and courage of her officers and crew." He made a similar but more impersonal observation of the bombardment of Fort Fisher: "Shot and shell could be heard screaming and bursting all around us but the *Malvern* seemed to be invincible." He recounted how the men laughed when a shell splashing near the bow drenched them with water, and how Porter coolly directed the fire of the fleet while shells flew about. Although *Under the Blue Pennant* rarely mentions how Grattan behaved and never how he felt under fire, he seems to have acquitted himself acceptably.[68]

In his diary, however, Grattan did express apprehension on one occasion. The original plans for the first Fort Fisher expedition called for the fleet bombardment and army landing to commence on 19 December 1864. On the eighteenth, Grattan wrote: "This is the night before the battle. As I sit here my thoughts wander to home, and to the fair girl who I have promised to make my wife. If I should be killed in this engagement my last breath will be to echo her name and to bid my father & mother, sisters & brothers good bye."[69] He never penned a similar admission again.

Grattan had no qualms about commenting on the spectacle of battle. Of the explosion of the powder ship *Louisiana*, he wrote: "Suddenly a bright flash was observed and a stream of flames ascended to a great height and spread out in an immense sheet of fire, illuminating for an instant the whole horizon. In a few seconds a loud report followed by a deep booming roar told us General Butler's experiment had been tried." One of *Under the Blue Pennant*'s most eloquent passages describes the bombardment of Fisher on 13 January 1865: "At sunset the firing was at its greatest fury. The scene from the *Malvern* was one of the wildest, the most exciting and at the same time most awful and sublime that the human imagination can possibly conceive." These passages, along with those devoted to heroic deeds, indicate that Grattan reveled in what J. Glenn Gray called the "secret attractions" of war: "the delight in seeing, the delight in comradeship, the delight in destruction."[70]

Despite its omnipresence during the Civil War, disease is absent from *Under the Blue Pennant*. So rampant was disease that one historian called it "natural biological warfare." Twice as many Union soldiers died of disease as of battle (Union battle deaths numbered 110,000; 224,580 died of disease). Disease struck soldiers in two waves. The first resulted from childhood diseases such as measles, mumps, and smallpox. City-bred soldiers who had developed immunities during youth fared better than country boys who had grown up in isolation and had never been exposed before joining the service. The second wave consisted of "camp diseases," such as dysentery, malaria, and diarrhea, which plagued soldiers throughout the war. The disease picture differed slightly for the navy. Some 2,784 sailors died of illness during the war; 1,804 were killed in action. The lower ratio of men who died from disease to those killed in battle in the navy might be attributable to better sanitary conditions on ships than in army camps, but yellow fever, malaria, and venereal diseases afflicted sailors throughout the war. Perhaps Grattan ignored disease in *Under the Blue Pennant* because there was no glory or heroism in it.[71]

Grattan recounted only one episode of noncombat death in his memoir. In January 1864, a sailor being punished in "double irons"—with both hands and feet manacled—fell from the bridge of the *Minnesota* into the water, striking his head against the muzzle of a gun protruding from a lower deck on the way down. He sank straight to the bottom and never surfaced. "By daylight next morning," Grattan noted, "the circumstance of the death of one of the ship's crew appeared to be almost forgotten."[72]

On the surface this comment seems cold, but it demonstrates the harsh reality of how Civil War fighting men dealt with death. Historian Gerald Linderman has observed that "nineteenth-century Americans were well acquainted with chronic illness and death, especially infant mortality, in ways that must have generated some emotional callus." Victorian Americans emphasized death as an escape from the trials, tribulations, and pain of life and an opportunity for a better life with God. Grattan and his shipmates reacted to the death of comrades with both anger and anguish, then bade them good-bye with the ritual of shipboard funeral services. Grattan noted that on one occasion, when Admiral Lee learned that Confederate sharpshooters had killed several of his men engaged in attempting to board a beached blockade runner, "he gave orders for the fleet to open fire and completely destroy the blockade runner and shell the beach." In describing the funeral for Charles Wilder, Grattan noted that "nearly every eye was filled with tears, and the old Admiral [Lee] who had faced death so many times and lost so many comrades could not restrain his emotion." Grattan and his shipmates felt the agony of their loss as much as anyone, but could do little to indulge their feelings beyond fighting back and holding funerals. They simply could not afford to dwell too long on dying, for duty demanded that they move on.[73]

Yet images of death must have haunted Grattan's thoughts long after the shooting stopped. Even though nineteenth-century Americans were more familiar than their twentieth-century successors with hunting wild animals and dressing their carcasses, slaughtering livestock, and killing, gutting, and plucking poultry, they still experienced profound shock during their initial encounter with human bodies mangled by bullets or shell fragments. Many soldiers and sailors never forgot the first time they saw a comrade die, or when they saw their first corpse. Of those killed at Shiloh, one veteran wrote: "I can never forget the impression those wide open dead eyes made on me." A veteran of Chancellorsville wrote: "Our line of battle extended over some eight miles and for that distance you see the dead bodies of the enemy lying in every direction, some with their heads shot off, some with their brains oozing out, some pierced through the head with musket balls, some with their noses shot away, some with their mouths smashed, some wounded in the neck, some with broken arms or legs, some shot through the breast and some cut in two with shells."[74]

While Grattan romanticized the dead in *Under the Blue Pennant*, he never romanticized death. In stark contrast to his romantic character sketches, he wrote of death with graphic realism. The brains of the "poor sailor" whose head struck the gun as he fell to his death from the *Minnesota*'s bridge "were undoubtedly dashed out before he reached the waves." When the rebel ironclad *Albemarle* put a shot through the *Sassacus*'s boiler, "instantly every part of the ship was filled with steam" and "above the din of battle the groans and screams of the wounded and scalded sailors could be distinctly heard." In recalling when he saw the bodies of Lieutenants Porter and Preston, he felt moved to write that "a calm peaceful smile played around [Porter's] mouth; but Preston wore a look of agony as his sufferings must have been terrible."

At Fort Fisher Grattan encountered death on a larger scale than anywhere else in his wartime travels. He and several shipmates walked the battlefield after Union forces captured the fort. "With some difficulty we managed to ascend the steep side of the fort nearest the sea, and stood upon the parapet from which a clear and uninterrupted view could be obtained of the interior and exterior of the immense earthworks. All around us in every conceivable attitude lay the dead and mangled bodies of both rebel and union soldiers." Grattan observed that several rebel cannon were still in good working order. "One of the guns was splattered with blood and brains of a Rebel gunner."[75]

Grattan's most grisly image of death was rendered not in prose but in paint. It is an image from his tour of Fort Fisher. The perspective is that of a Confederate defender inside the fort looking out toward the Atlantic. The background is a peaceful scene. One ship swings at anchor on a calm sea. Others sail or steam lazily by. Birds fly overhead. The foreground is a vision of hell. It is strewn with broken cannon, shell fragments, and unidentifiable debris. Scattered among the wreckage lay dismembered corpses and body parts; here a headless body, there an arm, a head nearby, a torso up on a mound. Red blood stains the sand near each fragment of humanity. It is a crude painting, but it conveys the reality of the Civil War's human cost like few others. Photographs of corpses by Mathew Brady, Alexander Gardner, and their contemporaries were shocking enough in their time, but they usually depicted whole bodies, often without the wound being visible.

Grattan's painting not only portrays combat death more graphically, but it also demonstrates that no product of the human mind, whether words, pictures, or anything else, can ever communicate what war is really like. Movies have attempted to replicate the sound of the battlefield, but no medium has ever reproduced its smell or its terror or its pain. Simply put, it is impossible for those who have experienced battle to convey what it is like to those who have not. A weak analogy is to try to explain to a nonparent what it's like to have a child. Words or pictures cannot convey how it feels to put your life on the line for cause and comrades or to watch brave and honorable people die painful, horrible deaths. To attempt to convey war's reality is noble and necessary. No politician should ever send American sons and daughters to war without having some sense of what they're asking. Every responsible American should read Eugene Sledge's *With the Old Breed* or some similar book to at least approach an understanding.[76] But to really know what war is like, there is simply no substitute for being there.

Walt Whitman recognized that the Civil War was no "quadrille in a ballroom."[77] For both Grattan and Whitman, "the real war" was the price paid by the dead and wounded. Whether Grattan brought alcoholism to the Civil War or developed the disease as a result of experiencing it cannot be known. But it is safe to say that he never recovered from either.

UNDER THE BLUE PENNANT was a fortuitous find. I discovered it in the midst of doing long-term research for a book about the combat experiences of Civil

Death and destruction inside Fort Fisher, by John W. Grattan (Naval Historical Center NH 50469-KN)

War sailors. Because *Under the Blue Pennant* is virtually a finished product, I opted to put my long-term research on the back burner and prepare Grattan's memoir for publication.

It is not clear when Grattan wrote *Under the Blue Pennant*, but the idea to write about the war occurred to him on the eve of the first Fort Fisher expedition. On 1 December 1864, he wrote his parents:

> I will give you a piece of information, which is *confidential* and not to go out of our family on any account whatever.
>
> General Grant is ready with his men and we will attack *Wilmington* in 5 days from now. . . . Keep your eyes open for newspaper accounts, and I wish you would keep every paper. Get Frank Leslies and Harpers Weekly every week and keep them home[.] I will pay for them. I am anxious to keep full account of this fight, which will be the grandest naval fight of the world either in ancient or modern history. If I come out all right I shall feel proud to say I participated in the splendid engagement.[78]

After the war Grattan evidently decided to expand this idea into a full account of his naval service.

Although Grattan did not cite his sources, it is obvious that he based *Under the Blue Pennant* on his own personal observations and opinions, his memory, the diary he kept during the war, and the official records of the North Atlantic

Blockading Squadron, to which he had access as the squadron commander's clerk. Several of Grattan's paragraphs closely resemble passages in the official correspondence, particularly Lee and Porter's dispatches to Secretary Welles. Either Grattan kept copies of the official records or did research after the war at the Navy Department, which held the squadron archives until they were published after Grattan's death in the multivolume series *Official Records of the Union and Confederate Navies in the War of the Rebellion.* I did not try to run down every bit of information in *Under the Blue Pennant,* but I did cite those documents in the *Official Records* that Grattan apparently used for particular passages. My editorial comments include a few extra details from his diary and, where necessary, explanations to clarify the text.

In editing the work, I intruded as little as possible on Grattan's organization and narrative style. I silently corrected his spelling and at times his grammar; inserted full names and ranks where individuals first appear in the text; and added dates to clarify certain passages. The organization of the text and the witty Victorian prose remain the work of John W. Grattan.

Under the Blue Pennant

or

Notes of a Naval Officer

John W. Grattan
Acting Ensign, United States Navy

Preface

Receiving an appointment in the United States Navy while the great Civil War was raging, I was attached to the staff of Acting Rear Admiral Samuel Phillips Lee who was in command of the North Atlantic Blockading Squadron, and upon his detachment I was ordered to report for duty on the staff of his successor Rear Admiral David D. Porter.

Having unlimited facilities at my command for observation and control over the archives of the squadron I availed myself of the opportunity by keeping a diary of the interesting events as they occurred from which I have compiled this volume.

To the survivors of the army and navy who participated in that terrible struggle as well as those who have forgotten or never knew of the incidents here recorded I trust will find the following pages interesting and instructive.

John W. Grattan
late Acting Ensign, U.S. Navy

1

The Baltimore steamer *Louisiana* ◆ Scenes on the passage to
Fortress Monroe ◆ Arrival at Norfolk ◆ The city after dark ◆
Ruins of the Gosport Navy Yard ◆ The U.S. Steamer *Florida* ◆
An agreeable exchange ◆ Ordered to the frigate *Minnesota* ◆
Newport News and the wrecks of the *Congress* and *Cumberland*
destroyed by the *Merrimack* ◆ The flagship *Minnesota* ◆
Admiral S. P. Lee ◆ The North Atlantic Blockading Squadron ◆
[October 1863]

IN THE MONTH OF OCTOBER IN THE YEAR 1863 the U.S. Mail and passenger
steamer *Louisiana* left her wharf at Baltimore bound for Fortress Monroe with
her decks crowded with as motley an assemblage of human beings as could be
brought together. All were going to the seat of war and many unconsciously yet
fearlessly were hastening to their grave. The most cheerful among the passengers were young, giddy, dashing officers who had never as yet experienced the
horrors of war, and the voyage to them was an excursion of pleasure. The laugh
and joke or witty repartee had the effect of banishing any gloomy forebodings
if any existed. Several others whose features bronzed by hard service proved to
be veterans returning to duty after recovering from the effects of disease or
wounds received in action, and a few whose pale, weak, and emaciated condition bore witness of long confinement and suffering in rebel prisons. Conspicuous for their color and the looseness of their wearing apparel were the
inevitable "contrabands" whose broad grin and grotesque movements were
source of constant amusement to all. Although the number of officers, soldiers,
and sailors was large, they did not appear to eclipse the swarm of sutlers, army
contractors, correspondents, and hospital nurses. Among the latter were a number of young ladies who had voluntarily abandoned the comforts of home in
order to attend to the wounded and dying soldier whose recovery or peaceful
exit from the world could only be soothed by a woman's tender and gentle
ministrations.

It was quite dark when the steamer entered the broad bosom of the Chesapeake and after supper violins, banjos and singing could be heard on the lower
deck accompanied with dancing by the happy darkeys who but a few months
previous were hoeing corn or picking cotton on the Southern plantations. In the
saloon a more quiet, but a far more dangerous spectacle was in progress. Every
table was crowded with officers and civilians "going it blind." An infatuated

55

View of Fort Monroe from the Chesapeake Bay (Courtesy of Robert M. Browning, Jr.)

player flushed with temporary success suddenly found his "flush" not worth a "cent," as a "full hand" held by a sutler whose rosy features denoted he was always "full" appeared against him. Many old soldiers watched the exciting play; but few were tempted to risk their hard-earned dollars. Throughout the entire night the game continued, and a large number were so infatuated as to regret when the gong sounded for breakfast.

After a very rapid and pleasant passage down the Bay, Old Point Comfort was reached and the *Louisiana* made fast to the wharf under the guns of Fortress Monroe. The U.S. Steamer *Florida*, to which vessel I had been ordered, was lying at the Gosport Navy Yard undergoing repairs, making it necessary for me to take passage on the Norfolk boat in order to report for duty. [Had Grattan sailed on the *Florida*, he might have spent his entire naval service on blockade duty.] While sailing up the Elizabeth River an excellent view could be obtained of the several objects of interest. In the distance at the mouth of the James River could be seen the flagship *Minnesota* surrounded by her formidable satellites, on blockading duty guarding the only navigable entrance to Richmond. After passing Craney Island the scenery would have been beautiful were it not for the ruin and desolation constantly before my eyes. On either bank of the river broken chimneys and charred timbers marked the spot where before the war had been elegant mansions. The fields and meadows were disfigured with abandoned earthworks and batteries without guns. In the river buoys marked the locality of sunken vessels and one in particular denoted the position of the ram *Merrimack* which had caused such terrible destruction and loss of life in the James River. These silent monuments of ruin and devastation on the banks of the Elizabeth made everyone realize to a certain extent the effects resulting from the bloody war.

Arriving in Norfolk after sunset not a light could be seen. Owing to the absence of gas the city was in total darkness. A few solitary candles here and there only served to increase the gloom. After considerable difficulty the Atlantic Hotel was discovered and I was made as comfortable as the landlord's limited facilities would allow. The city being under martial law, the streets were quite deserted except by the patrol guard; but for all the care and protection which I knew was extended by our troops I felt about as cheerful as if I was passing the night in a graveyard.

A bright morning changed the dreary scene, and after a breakfast of hoe-cake [a small cake made of cornmeal] and coffee, I crossed the river to Portsmouth and arrived at the Navy Yard. Upon passing the marine guard at the entrance a scene of utter ruin and destruction burst upon my view. In every direction brick and stone walls and broken chimneys were all that remained of handsome large buildings and workshops. The only house remaining was the one occupied by the commandant. Before the war this navy yard was considered to be the finest and most complete of any in the country, but upon the evacuation of Norfolk the enemy left it a mass of ruins, and sank, burned and totally destroyed several men-of-war lying at the docks. Temporary repairs had since been made and the facilities, although limited, were sufficient to enable our vessels to be kept in fighting order and in a seaworthy condition.

The U.S.S. *Florida* was undergoing considerable repairs preparatory to making her appearance upon the Wilmington blockade. She was formerly in the merchant service; but with a few alterations and a number of guns made a very fair warship. My stay upon her was very short. A young officer being then attached to the *Minnesota* having a great desire for prize money was willing to leave that splendid frigate and offered to exchange his position for mine. Nothing could have pleased me better, and as no objections were made by our respective captains I was appointed to the *Minnesota*.

The North Atlantic Squadron at that time was under the command of Acting Rear Admiral Samuel Phillips Lee, an old veteran of the sea, whose hair had grown gray in the service. He was a strict disciplinarian but in his cabin would occasionally unbend his solemn features and laugh heartily at a good joke or yarn. Nothing escaped his sharp penetrating eye, and it is believed by many he never slept, as it was a very common occurrence to see him come on deck after midnight and walk for hours upon the bridge, in deep thought and meditation. His pipe was his constant companion, and upon one occasion after breakfasting with him he invited me to try one of his pipes and some tobacco presented to him by friends in Virginia. Although young in years I was a great smoker and after giving the tobacco a fair trial and filling the cabin with smoke I informed him it was the best I had ever smoked, which so pleased him that he told me to load up again.

The *Minnesota* was a first class frigate of 3,307 tons and mounted a battery of fifty-two heavy guns. She was entitled to a complement of about seven-hundred

Rear Admiral Samuel Phillips Lee (Courtesy of Robert M. Browning, Jr.)

men, and being the flagship of the squadron had many more officers on board than she would have required as a regular man-of-war.

Being anchored near Newport News we lay but a short distance from the wreck of the *Congress* whose burned hull could be seen near the beach, and a few yards farther up the river the water covered the *Cumberland* and her gallant crew who sank with her, firing the guns as she went down, both vessels having been destroyed some nineteen months previous by the *Merrimack*.

The exigency of the service required the presence of every available seaworthy vessel upon the Wilmington Blockade and consequently the naval force at the mouth of the James River was not very large. The three-turreted razeed frigate *Roanoke* [to "razee" a ship was to cut down or reduce the number of decks; the *Roanoke* was the Civil War's only three-turreted ironclad, converted from a *Merrimack*-class frigate] lay a short distance up the river with steam always up and ready to move and try her heavy guns on the rebel rams which

USS *Merrimack*, circa 1856. The *Minnesota* resembled her sister ship. (Naval Historical Center NH 46248)

were known to be at Richmond. Several other vessels with heavy batteries but no speed were kept on the station and all were anxiously waiting for the enemy to come down the river.

The North Atlantic Blockading Squadron was composed of fifty-six vessels; but only twenty could be pronounced in a seaworthy condition. These were kept constantly on the Wilmington blockade and the others were stationed in the sounds of North Carolina, Hampton Roads, Chesapeake Bay, and the James, Nansemond, Elizabeth, and York rivers. To keep this small squadron in working order, the greatest energy and increasing vigilance of the admiral was required. The great demand for naval vessels at Charleston, Mobile Bay and in the Mississippi where hostilities were in progress was the principal cause which impaired the efficiency of our squadron; but in spite of the many disadvantages and the limited facilities for repairs at the Norfolk Navy Yard the vessels on the Wilmington blockade inflicted great damage to the blockade running interests of foreign and rebel capitalists.

2

Life on a man-of-war • The jolly boatswain • My experience on the main top • General Butler ordered to assume command of the Department of Virginia and North Carolina • His interview with the admiral • An inspection of the defenses in the sounds of North Carolina • The rebel ram • The admiral inspects the Wilmington blockade • Floating torpedoes discovered in James River • The return of the admiral • Captain Upshur in command of the frigate • The officers attached to the vessel • The admiral again starts for the blockade in the *Fahkee* • The *Minnesota* directed to prepare for sea and join him off Fort Fisher • [October–December 1863]

IN SPITE OF THE MANY trials, hardships, and vexations upon a man-of-war, there were seasons of relaxation which presented much pleasure and happiness, and the longer a man was in the service the better he liked it. From sunset to eight o'clock, all hands except those on watch assembled in groups on the forecastle [forward end of the upper main deck between the foremast and head] and sang or listened to the violin or guitar. The young men gathered around the old salts who were proud to give them a song or a yarn. Upon the frigate were several plantation darkies and many of them could sing and dance. Almost every night their services were brought into requisition and the roars of laughter which greeted their comical efforts could be heard in the admiral's cabin. In the wardroom [the space in a warship allotted for living and messing quarters for the commissioned officers, except the captain of the ship and the commander of the squadron], the officers who by right of rank are entitled to enter that *sanctum sanctorum* throw off their quarter-deck dignity and reserve, and if not as noisy are as free easy and jolly as the bluejackets on the forecastle. [The quarterdeck is the upper deck to the rear of the mainmast. Naval etiquette required all persons to salute upon coming on the quarterdeck and to behave correctly while on it. The starboard side in port and the weather side at sea were reserved for the commanding and executive officers and the officer of the deck.] If it was a clear moonlight night many ascended to the spar deck [the uppermost deck that extended the length of the vessel], and for hours the clean white quarter-deck resounded with the measured tread of the officer of the deck and his volunteer watch.

The boatswain [a warrant officer in charge of the ship's deck force, rigging, boats, cargo gear, deck gear, deck stores, and general maintenance work] of the *Minnesota* was a perfect specimen of an American man-of-wars-man. Born in New England Mr. William Bunker at an early age entered the service and for nearly thirty years he had known no home but a man-of-war. The appearance of the frigate proved him to be a master of his profession. After the day's duty was over he would join the steerage officers in their games or songs and for hours would keep the table in a roar of laughter at his dry yarns. [The steerage was that part of the berth deck, usually forward of the wardroom, reserved for junior officers.]

A few days after I had joined the ship I made the acquaintance of the boatswain under very peculiar circumstances; but we were ever afterwards great friends. He entered the steerage one evening and with a very solemn face informed us the enemy were firing musketry and burning buildings only a short distance up the river near the army lines, and as I afterwards found for my own benefit, said an excellent view of the conflagration could be obtained in the main top [a semicircular platform resting upon the trestle trees of the lower main mast; it served as a working floor and a vantage point for sharpshooters]. Being very young and full of curiosity I went on deck and began climbing the shrouds [ropes belonging to the standing rigging of a ship, used to support masts and spars and as a means for climbing aloft]. Before I had proceeded far up the ratlines [small lines traversing the shrouds parallel with the water, which serve as a series of steps in a ladderlike arrangement for climbing aloft] all my messmates including the colored steward and our boy Robert E. Lee who was as black as the ace of spades were on deck watching my agility as I thought. I was soon standing on the main top; but although it was a beautiful moonlight night, could see nothing of the terrible destruction. The thought at once flashed upon me that I was the victim of a practical joke as none of my companions had accompanied me. As I was about to descend to the deck my attention was called to a number of bluejackets [seamen as distinct from marines] rapidly coming up the shrouds on both sides, and in a moment I was surrounded. The leader expressed himself as glad to see me in such an elevated position and asked me if I had paid my footing. Being in total ignorance of the meaning of his remarks I asked him for an explanation, and informed that it was the custom for every officer to pay his footing or initiation when he honored the main top with a visit for the first time. Not wishing to render any of the sailors incapacitated for duty which would result from intoxication I regret to say I tried to escape by sliding down one of the stays. I was quickly secured and bound with rope yarn when I begged for quarter and promised to pay my footing. I was then allowed to descend to the deck with many thanks for my *liberality*. None of my messmates were present but the broad grinning face of Robert E. Lee beamed upon me from the hatch way, who seeing me coming made a hasty retreat before I could make any impression upon him.

The dull and monotonous life incidental to the blockading service began to be felt by the officers and crew when we learned with pleasure that Major General Benjamin F. Butler was ordered to Fortress Monroe to assume command of the department of Virginia and North Carolina [departments comprised the basic territorial subdivisions of Union forces], and it was anticipated that active operations would soon be resumed. Upon the arrival of the general he called upon the admiral and a plan was arranged for a military and naval inspection of our forces in the sounds of North Carolina and on the Wilmington blockade.

The *Minnesota* being too heavy a vessel to be used on coast or river service the admiral temporarily transferred his flag to the U.S. Steamer *Fahkee*, and General Butler and staff established themselves on board the Army transport *Spaulding* [the Union army had its own transport and logistics vessels]. All the preparations being completed, on the 18th of November 1863 the two vessels put to sea.

On the evening after the departure of the admiral the enemy began to show signs of activity in the James River. Several suspicious objects were discovered floating with the ebb tide past the *Minnesota*. The *Roanoke* being a considerable distance up the river appeared to take no notice of them as they floated by her. A cutter was lowered and one of the strangers was picked up and towed ashore, where our suspicions were verified. It proved to be a torpedo containing about seventy-five pounds of powder and intended to explode by striking against the bows or sides of a vessel. No accident occurred to the fleet; but the attempt had a very beneficial effect as greater vigilance was maintained on every ship.

New Bern, Washington, Plymouth and Roanoke Island were visited and inspected by the admiral and General Butler. To maintain possession of these important points a strong military and naval force was necessary. The naval vessels had to be constantly on the alert as it was known by the admiral and his officers the enemy were engaged in constructing a formidable ironclad ram [the CSS *Albemarle*] for the purpose of driving the wooden vessels out of the sounds and assist in recapturing the fortifications held by our troops. The admiral informed General Butler of the preparations being made by the rebels, and suggested that a few old hulks should be sunk in the channel above Plymouth to prevent the ram from coming down the river; but the general did not deem it necessary, and expressed his unconcern about the ram as the only evidence of its existence was the unasked testimony of rebel deserters. This may have been very wise reasoning of the learned Massachusetts lawyer, but subsequent events proved that if the admiral's simple advice had been carried out the terrible disaster and loss of life which followed would not have occurred.

After a very hasty inspection of the troops and defenses General Butler did not think it necessary to visit the blockading fleet and view the rebel fortifica-

Major General Benjamin
Franklin Butler (Library of
Congress LC-B8172-1406)

tions. At that time Fort Fisher swarmed with men and was being rapidly
pushed to completion, and it might have been of great benefit to the general if
he had seen the work, to guide him in future operations against it.

The admiral continued the inspection of his fleet and then returned to the
mouth of the James River.

Lieutenant Commander John H. Upshur arrived a few days after with
orders to take command of the frigate *Minnesota* and under direction of the
admiral we commenced preparations for sea. The new captain soon made himself a favorite of the officers and men, and it was the unanimous opinion a more
affable gentleman or better officer never graced the quarter deck. The crew
were soon brought into a high state of discipline, and their happiness and comfort as well as his officers' were his constant studies.

As it may gratify the curiosity of the uninitiated to know the personnel of
the officers on board of the flagship I will insert it here [the list includes a few
of the *Minnesota*'s personnel as well as the squadron commander's staff]:

Executive Officer: Lieutenant Joseph P. Fyffe
Fleet Surgeon: William Maxwell Wood
Fleet Paymaster: Charles C. Upham
Fleet Engineer: Benjamin F. Garvin

Admiral's Secretary: Mr. Van Blunt

Assistant Surgeons: Gustavus S. Franklin, William S. Fort, and Arthur
    Matthewson

Chaplain: Thomas G. Salter

Marine officers: Captain John Schermerhorn, Second Lieutenant Charles F.
    Williams

Acting Masters: Robert Barstow, Abraham B. Pierson, and Woodbury H. Polly

Acting Ensigns: John W. Grattan, John M. Cowen, James Birtwistle,
    E. R. Olcott, and Richard Bates

Acting Masters Mates: Frederick A. O'Conner, John Brann, James M. Skarden,
    George W. Kellogg, and Silas A. Tabor

Chief Engineer: John H. Long

Second Assistant Engineers: George W. Sensner and James Renshaw, Jr.

Third Assistant Engineers: Guy Samson, Robert D. Taylor, Frank W. Nyman,
    William Bond, and James D. Lee

Boatswain: William Bunker

Gunner: Charles W. Horner

Carpenter: John W. Stimson

Sailmaker: Thomas O. Fassett[1]

On the 22nd of December 1863 the admiral put to sea again in the *Fahkee*, leaving orders for the *Minnesota* to follow as soon as possible and join him on the Wilmington blockade.

3

Arrival of the Russian fleet at Hampton Roads • Salute •
Preparations for sea • "All hands weigh anchor" • Off for the
blockade • Frying Pan Shoals and a gale of wind • Heavy firing
down the coast • The *Fahkee* under the orders of the admiral
destroys the blockade runner *Bendigo* • The blockading service •
An attempt to save the *Bendigo* • Loss of the U.S. Steamer *Iron
Age* • Rebel signal lights • [December 1863–January 1864]

T HE FRIGATE *MINNESOTA* weighed anchor on the 24th of December 1863 and
proceeded as far as Fortress Monroe where she began taking in stores. Christmas eve was spent in preparing for sea. On the following day the Russian fleet,
which had been so warmly welcomed and entertained by the several Northern
cities, arrived, intending to anchor in Hampton Roads for the winter. Fortress
Monroe and the frigate gave the representatives of the Czar a magnificent
salute, which was promptly acknowledged and returned by the Russian flagship. Our officers were soon on intimate terms of friendship with their foreign
brothers in arms, and for a few days dinners and receptions were given where
the Russian bear and the American eagle were duly toasted and moistened with
all the honors. But these festivities soon came to an end, and at last the order
was given "all hands weigh anchor."

The boatswain and his mates gave their whistles the full power of their
lungs, and the crew were soon on deck. A marine with his fife struck the tune
of "The girl I left behind me," as the sailors manned the capstan [a vertical
drum revolving on a spindle, used for lifting the anchor and other heavy
weights; sailors turned the capstan with bars inserted into holes around the capstan head], and kept step to the music until the anchor was at the bow. The
engineers were at their post and in a few seconds the powerful machinery was
in motion, and the beautiful frigate was underway. With the order "All hands
make sail," the bluejackets were in the rigging and aloft and in a few minutes
the white canvas was stretched to the breeze. Like a horse feeling the spurs,
she plunged through the waves, and in a few hours we were on the blue waters
of the Atlantic with the lighthouse at Cape Henry gradually fading in the distance.

The weather continued favorable until after we had passed Cape Hatteras.
The captain deeming it a good opportunity to drill the crew, came on deck at
midnight and ordered the drums to beat to quarters. The officers and sailors

Russian sailors on the Imperial Russian frigate *Osliaba*, Alexandria, Virginia, circa 1863 (National Archives 64-CV-210)

came tumbling up on deck and in about five minutes the guns were cast loose, magazines opened, everyone at their stations and ready for action. After inspection and a few complimentary words by the captain they were "piped down" after securing the guns.

The last day of the year set in stormy with a heavy sea running, wind dead ahead, and we were soon plunging and rolling in a manner which prevented many from having an appetite for breakfast. As we were approaching Frying Pan Shoals the gale increased and the captain ordered the vessel's course to be changed for deeper water. As evening advanced we steered for the New Inlet entrance of the Cape Fear River and within twenty-five miles of the coast dropped anchor for the night in sixteen fathoms of water. The following day we were favored with a clear sky but the wind blew fiercely and the frigate remained at anchor all day and night. On the 2d of January 1864 we again weighed anchor and turned the point of the shoals and under full sail and steam arrived the following morning at the Western Bar entrance to the Cape Fear River, where we awaited the coming of the admiral.

A few hours after our arrival heavy firing was heard down the coast, and after considerable anxiety we discovered the *Fahkee* rapidly approaching us. The admiral was quickly transferred and the blue pennant again floated at our mast head.

The guns which we had heard were fired by the *Fahkee* which had chased and driven ashore a blockade runner; but her crew escaped. Shot after shot were fired into the stranger and she was soon in flames. With the exception of her iron hull and machinery everything on board was destroyed. She proved to be the anglo-rebel steamer *Bendigo* from Bermuda bound for Wilmington with a cargo of freight. [Admiral Lee's report of 4 January 1864 to Secretary Welles states that the *Bendigo* operated out of Nassau and had "no cargo or freight of any description on board."[1]]

Violations of the blockade were very rarely attempted in the daytime. The vessels engaged in this hazardous occupation took advantage of the darkest nights to run in or out; but in many instances where they escaped the vessels blockading the entrance, they were caught after daylight by our fast outside cruisers.

During the daytime the blockading fleet would anchor about three miles from the entrance to the harbor; but after dark would move in very close to the beach. The light draughts cruised up and down all night while the larger vessels remained a little farther off with everything ready to move at a moment's notice. On the bar and sometimes inside the harbor small picket boats were stationed ready to signal to the fleet whenever a vessel ran out. Rockets indicated the direction which the stranger was moving and the exciting chase would begin.

Almost every night the rebel forts and batteries would suddenly open fire and rake the bar and the blockaders within range; but our gallant sailors became so accustomed to these midnight salutes and evinced so much daring as to call forth even the admiration of the enemy.

Believing there was a reasonable chance of saving the hull of the *Bendigo*, the admiral ordered the *Minnesota* and five of the blockading vessels to proceed down to Lockwood's Folly Inlet where the runner was beached and make the attempt. All was quiet upon our arrival, and officers and men were sent on board the *Bendigo* to prepare her for being hauled off. Shot holes were plugged, the water bailed out and fires started under the boilers.

Lieutenant Commander Edward E. Stone commanding the *Iron Age* was ordered to move closer to the beach and pass a hawser to the wreck. When all was ready the *Iron Age* with the assistance of the other vessels started ahead; but the *Bendigo* remained immovable. The tide having fallen all further attempts to haul her off were deferred until next high water which would be a little after eight o'clock the following morning. In the meantime everything that could be devised to insure the success of the undertaking was completed. The weather was very fine and the water smooth. When all were ready to make the last pull at the wreck an unfortunate and quite unexpected accident occurred. The *Iron Age* did not move, and soon after she signaled she was fast aground and asked permission to throw her guns overboard. After sending the other vessels to her relief the admiral went on board of her. She had but five feet of water on her starboard and four feet on her port side. Her draught was nine feet six aft and eight feet forward. Captain Stone was directed to get ready to haul off at next high water; to lighten the vessel of her stores and ammunition, removing her guns last; to get out an anchor to prevent her from being set further up on shore as the tide made, and her consorts the *Daylight* and *Governor Buckingham* were ordered to pull her off at high tide that evening. Towards evening the weather looked threatening; but the sea still remained smooth. At high water Captain Stone reported he had only seven feet of water alongside and in compliance with his request the admiral directed him to throw his guns overboard; but even then the combined efforts of the other vessels failed to draw her off in deep water. Finding the ship did not move and knowing the tide was falling, all hopes of saving her were abandoned. It now became necessary to decide whether to run the risk of a gale of wind and the probable capture of the whole ship's company by the enemy or abandon and destroy the vessel. After consulting his officers Captain Stone decided to fire the ship. At midnight the officers and men were taken on board the other vessels. The captain and his gig's crew only remained on board the *Iron Age*. At 4:00 A.M. the torch was applied. The light of the conflagration was reflected on shore and far out to sea, and the enemy could be plainly seen with their signal lights warning off blockade runners which might be in the vicinity.

The burning vessel afforded a sad but at the same time a magnificent spectacle, and after nearly everything of value on deck had been destroyed, the fire communicated with the magazine. Instantly an immense flash and volume of smoke and flames leapt toward the heavens, and a deep booming roar told us the *Iron Age* was no more. The air was full of bursting shell and glowing firebrands which fell hissing in the water. With the explosion darkness threw its somber mantle over the scene.[2]

4

The blockade runner *Ranger* discovered on the beach ◆
Boats board her under fire of rebel sharpshooters ◆ Loss of life ◆
The *Minnesota* opens fire ◆ Destruction of the blockade runner ◆
Black smoke on the horizon ◆ The *Aries* gives chase and
destroys the blockade runner *Vesta* ◆ The flagship returns to the
blockading fleet ◆ Rebel battery opens fire on the vessels
guarding the wrecks ◆ "All hands bury the dead" ◆ Funeral
ceremonies at sea ◆ Bound for Hampton Roads ◆ The frigate in
a storm ◆ Arrival in James River ◆ Wardroom amusements ◆
"A man overboard" ◆ Drowned in double irons ◆ [January 1864]

AT DAYLIGHT ON THE MORNING following the destruction of the *Iron Age* a large side-wheel double smokestack blockade runner was discovered on the beach near the wreck of the *Bendigo*. Boats were quickly manned by the different vessels and started to board her; but were driven off by rebel sharpshooters who opened fire behind the sand hills. The flagship sent three boats under the command of Acting Masters Mate Frederick A. O'Conner with orders to board the steamer. The boats from the other vessels were compelled to retire after losing one man killed and several wounded. Mr. O'Conner was soon underway for the runner, which was then discovered to be on fire. The *Minnesota* stood in for the beach and anchored in four and one half fathoms, her draught being twenty-four feet. As the boats drew within range a galling fire of musketry commenced and was continued until our boats dashed alongside of the vessel. Several men were severely wounded and remained in the boats. Mr. O'Conner and a few of his men jumped on board and again received warm attention by the enemy; but without accident they entered the cabin and were out of immediate danger.

The blockade runner proved to be the *Ranger* from Bermuda, and made our coast on the 10th of January about five miles northeast of Murrell's Inlet where she landed her passengers. [Grattan noted in his diary that the boarding party found the *Ranger*'s cabin "handsomely & expensively furnished."[1]] The next morning, finding her course to Wilmington intercepted by the flagship, *Daylight*, *Governor Buckingham* and *Aries*, she was beached and fired by her crew.

Mr. O'Conner carefully examined her and found she was too firmly embedded in the sand to warrant an attempt to haul her off, and securing her log book, azimuth compass, and her colors jumped into his boat and shoved off.

Naval scene off Lockwood's Folly Inlet, coast of North Carolina, 1864, by John W. Grattan (John W. Grattan Papers, Library of Congress)

The firing of the rebels was renewed, several bluejackets were badly wounded; but just as the boats were nearly out of range John McAllister, the coxswain of Mr. O'Conner's boat, fell forward with a bullet in his brain. He was laid down in the stern sheets and covered with the captured flags while the boats fell in line and slowly pulled for the frigate. [According to Grattan's diary, "one of the rebel flags found on the vessel was put over (McAllister's) face to keep the horribly mutilated face from view."[2]]

The loss of life and a man-of-war, together with the inability of the vessels to make prizes of the *Bendigo* and *Ranger* had a very depressing effect upon the admiral. When he heard Mr. O'Conner's report he gave orders for the fleet to open fire and completely destroy the blockade runner and shell the beach.

A rebel battery of light artillery could be seen out of range; but the sand hills along the coast were full of sharpshooters. After a few shell had been fired the enemy scattered in every direction and a large house on shore and the two blockade runners were completely destroyed. While the firing continued black smoke was rising in the direction of Shallote Inlet, and the *Aries* was ordered to chase; she soon returned and reported a handsome double propeller blockade runner, which proved to be the *Vesta*, was beached and on fire near Little River Inlet; but owing to a strong force of sharpshooters the boats were prevented from boarding her. This was the twenty-second steamer lost by the rebels and the blockade runners in their attempts to violate the Wilmington blockade for the period of six months.[3]

Two days previous to the destruction of the *Vesta*, the *Aries* and *Montgomery* chased the Confederate steamer *Dare* during a thick fog. After six hours spent in endeavoring to overhaul her, the *Montgomery* and *Aries* were within range when the runner struck the sands. Boats were sent in to board her; but nothing could be done to haul her off and she was set on fire in three places. The surf was running high and when the men returned to their boats several of them were swamped, and their occupants were captured by the enemy. The *Aries* lost two officers and seven men and the *Montgomery* two officers and fourteen men.[4]

Having fully satisfied himself of the total destruction of the *Bendigo* and *Ranger*, the admiral ordered the flagship to return to the Western Bar. While approaching our anchorage we heard heavy firing in the vicinity of the wrecks, and subsequently learned that a battery of rebel artillery had opened upon the vessels we had left there; but after a rapid exchange of shot and shell the enemy retired.

A melancholy duty was performed on the frigate on the following day. The solemn tones of "All hands bury the dead" resounded throughout the ship. The bell tolled, the wind moaned through the rigging and all voices were hushed. The sailors mustered on the gun deck by the gangway. Near the admiral's cabin the body of the brave coxswain lay swinging in a cot, covered with the Union Jack [a small flag corresponding in appearance to the union of the national flag; in this case, white stars on a blue field]. The day was very appropriate for the ceremony; the sky was dark and cloudy and the long-threatening storm would soon burst upon us. After the admiral and his officers were seated the venerable chaplain with a trembling voice commenced the affecting funeral sermon for the dead, followed by an earnest prayer. The order was then given to clear a passage for the pall bearers, and accompanied by the marines' muffled drum and shrill fife performing a dead march, the body was slowly carried along the deck. The officers followed the procession with uncovered heads. Arriving at a port hole, the marines presented arms and the dead sailor was lowered in a boat and transferred to the *Fahkee* where another poor bluejacket killed in action lay ready for burial. When the concluding ceremonies were finished both bodies were consigned to the deep.

A few hours after the burial scene, the flagship put to sea bound for New Inlet, necessitating a long detour in order keep clear of the dangers of Frying Pan Shoals. Several new vessels having arrived the admiral placed them on the blockade and finding the fleet at New Inlet in excellent working condition ordered the frigate to proceed to Hampton Roads. We were soon under sail and steam when the long-expected storm burst upon us with great fury. The orders on deck could scarcely be heard. The rain poured in torrents and the wild wind groaned and shrieked and roared through the rigging. Towards midnight the gale increased, and at one time it was feared some of the heavy guns would break loose; if such an accident had occurred the consequences would have been terrible. Only a short time previously the *Governor Buckingham* had such an affair happen but fortunately it was a heavy bow gun, and when it broke loose, it plunged into the sea.

The storm continued with great violence for three days and for safety the *Minnesota* kept far out to sea; but on the evening of the 20th of January we sighted Cape Henry and anchored on our station in the James River on the following morning.

The Russian fleet being still at anchor at Hampton Roads, numerous visits were interchanged between the officers and for a time we ceased to trouble ourselves about the war. General Butler and staff called upon the admiral and the best of feeling appeared to prevail.

A few evenings after our arrival a circumstance occurred which will give a pretty fair idea of life and death, amusements, and sorrows upon a man-of-war. As was our usual custom the officers in the wardroom who were not on duty were assembled around the long table or on the sofas reading or engaged in conversation when a universal demand was made on Lieutenant Williams, the young dashing officer of marines, to produce his violin. He was an excellent musician and his fascinating executions with the bow generally had the effect of setting not only the officers a dancing; but in the stern of the ship where the colored steward and the servants were stationed when their services were not required, would as softly as their government shoes permitted keep step to the music. In the absence of ladies for partners we would be compelled to select the most light and airy to fill their place. Mr. Cowan always insisted upon being a lady; he was about fifty years of age; with a waist and other general dimensions about the size of the butt of a XV-inch gun [Mounted on monitors, the XV-inch Dahlgren gun was the largest Union naval cannon to see service during the war. Its maximum diameter measured forty-eight inches. Roman numerals were used in the nomenclature of Dahlgren guns to differentiate them from other types of cannon.]; but with all this mass of flesh and blood no more graceful dancer could be found in the wardroom. Several round dances had been very well executed when Lieutenant Fyffe who was the life of the mess said he would give us a specimen of his choice steps which he had learned while dancing with the black-eyed belles of Cadiz, and by his graceful motion led our imaginations to wander to the beautiful ladies whose waists he had encircled in that far off clime, when the poetry of motion was roughly dispelled by his giving us an imitation of an Indian war dance, and during its continuance war whoops and yells of laughter resounded throughout the wardroom. Even the old chaplain was compelled to add to the noise by making a very unnatural "haw, haw," while tears rolled down his cheeks.

We were thus pleasantly engaged when suddenly the dreaded cry of "a man overboard" was heard. Everyone rushed on deck, the life buoy had been promptly cut away, and the boats manned and lowered; but nothing could be seen of the poor fellow. It was soon learned that he was one of the sailors who had been placed on the bridge in double irons for punishment. In falling he

Union naval officers enjoying leisure time outside their staterooms. Note the carpet slippers on the man at the right. (National Archives B-598)

struck his head against the projecting muzzle of a gun on the lower deck and instantly sank to the bottom. While we were engaged looking at the dark waters which had covered over from sight the remains of the poor sailor whose brains were undoubtedly dashed out before he reached the waves, it struck eight bells and the sentries at the gangways sang out "eight o'clock and all's well." It seemed mockery; but still we knew it was only carrying out the rules and regulations of the service, and by daylight next morning the circumstance of the death of one of the ship's crew appeared to be almost forgotten.

5

Army and navy expedition up the James ✦ Caught in a trap ✦
General Graham asks for reinforcements ✦ The army gunboat
Smith Briggs and army detachment captured by the enemy ✦
The bluejackets under fire but escape ✦ The wounded ✦
Return of the survivors of the expedition ✦ General Butler asks
the admiral's cooperation in a grand advance ✦ The naval
preparations completed ✦ General Butler abandons the expedition
and charges Captain Upshur with treachery ✦ A court of inquiry
demanded by Captain Upshur ✦ His character vindicated and
the secret of the expedition divulged by an army officer ✦
All quiet on the James ✦ Wardroom festivities ✦
Sam the contraband dancing for punishment ✦
[February–March 1864]

B RIGADIER GENERAL CHARLES KINNARD GRAHAM commanding the Naval Brigade in General Butler's Department came up the river from Fortress Monroe on the 1st of February with several army transports and gunboats, and in the absence of the admiral who was at Norfolk Navy Yard, applied to Captain Guert Gansevoort, the senior naval officer on the station, for naval assistance to accompany him a short distance up the James and capture a body of rebel troops and a quantity of tobacco. [Brigadier General Graham, USV, commanded the Naval Brigade of the Union Army of the James (28 April 1864–17 February 1865) on expeditions up the James and adjacent waters. Near Fredericksburg, Virginia, he shelled the house of the brother of the Confederate Secretary of War, James Alexander Seddon, in retaliation for Jubal Early's burning of Montgomery Blair's house in Silver Spring, Maryland. Captain Guert Gansevoort was skipper of the steamer *Roanoke*.] The general could not wait for the return of the admiral and in compliance with his request the heavily armed gunboat *Commodore Morris* was ordered to cooperate and render any service that might be required. [The *Commodore Morris* was a converted New York side-wheel ferryboat armed with a 9-inch Dahlgren smoothbore, a 100-pounder Parrott rifle, and two 30-pounder Parrott rifles. After the war she returned to New York and remained in service as a ferryboat until 1931.]

The expedition started and soon afterwards the admiral returned; when he ordered the *Shokokon* and *Commodore Barney* to follow General Graham and render any assistance that might be required.

Early the following morning a message was received from the general asking for more naval reinforcements, and as quickly as they could be manned the two launches of the *Minnesota* armed with howitzers were sent to his aid, and a telegram sent to General Butler. Later in the day we learned that a detachment of cavalry, infantry, and a howitzer squad, in all about one hundred men, had been landed by General Graham at Smithfield and were met by a larger force of the enemy. The two launches under the command of Acting Master Abraham B. Pierson were towed by the *Shokokon* as near as the depth of water would allow, and the light draught army steamer *Smith Briggs* then took the launches in tow and cautiously ascended Pagan Creek as far as Smithfield. When they were within two thousand yards of the town it was discovered that our troops were hotly engaged with the enemy who had brought a battery to bear upon them. The *Smith Briggs* and the launches at once opened fire, when it was observed our troops were seized with panic and confusion. They rushed down to the wharf and sang out for the *Smith Briggs* to come alongside. As quickly as possible the request was complied with and the troops crowded on board. The greatest excitement prevailed, and before the vessel could leave the wharf the rebels rushed down upon them with a yell and captured the boat and all on board.

The launches had been keeping up a steady fire with canister and shrapnel; but after the capture of the *Smith Briggs* and the soldiers the enemy opened a very rapid fire of musketry, and before the launches could drop down the creek Acting Master Pierson and three sailors were seriously wounded. Thus ended an expedition hastily organized and with no definite co-operating orders or instructions. When the disastrous result became known the admiral sent a short but respectful note to General Butler with the suggestion that all future expeditions requiring naval co-operation, or passing the lines of the blockade should be arranged between the general and himself personally before they were undertaken.[1]

A few days after this affair, Commander Dominick Lynch, the senior naval officer at Hampton Roads, came on board the flagship and held a long consultation with the admiral. He brought a message from General Butler requesting naval co-operation as he intended to move on the city of Richmond as soon as his plans were arranged. All the available vessels were sent to the Norfolk Navy Yard to fill up with coal and ammunition and with orders to hold themselves in readiness to sail at a moment's notice.

On the following day, Sunday, every vessel was ready for service. The admiral and staff were very busily engaged in writing and receiving dispatches. On deck the chaplain and crew were assembled at divine service, totally ignorant of the occupation and preparations going on in the cabin.

The contemplated expedition was kept a profound secret, and outside of the cabin of the flagship nothing was known of the intentions of the admiral and the general. During the day a strong reconnoitering party was sent out by

General Butler and reported the enemy to be very strongly intrenched near Williamsburg and Yorktown.

While the preparations for war were going on, quite a different scene was transpiring on the gun deck of the frigate. At the request of a number of old sailors the chaplain gave an evening service. A desk was covered with the American ensign and placed between the butts of two IX-inch Dahlgren guns. Lanterns hung from the hammock hooks and spread a weird glare over the polished guns and the solemn faces of the assembled throng. Capstan bars placed across inverted buckets were occupied by the bluejackets as seats, and when they had taken their places the officers filled the vacant space in the rear. When the sailors sang the simple hymns the scene was highly impressive, and when the gray haired chaplain preached the sermon in language which poor Jack [short for "Jack Tar," a nickname for enlisted sailors] could understand, a more attentive and serious congregation could not be imagined. At eight bells the meeting quietly broke up and all retired to their hammocks or staterooms with lighter hearts and better resolutions for their future conduct. ["For all these primitive contrivances for comfort of the poor and much abused 'Jack,'" Grattan commented in his diary, "there is more earnestness and Christian feeling manifested that would shame many a fashionable congregation [ashore]."[2]]

When the naval preparations were completed the admiral notified General Butler he was ready to co-operate with him; but to his surprise and mortification and exceeding regret the general informed him he had abandoned his intentions, alleging as his reasons that the enemy were fully prepared to meet him; having been informed of the contemplated movement and he charged Lieutenant Commander Upshur, the captain of the *Minnesota*, with treachery in having divulged the secret to his wife who resided at Norfolk, and she in turn informing her neighbors who forwarded the news to the enemy. In conclusion the general stated that "naval officers were more leaky and untrustworthy than their poorest vessels." Upon receipt of this dispatch the admiral handed it to Captain Upshur who after reading it, indignantly and with emotion denied the foul charge in every particular and demanded a court of inquiry and a rigid investigation. The demand was sent to General Butler with a request that the court be held on board the *Roanoke* to which he agreed. A very careful and searching inquiry was made and it was proved positively that the secret of the contemplated army and navy expedition was divulged by an army officer connected with a Connecticut regiment who had received his information at General Butler's headquarters. The facts were so clear that the general acknowledged his regret at making such an unfounded charge and Lieutenant Commander Upshur was most honorably acquitted of the foul and infamous slander.

As the advance to Richmond had been indefinitely postponed the officers and crew of the frigate tried to make the best of their disappointment, and every evening could be heard singing or music fore and aft. The admiral with

Sailors enjoying leisure time on board USS *Hunchback* in the James River, circa 1864. One sailor smokes a pipe, another holds a dog, several are reading, many are barefoot, and a few are peeling potatoes or apples. Their officers stand imperiously above them. (National Archives B-2011)

his pipe would spend hours playing back-gammon and no doubt he would imagine his opponent was General Butler and with that idea in view he would always win.

In the starboard steerage the masters mates, paymasters and captain's clerks, with an occasional visit from the warrant officers, strove to enjoy themselves as well as the small confined room would allow, and in the port steerage the assistant engineers would on rare occasions let off steam and vie with their brother officers in songs and yarns. But the wardroom, being very large and comfortable, was the place where unrestrained mirth had full vent. One evening we were favored by a grand ballet divertissement with the graceful Mr. Cowan as premier. Mr. Fyffe done very well except towards the last when he finished with an Indian war dance. The other younger officers made as respectable an appearance as their scanty feminine wardrobe would permit. When Mr. Williams gave the opening overture of "Old Dog Tray" amid the broad smiles and almost choking laughter of the chaplain and other old officers of the mess, the gong was sounded and from the different state rooms emerged the most ludicrous band of Amazons that could be formed. Their costume consisted of a very short dress made of coffee bags. Several wore in addition tarpaulin hats and heavy sea boots. They were soon hard at work, for it was work, and the fun was fast and furious; until Mr. Cowan tried to cut a pigeon wing when he slipped and fell flat on the deck jarring the ship from stem to stern.

The laughter was excessive; but one particular voice between a chuckle and a yell was traced to one of our plantation darkies who was in paroxysms of delight and watching the comical scene from the rear room. He was ordered to appear and show cause why he should not be punished as it was against the rules for waiters and servants to make any unnecessary noise. Not giving a satisfactory excuse for his misdemeanor he was ordered to dance for punishment, and then we had without the aid of music one of the genuine Southern plantation break downs. After dancing until we were tired of the sport Sam retired with many substantial compliments and no doubt felt as happy as a king.

6

Acting Master Charles B. Wilder • Rebel raids on the oyster boats in the Nansemond • Mr. Wilder volunteers to capture the guerrillas • A rainy night expedition • A light in a farmer's window • An unwilling guide • March through the swamps • The headquarters of Lieutenant Roy's guerrillas surrounded and the gang captured • Safe return of the expedition with the prisoners • Instructions to the fleet to be on guard for torpedo boats • A strange boat seen approaching the flagship • An attempt to sink it • The *Minnesota* struck by a torpedo • Excitement and confusion on board • The injury inflicted on the vessel • A narrow escape from destruction by the explosion of the infernal machine • The torpedo boat escapes uninjured • [March–April 1864]

LIEUTENANT FYFFE AT HIS OWN REQUEST was detached from the *Minnesota* and placed in command of the gunboat *Commodore Morris*, and Acting Master Charles B. Wilder having a short time previously been ordered to the frigate and being senior in rank assumed the duties of executive. He was a very modest, pleasant man and a thorough sailor, and by his own merits had risen step by step in the service until he achieved the proud position of first lieutenant on board as fine a man-of-war as was in the navy.

The rebels in the vicinity of the Nansemond River after the capture of the army steamer *Smith Briggs* and the detachment of troops, began committing depredations on the numerous small vessels engaged in gathering oysters. Several were captured and destroyed and others were robbed of everything of value. In addition to these outrages a rebel mail route between Norfolk and Richmond was discovered to be in operation.

Conceiving an idea he could capture the mail agent, Acting Master Wilder applied to the admiral for permission to make the attempt which was granted. A dark and rainy night was selected and on the 28th of March 1864 four of the *Minnesota*'s launches and cutters were manned with volunteers armed with cutlasses and rifles. The *Commodore Barney* under the command of Acting Master James M. Williams who had arranged the expedition with Mr. Wilder, took the boats in tow. It was very dark and raining hard when they arrived in the Nansemond; but without accident proceeded several miles up the river and landed the men near a dense wood. Leaving a few sailors to take care of the boats, the

Boat crews patrolling the James, circa 1864 (Courtesy of Robert M. Browning, Jr.)

bluejackets and a few marines who accompanied them marched cautiously through the forest. A short distance ahead a light could be seen dimly burning in the window of a farm house. Mr. Wilder placed his men so as to prevent the inmates from escaping and then knocked at the door. The farmer upon making his appearance was struck with terror and for a few moments could not speak. He professed total ignorance of the location of the enemy's pickets; but upon being threatened with instant death he offered to lead them to the rebel headquarters. The old farmer informed Mr. Wilder that the troops in the vicinity were known as "Lieutenant Roy's guerrillas," and said the neighbors were as afraid of them as they were of the "Yanks." Without a guide it would have been impossible to proceed as the rain continued to pour in torrents; but the farmer knew every foot of the ground and faithfully led the way. After a long march he whispered, "There is the house." A large building could be faintly seen; but there were no signs or lights to show that it was inhabited. It was then near midnight and nothing but the noise of the storm disturbed the deep solitude. Slowly approaching the house it was quietly surrounded, and a sleepy sentry captured. When all were ready the door was burst in, lanterns were uncovered, and scattered around the room were "Lieutenant Roy's guerrillas." The assault was quickly accomplished and all were captured before many of them were fairly awake. A few made a slight resistance but were knocked down and disarmed. Unfortunately the chief of the gang was absent but all his men, numbering twenty, as hearty a lot of gray backs as could be found in the Confederate army, were ordered to fall in line. A large quantity of ammunition, muskets, and revolvers were secured when the command was given to return to the boats, which was safely accomplished after a rapid march through cane brake, swamps, rain and mud, and at daylight the officers and men with the prisoners were on the deck of the *Minnesota*.[1]

The admiral was greatly pleased with the success of the expedition especially as no lives had been lost, and immediately recommended Acting Masters Wilder and Williams to the Navy Department for promotion as Acting Volunteer Lieutenants. The news of this daring raid created a profound sensation in this section of the enemy's country and we felt confident they would in some measure retaliate.

The rebels had been experimenting for some time with torpedoes and torpedo boats, and at last had met with success. A boat called a "David" was constructed, and when afloat was almost submerged. It was covered with boiler iron and operated by a low pressure steam engine; the torpedo being attached to the end of a swinging boom. The admiral anticipated the enemy would use this infernal machine on some of his vessels, and to guard against a repetition of the catastrophe following the meeting of David and Goliath issued very stringent orders to the fleet to be always on the alert for this new danger. Many ridiculed the old admiral for his extreme cautiousness; but the result proved he had not overrated the power of this new element in modern warfare. At night picket boats were thrown out, and the steam tug boats were ordered to be ready to move at a moment's notice, and were directed to run down and sink any boat or suspicious object found inside the picket line after dark.

At two o'clock in the morning on the ninth of April Mr. Birtwistle, the officer of the deck of the *Minnesota*, had his attention called to what appeared to be a boat adrift about one hundred and fifty yards from the flagship. The sentry of the gangway hailed it, and in reply received the word "Roanoke." Mr. Birtwistle having his suspicions aroused ordered the stranger not to come alongside, and was answered "Aye aye, sir." [Grattan noted in his diary that at first, the officer of the deck mistook the Confederate vessel for a "common row boat" and took no action until it closed within hailing distance.[2]] The picket tug *Poppy* lying astern of us was ordered to overhaul the boat; but through carelessness and neglect of duty her steam had run down and she was unable to move. In the meantime the torpedo "David"—as she proved to be—began approaching the frigate. [The vessel that attacked the *Minnesota* was actually the *Squib*, one of four torpedo boats built in Richmond. The *David*, the world's first torpedo boat, operated in Charleston. She attacked the USS *New Ironsides* off that city on 5 October 1863. Thereafter "David" became a generic term for Confederate torpedo boats, just as "monitor" was for Union turreted ironclads with low freeboard.]

The captain was called and sprang on deck just as Mr. Birtwistle saw a glimmer of light and heard the puff of steam on board the rapidly nearing torpedo boat. He ordered the sentries to fire their muskets into her and springing to a convenient gun called the watch to train it; but before it could be brought to bear the David dashed forward inside of range and exploded a torpedo under the port side and abreast of the after magazine. In a second the frigate was thrown over on her beam ends, the main yard arms touching the water. Hundreds of seamen were thrown violently out of their hammocks; ladders and gratings came crashing down the hatchways; capstan bars, sponges, rammers, shot, and shell were displaced and set rolling about the decks. Amid the greatest confusion and excitement the drums beat to quarters; but owing to the absence of ladders and the extinguishment of all the lights by the shock, the officers and crew could not get on deck. During the confusion the torpedo boat succeeded in escaping unobserved. A gun was fired in the direction she was supposed to be; but the only effect it had was to increase the excitement below where half-naked officers and sailors were struggling to get on deck.

[Grattan described his own experience during the attack in a letter to his parents: "I can feel very thankful that I am alive to relate the narrow escape we have had from destruction. About 2.15 A.M. this morning, I was thrown out of my bunk by the concussion of an immense torpedo. I heard the sound and in a second afterwards the hatch gratings and gangway ladders came tumbling down the cock-pit. I immediately guessed what was the matter, as I could hear the ring of the torpedo striking the side of the ship, below the water line. The ship tottered and rolled like a small boat in the sea. The whole ship was lifted completely out of the water and came down with a tremendous jerk. As soon as the gratings and heavy hatch-braces had stopped tumbling down the hatch, I picked myself up, being pretty severely bruised, and managed to hobble to within a few feet of the cockpit ladder, when I struck my shin and had just got from under the hatch when a heavy iron bar from the spar deck came rattling down, just grazing my head. There was no light every thing dark as midnight, and I could hear the rush and heavy tread of five hundred men on the decks above. Every one thought the ship was sinking. In about five or ten seconds after the explosion I was on deck with all the officers and men, not one in fifty being dressed. . . . I looked out towards the port quarter and could see a small sigar [sic] shaped steamer, about the size of the Captain's Gig, moving very rapidly towards the rebel shore. . . . I never saw such excitement and confusion before. . . . The torpedo went off within 10 feet of the magazine bulkhead. The Gunner says it is a miracle that the ship as not blown into a thousand atoms."[3]]

Above the din could be heard the agonized voice of the paymaster's clerk whose state room was in the cockpit [space located aft on the lowest, or "orlop," deck used for junior officers' quarters] and immediately opposite where the torpedo had exploded. Although there was on duty a marine sentry stationed within ten feet of his door, the clerk always kept it fastened and it appeared that the key was thrown out of the lock rendering it impossible for him to open the door. In spite of the danger we could not help but smile at the ludicrous position of Mr. Moody. He prayed and swore in the same breath, "Save me you damn marine. Help, oh help my good Lord. On deck there, somebody. Mr. Moody is dying." But after a while Mr. Moody found his key and joined us on the berth deck with nothing but his shirt. [Grattan noted in his diary that after the explosion he agonized for a moment on whether to dress or to try to reach the spar deck in his underwear. He decided to dress.[4]]

After considerable difficulty all hands were on deck except a few who were very badly bruised and injured by falling out of their hammocks. The pumps were sounded; but no water was found. Had the torpedo been properly adjusted and not exploded so near the surface the attempt to destroy the frigate would have been more successful. The result however was very serious; several heavy timbers and the decks were badly sprung; bulkheads splintered and knocked down; guns were lifted from the carriages, crushing and splintering the ports and a number of elevating screws broken, bent, or rendered useless. The masts were thrown out of line and the shaft alley of the propeller was crushed in, preventing the machinery from working. In the magazine and shell room was a mass of rubbish, loose powder being scattered in every direction, and the wooden boxes which had contained shot and shell were broken to splinters. Those who saw the magazine expressed their surprise that it had not exploded from the concussion and friction.

It was subsequently ascertained that Hunter Davidson, formerly a lieutenant in our navy, had command of the torpedo boat and in addition had general supervision of all the torpedoes and obstructions in the James River.[5]

This daring attempt to destroy the flagship had the effect of infusing some life and activity in General Butler's department and preparations were at once commenced to punish the rebels for their audacity.

7

The admiral visits General Grant at Fortress Monroe ◆
An important movement contemplated ◆ Activity of the enemy ◆
Another expedition by General Graham ◆ The admiral does not
approve of his plan ◆ Naval cooperation and advance of the
troops ◆ The enemy retire ◆ The naval launches ascend Pagan
Creek beyond Smithville ◆ Engagement with the enemy ◆
Death of Acting Master Wilder ◆ Failure of the expedition ◆
Funeral service on the flagship ◆ [April 1864]

A FEW DAYS PREVIOUS to the attempt to destroy the *Minnesota* the admiral
had a consultation with Lieutenant General U. S. Grant at Fortress Monroe and
arrangements were made for a grand military and naval movement up the James
River. Two days after the torpedo explosion Major General William F. (Baldy)
Smith came on board the flagship and informed the admiral he was to have a
column to move on Richmond and desired a naval co-operating force.[1] [Smith
then commanded XVIII Corps in the Department of Virginia and North Carolina. Although he had more hair than most men his age, he had retained his
cadet nickname "Baldy," given to him because he had less hair than most of
his classmates at the Military Academy. Smith spent most of his time criticiz-
ing the plans of other generals, particularly superiors.] Charts of the river and
maps of the surrounding country were examined and a plan of operations was
agreed upon. Dispatches and telegrams in cypher were sent to and received
from General Grant and preparations were commenced for a simultaneous
advance with the Army of the Potomac.

In the meantime the enemy showed signs of increased activity in the vicinity of Smithfield and Chuckatuck, and the woods were known to be infested
with guerrillas, who had boats concealed in the creeks. The admiral informed
General Butler of the condition of affairs and suggested that a military force be
sent to capture the rebels and destroy their boats. [Grattan recorded in his diary
that part of the purpose of this expedition was "to find out where the 'torpedo
boat' that recently paid us a visit was stationed."[2]]

In accordance with the request General Graham was directed to cooperate
with the navy and charged to make such disposition of his forces as the admiral might suggest. After a consultation General Graham proposed moving up
the creeks with his light armed transports; but the admiral did not approve of
this plan, and called upon General Butler the same evening and urged him to

send a suitable force to the rear and envelop the rebels so as to capture them between the Blackwater, James, and Nansemond Rivers, and to prevent them from escaping by water a naval force would be stationed at Pagan and Chuckatuck Creeks. The general appeared to be pleased with the admiral's plan and promised to have his suggestions carried out; but subsequent events went to show that General Graham's original proposition was substantially attempted.

The gunboats ordered to participate in the expedition were the *Commodore Jones*, *Commodore Morris*, *Commodore Barney*, and *Stepping Stones*. The two launches that had accompanied the previous expedition were armed with howitzers and manned by a picked crew under the command of Acting Master Wilder. On the evening of the 13th of April the army transports arrived and shortly before midnight the expedition was underway.

The light draughts and the launches proceeded up Pagan Creek and landed a detachment of troops at Smithfield without opposition. The other vessels entered the Nansemond and arrived at Chuckatuck Creek. General Butler had sent a force of cavalry from Norfolk but they were too far away and arrived too late to be of any advantage. As the admiral expected, the enemy fell back and our troops advanced, and all hopes of capturing them were abandoned. Inquiries were made of the inhabitants of Smithfield concerning the torpedo boat when it was learned that she had been there a few days before but had since gone to Richmond. [According to Grattan's diary, the men of Smithfield hid but the women talked to the Northerners. Several soldiers looted a grocery store and a hat store.[3]] The intended co-operation at Pagan Creek failed of being fully carried out owing to the grounding of the transports and delay in landing troops, and that part of the expedition intended to explore the creek did not begin to ascend it until about noon.

The troops at Chuckatuck were reinforced by a regiment under the command of Colonel Oliver Keese, Jr. and about 1:00 P.M. the march began. [Keese commanded the 118th Regiment of New York Infantry.] A number of large mills and barns filled with grain were soon in flames. Guerrillas assisted the farmers in driving off their cattle, a few shots were exchanged; but the enemy were too weak to make any open resistance and as our troops advanced they of course fell back.

In the afternoon heavy firing was heard in the direction of Smithfield but did not continue long, and as darkness set in the sky was illuminated with the glare of burning buildings; but no sounds indicating an engagement were heard.

The result of the movement was not known until the next morning. About nine o'clock several vessels were seen coming down the river; one of them, the *Stepping Stones*, had her flag at half mast and in a boat at her davits lay the body of Acting Master Wilder. The remains of the gallant officer were carefully transferred to the *Minnesota* and placed in a cot on the gun deck. When it became known our brave executive officer was dead not a dry eye could be found in the ship. [In his diary Grattan noted that Wilder had been a splendid officer,

Killed in Action

Lieutenant Charles B. Wilder. Grattan made the notation on the bottom of the picture. (John W. Grattan Papers, Library of Congress)

considered one of the navy's best, and "full of fun and a good friend to all of his acquaintances." Wilder's death left his bride of a year a widow.[4]]

It appeared that when Mr. Wilder had proceeded with the launches a short distance up the creek beyond the town, a body of rebels concealed by the dense shrubbery opened fire. Our men were prepared and immediately returned the compliment with their rifles and howitzers. After several volleys had been exchanged the enemy were driven from their position. Mr. Wilder was in the act of sighting the howitzer for the last shot when he was struck with a minie rifle ball, which pierced his skull and resulted in instant death. As he fell Mr. O'Conner quickly seized the lock string and discharged the gun. The launches then returned to Smithfield and the body of their brave commander was placed on board the gunboat.

The troops having accomplished nothing evacuated the town and returned down the river, landing at Newport News where they were afterwards joined by the balance of the detachment. The expedition proved to be a complete failure, the results being the capture of four prisoners, one howitzer, belonging to the navy and captured by the rebels from the army boat *Smith Briggs*, and a few wagons taken by the soldiers from the farmers; and the loss of a valuable officer and one sailor badly wounded.[5]

At the time the launches were engaged with the enemy dispatches were received from the Navy Department containing the promotion of Acting Master Wilder to the grade of Acting Volunteer Lieutenant; but the poor fellow never saw the document.

The officers and crew of the flagship assembled on the following day to pay the last sad tribute of respect to the dead hero. The coffin was placed on the quarter deck and covered with the national flag. A guard of marines in full uniform took position alongside, while the officers collected together on the starboard and the crew on the port side of the deck. Upon the appearance of the admiral all heads were uncovered. Not a sound could be heard and all were impressed with the solemnity of the occasion. The venerable chaplain read the funeral service for the dead and finished with an eloquent and very pathetic prayer. Nearly every eye was filled with tears, and the old admiral who had faced death so many times and lost so many comrades could not restrain his emotion. The sharp, quick orders of the marine officer was followed by three volleys over the remains thus closing the ceremony. The coffin was then carried slowly along the deck, down the gangway to the barge which conveyed it to the *Stepping Stones* and in a few hours the body of Lieutenant Wilder found rest in the Naval Cemetery at Norfolk.

8

Naval operations in the sounds of North Carolina ◆ Attack of
the enemy on Plymouth ◆ The gunboats open fire and drive
them back ◆ Gallant conduct of Lieutenant Commander
C. W. Flusser ◆ Appearance of the Rebel ram *Albemarle* ◆
The engagement ◆ Sinking of the *Southfield* ◆ Death of
Captain Flusser ◆ The gunboats retire from action ◆ The enemy
storm and capture Plymouth with its garrison of two thousand
soldiers ◆ The admiral sends reinforcements to the sounds ◆
Renewal of the conflict with ram ◆ Capture of a Rebel gunboat ◆
Sassacus rams the ironclad ◆ Loss of life ◆ The ram retires
uninjured ◆ Wood versus iron ◆ [April–May 1864]

NAVAL OPERATIONS IN THE SOUNDS of North Carolina were beginning to be
of a very interesting and important character. For several months the enemy
had been preparing a grand movement, whose object was the re-capture and
occupation of the towns and fortifications held by our troops, and the command
of the waters. Their ram, the *Albemarle*, had been launched and heavily armed.
At that time the military force was too weak to resist a formidable movement
of the rebels and there was nothing but wooden vessels to oppose the descent
of the powerful iron-clad. The gunboats *Miami* and *Southfield* with heavy guns
were stationed at the mouth of the river, under command of Lieutenant Commander Charles W. Flusser.

About 4:00 P.M. on the 17th of April 1864 the enemy opened fire upon
Plymouth. Driving in the pickets, they planted a battery on the river bank
which commanded our soldiers. Captain Flusser ordered a tug to go up the river
and communicate with the gunboat *Whitehead* then guarding the upper obstructions. At 10:00 P.M. the rebels ceased firing; but at day's dawn opened a furious
bombardment and at six o'clock made a general assault. The *Miami, Southfield,*
and *Ceres* took up position to assist our troops who were fighting desperately
with a greatly superior force, and opened a rapid and severe cross fire on the
enemy driving them back with considerable slaughter; but this victory was only
temporary.

About sunset the *Whitehead* came down the river and reported having seen
the ram pass through the obstructions followed by two small gunboats. All was
quiet until about three o'clock next morning when the *Ceres* reported the ram
was coming. Captain Flusser then gave orders for the *Miami* and *Southfield* to

Lieutenant Commander Charles W. Flusser (seated, reading) and officers on board the USS *Miami* after a hunting trip ashore. Note the hunting dogs and game bag. (Courtesy of Robert M. Browning, Jr.)

steam ahead and engage the iron clad. In less than two minutes from the time she was reported, she struck the *Miami* on the port bow near the water line; and at the same time struck the *Southfield* on the starboard bow causing her to sink rapidly. Up to this time the two vessels had been firing solid shot from 100-pound Parrott rifles and IX-inch Dahlgrens; but no impression was made on the *Albemarle*. [The IX-inch Dahlgren smoothbore fired a 72-pound shell and a 93-pound shot; the bore diameter of the 100-pounder Parrott measured 6.4 inches.] But a sad accident occurred which cast a gloom over the bluejackets. Captain Flusser fired the first three shots from the *Miami*. The third was a IX-inch Dahlgren shell which, upon striking the ram, exploded. Several pieces rebounded and struck the brave captain in the breast and wounded several of the gun crew. Captain Flusser was carried below to his cabin where he died in the arms of an officer. Poor Flusser, to quote the words of the admiral, "was generous, good, and gallant, and his untimely death is a real and great loss to the public service."[1]

When the surviving officers of the *Southfield* succeeded in reaching the *Miami*; it was deemed best to drop down the river. The ram in the meantime kept up a steady fire with her powerful guns.

At daylight in the morning following the disastrous encounter with the iron clad, the rebel forces made another assault with overwhelming numbers and carried the defenses and captured the entire garrison, comprising two thousand two hundred men under the command of Brigadier General Henry W. Wessells, and a large quantity of stores, guns and ammunition. [Brigadier General Henry W. Wessells, USV, commanded the Union army's Sub-District of the Albemarle.] This victory gave the enemy possession of the upper sound.[2]

Upon the receipt of the official reports relating to the disaster the admiral sent Captain Melancton Smith to the sounds and directed him to make every preparation to attack and destroy the *Albemarle*. [Smith replaced Flusser as senior naval officer in the sounds.]

The new double-ender gunboats *Sassacus*, *Mattabesett*, and *Wyalusing* had just arrived from the north, intended for chasing blockade runners; but for the time being they were ordered to proceed at once to the sounds and prepare for action. When Captain Smith arrived the ram was in quiet possession of the upper sound. The steamer *Cotton Planter* and the armed tug *Bombshell*, which had been captured from our troops, were in her company. [The *Bombshell* had served as an Erie Canal steamer before the Union army acquired her as a transport. Confederate batteries sank her on 18 April 1864. The Rebels subsequently raised her and armed her with four light guns. The *Cotton Planter*, usually called *Cotton Plant*, was a small screw steamer operating in the sounds before the war. The Confederates used her throughout the conflict.]

All the preparations that it was possible to make were completed by the 5th of May. At 2:00 P.M. on that day the rebel vessels were underway. The double-enders and the *Whitehead* formed in designated order, and the other vessels under the lead of the *Miami* formed another line of battle. After considerable time occupied in maneuvering, the ram opened fire, her shot striking the launch of the *Mattabesett* and wounding several of her crew. Another shot cut away a portion of her standing rigging.

The *Mattabesett* then opened fire and advanced rapidly toward the rebel vessels. The *Bombshell* tried to escape but was soon captured with her crew of thirty-seven men. She was then placed in the line and her gun trained upon the ram. At a distance of one-hundred yards the *Mattabesett* fired a broadside at the *Albemarle*, which was repeated by the *Sassacus*; but the shot left no impression whatever on the formidable vessel. The engagement then became general with every vessel firing rapidly, but the ram defied them all.

At about 5:00 P.M. the *Sassacus* hauled off a short distance and then went ahead under full steam and open throttle towards the broadside of the *Albemarle*. The firing had ceased, and everyone was watching the movements of Captain Francis A. Roe who had determined to ram the iron clad. In a few seconds she struck with terrific force, her wheels continuing to revolve. The ram careened over at an angle of forty-five degrees and the water submerged one side so deeply as to cause the impression she was sinking; but she soon righted and floated on an even keel. [Lieutenant Commander Francis A. Roe, skipper

Sassacus-class double-ended gunboat (Courtesy of Robert M. Browning, Jr.)

of the *Sassacus*, was advanced five numbers in grade for his action against the *Albemarle*.]

Simultaneously with the collision, the *Albemarle* sent a 100-pound rifle shot crashing through and through the *Sassacus* from the starboard bow to the port side. [The *Albemarle* carried two 6.4-inch Confederate-produced Brooke rifles, which fired a 95-pound shot.] For the space of ten minutes the *Sassacus* kept forcing her bow into the ram, and her crew were firing hand grenades upon her casemate and an attempt was made to throw powder down her smoke stack. A rapid musketry fire was kept up by the enemy in addition to her two heavy guns. Finding it impossible to sink the formidable vessel, the *Sassacus* began to swing around when another heavy shot struck her, and instantly every part of the ship was filled with steam. Above the din of battle the groans and screams of the wounded and scalded sailors could be distinctly heard. The iron clad taking advantage of the excitement and confusion began to retreat. Solid shot were rapidly fired at her by the other vessels; but with the exception of having her boats shot away and her smoke stack riddled she escaped uninjured, her machinery in particular being in excellent working order.

The engagement continued until darkness set in, when the fleet anchored and began repairing damage. Our loss was thirty men killed and wounded, many of whom being scalded to death.[3]

It was a gallant action, but demonstrated that wooden vessels were no match against iron clads. Had the admiral's advice been taken by General Butler the *Albemarle* would never have been able to enter the sounds and under the protection of the gunboats the garrison of Plymouth could not have been captured.

9

Military and naval movements on the James River ◆ Arrival of
the monitors ◆ The admiral transfers his flag to the U.S. steamer
Malvern ◆ Adieu to the frigate *Minnesota* ◆ The new flagship ◆
The vessels engaged in the expedition ◆ The advance up the
James ◆ Arrival at Wilson's Wharf ◆ The monitors crossing
Harrison's Bar ◆ Dragging for torpedoes ◆ The transports coming
up the river ◆ City Point and Bermuda Hundred occupied by the
troops ◆ The gunboats advance to Deep Bottom ◆ Destruction
of the *Commodore Jones* by a torpedo ◆ Her destroyers trying
to escape ◆ One shot dead and the others captured ◆
Galvanic batteries and torpedoes found ◆ The fleet at
anchor along the river ◆ [May 1864]

WHILE THE EXCITING SCENES narrated in the last chapter were being
enacted in the sounds of North Carolina, a combined military and naval movement had commenced in the James River and on the old battle grounds of Virginia [Grattan is referring to General Butler's Bermuda Hundred campaign and
the beginning of Grant's 1864 odyssey].

Owing to the great draught of water and impossibility of maneuvering a
frigate in the river, the admiral transferred his flag to the U.S. Steamer *Malvern*.
This vessel had been captured while attempting to run the blockade, and after
condemnation was purchased by the government. She was a beautiful large
side-wheel steamer, and had been fitted out for the special accommodation of
the admiral and staff, whose quarters were situated aft, and wardroom and
steerage for the ship's officers were located forward under the forecastle. The
commanding officer had a very comfortable stateroom on deck aft of the wheel
house. In addition to a large cabin, the admiral had several handsomely furnished staterooms, one of which was occupied by his fleet captain and another
by his secretary. Another large room contained the archives of the squadron and
was the office for transaction of business. On the sides of the room were situated four staterooms occupied by the ordnance officer, fleet surgeon, fleet paymaster and fleet engineer, and another large room adjoining the office was the
mess dining apartment, with several other large staterooms on the side occupied by members of the staff not below the grade of ensigns. The fleet paymaster, fleet captain, and admiral's clerks messed forward with the ship's
officers.

USS *Malvern*, by John W. Grattan (John W. Grattan Papers, Library of Congress)

Upon her arrival the new flagship was sent to the Norfolk Navy Yard and received a battery of twelve 24-pounder howitzers and a full crew of two hundred and fifty sailors.

On the 4th of May 1864 she returned to Fortress Monroe where the *Minnesota* was lying and the admiral and staff were transferred. Orders were given to Acting Volunteer Lieutenant W. K. Cressy who was in command to proceed to Newport News, and the staff was directed to assemble in the office. For the first time and without the slightest knowledge of the intentions of the admiral we were informed the advance up the James River would commence at midnight.

Five iron clads had arrived and the vessels slated to participate in the movement were all ready at Newport News waiting for special orders. The fleet was composed of twenty-three vessels mounting in all 107 guns, and as some of them were destroyed or performed extraordinary service I will here insert the names of all: viz.-

Malvern. flagship. 12 guns
Tecumseh. iron clad. 2 guns
Saugus. iron clad. 2 guns
Canonicus. iron clad. 2 guns
Onondaga. iron clad. 4 guns
Atlanta. iron clad. 4 guns

Mackinaw. paddle wheel. 10 guns
Eutaw. paddle wheel. 10 guns
Hunchback. paddle wheel. 7 guns
Commodore Jones. paddle wheel. 6 guns
Commodore Morris. paddle wheel. 6 guns
Shokokon. paddle wheel. 6 guns
Stepping Stones. paddle wheel. 5 guns
Delaware. paddle wheel. 3 guns
General Putnam. paddle wheel. 2 guns
Shawsheen. paddle wheel. 3 guns
Dawn. screw. 3 guns
Hydrangea. screw. 2 guns
Poppy. screw. 2 guns
Cohasset. screw. 2 guns
Rose. screw. 1 gun
Young America. screw. 2 guns

[The *Tecumseh, Saugus,* and *Canonicus* were *Canonicus*-class monitors launched in 1863. Each carried two 15-inch Dahlgren guns. The *Tecumseh* sank on 5 August 1864 after striking a torpedo during the Battle of Mobile Bay. The *Onondaga*, a double-turreted monitor, served for many years after the war in the French navy. The *Atlanta* was a Confederate ironclad captured by the monitors *Weehawken* and *Nahant* on 17 June 1863. The *Mackinaw* and *Eutaw* were *Sassacus*-class double-enders. The gunboats *Hunchback* and *Shokokon* were ex-ferryboats; the gunboats *Dawn, Delaware,* and *Shawsheen* converted merchantmen. The rest were tugboats.]

It was near midnight before all the vessels had received their orders;[1] but at the break of day every one were underway, and presented an imposing appearance.

The troops were already on the march up the peninsula and gathering on board the transports. At sunrise every man-of-war with the exception of the *Roanoke* and her tender were moving rapidly up the James, the flagship leading the van.

The weather was all that could be desired, nothing disturbed the unbroken solitude; but in the distance dark clouds of smoke could be seen indicating the line of march of our soldiers.

The iron clads were being towed by some of the vessels and came along in fine style. About 10:00 A.M. we arrived at Wilson's Wharf, which we expected to find our troops in possession of, but they had not made their appearance as yet. The *Dawn* and *Young America* which had been towing the *Atlanta* cast off and the three vessels took up a position to cover and assist the soldiers when they arrived. Approaching Fort Powhatan we looked for our flag; but could not see it or any signs of the presence of our troops whom we expected to find in full possession. It was one of the strongest points on the river and not knowing

USS *Commodore Barney*, formerly a New York ferryboat. The walking beam machinery, the paddlewheels, and anyone standing atop the wheel house were vulnerable to enemy gunfire. (Courtesy of Robert M. Browning, Jr.)

whether it was occupied or not the vessels cautiously approached it ready for action; but passed on unmolested. [A small earthen Confederate fort on the James twenty-five miles below Richmond, Fort Powhatan was purportedly built on the site of an old Indian fort.]

Arriving at Harrison's bar the *Malvern* anchored and awaited the arrival of the monitors. At high water they safely crossed the bar and the gunboats went ahead dragging the channel for torpedoes. When within a short distance of City Point a rebel battery opened fire; but was quickly silenced by the vessels in advance. The fleet slowly moved towards City Point and when within range, the army transports filled with soldiers came up the river and greeted the flag-ship with hearty cheers, which the bluejackets returned. Meeting with no opposition they landed under cover of our guns, and pickets were thrown out. In a short time the army signal flag was waving from one of the house tops, and the first message was to the admiral informing him that City Point was in full possession of our troops and the enemy was nowhere in sight.

The fleet continued on as far as Bermuda Hundred where another landing was made by the soldiers. For several hours the transports continued to arrive, and at night thousands of camp fires were brightly burning. Earthworks were thrown up during the night and by daylight the army was strongly intrenched.

USS *Commodore Morris*, formerly a New York ferryboat. Visible armament, from left to right, includes a IX-inch Dahlgren smoothbore, a 100-pounder Parrott rifle, and a 24-pounder Dahlgren boat gun. (National Archives 111-B-411)

After the landing had been accomplished General Butler arrived and issued orders for the troops to advance on the following day.

At 9:00 A.M. the iron clads and gunboats were underway. After communicating with General Butler the admiral came on board with information that the enemy were in force about three miles up the river. The advance vessels had boats out and were themselves dragging for torpedoes. All was working well until they arrived at Deep Bottom. Several torpedoes had been discovered and being too heavy to raise, the wires which connected them with galvanic batteries on shore were cut. The *Commodore Jones* was engaged on this duty when without a second's warning a torpedo was exploded under her and she was blown to fragments, more than one half of her crew being killed or wounded. It was fortunate that all her boats were out dragging for the infernal machines or the loss of life would have been greater.

Immediately after her destruction three men were discovered running from a clump of bushes on shore. A coxswain in one of the cutters shot one of them dead and the others were captured. Upon being examined they gave their names as P. W. Smith, an Acting Master in the Confederate Submarine Battery

Service under command of Lieutenant Hunter Davidson of the boat *Torpedo* [Davidson commanded the Submarine Battery Service from the summer of 1862 to late 1864; the *Torpedo* was a 150-foot torpedo boat tender armed with two guns], and Jeffries Johnson, a private in the same service. The torpedo which blew up the *Commodore Jones* was exploded by them with a galvanic battery. A party of sailors and marines were sent on shore and discovered three galvanic batteries sunk in pits in the ground from which wires were attached to torpedoes which were not exploded. From Smith it was learned that there were a great number of torpedoes in the channel of the river; but would not indicate their location. Johnson said he was a conscript and procured his exchange from the army into this branch of the service as it would enable him to be nearer home, which was at Deep Bottom. He would not at first give any information with regard to torpedoes; but when he was informed he would be placed on board the advance vessel and share her fate if she was destroyed he consented to communicate all the knowledge he possessed. He stated that the torpedo which blew up the *Commodore Jones* had been placed in the river in the fall of the year previous, and contained two thousand pounds of powder. A number of others were pointed out and the wires cut. The smallest torpedo which was exploded by a galvanic battery contained four hundred pounds of powder. Those containing a less quantity of powder were intended to explode by striking the bottom or sides of a vessel as she passed over them, or by means of a trigger and line from the shore.

It was a very fortunate circumstance that led to the capture of this man, as it no doubt prevented the destruction of other vessels in the fleet. Through his forced assistance a large number of these terrible engines of ruin and death were discovered and rendered harmless.[2] [According to Grattan's diary, the executive officer of the *Commodore Jones* was "badly wounded, but he had the honor & pleasure of shooting one of the men who set the torpedo off." After the torpedo exploded, "four men were seen running up the banks. One of them was recognized as being the notorious Lieut Davidson." The diary reflects the hatred that navy men had for those in the Submarine Battery Service. Although Grattan's diary differs in the details regarding the number of rebels seen running, who did the shooting, and the presence of Davidson, Grattan used the official accounts to reconstruct this incident in *Under the Blue Pennant.*[3]]

Not deeming it prudent to advance any further until the torpedoes were cleared out of the channel, the admiral directed the vessels to anchor in line at convenient distances from each other along the river. The *Shawsheen* under the command of Acting Ensign Charles Ringot had discovered some torpedoes at Turkey Island Bend over which the other vessels had safely passed. He was left there with orders to destroy them or render them harmless.

10

The Union pickets abreast of the flagship ✦ Heavy firing heard
down the river ✦ The *Malvern* aground ✦ Destruction of the
gunboat *Shawsheen* by a rebel battery of light artillery ✦ Two of
the survivors rescued ✦ The monitor *Canonicus* stationed at
Turkey Island Bend ✦ Floating torpedoes discovered ✦
The monitor sweeps the shore with her guns ✦ The *Malvern*
assists in dislodging the enemy concealed back of the river ✦
The admiral directs the vessel to proceed to City Point ✦
All hands at supper and a very few on deck ✦ The scenery from
the wheel house ✦ Rebel sharpshooters open fire on the flagship ✦
A narrow escape and some grand and lofty tumbling ✦
Information from the army ✦ The troops engaged ✦ A visit to
General Butler's intrenchments ✦ The monitors and
heavier gunboats advance to Trent's Reach ✦ The enemy
at work on a formidable battery at Howlett's house ✦
The monitors open fire ✦ [May 1864]

AT DAYBREAK ON THE FOLLOWING MORNING, MAY 7, the Union pickets were
discovered abreast of the *Malvern* and thus far they had met with no serious
opposition. After breakfast the admiral went on board the *Commodore Morris*
and made a formal inspection of the fleet; but he had not been absent long,
when heavy artillery firing was heard down the river. The *Malvern* quickly got
underway but unfortunately ran aground. The admiral came down from the
advance vessels; but seeing our condition remained on board the gunboat and
ordered the flagship to follow as soon as she was afloat. In the meantime the
firing continued with rapidity. We kept our wheels moving under full steam,
and was soon clear of the muddy bottom. Upon rounding the bend of the river
we discovered the *Shawsheen* to be on fire and a rebel battery on the bluff. In a
few moments her magazine exploded and the vessel was a complete wreck.
The *Commodore Morris* had opened fire; but her guns were too heavy for the
enemy and they retreated with their light artillery.

Two of the crew of the unfortunate vessel were picked up in the water, when
it was learned that while engaged in dragging for torpedoes they were surprised
by the rebel battery. The first shot passed through her boiler and left her at the
mercy of the foe; shot and shell were poured into her and she was soon on fire.
Captain Ringot and several of his men tried to escape by swimming to the

Destruction of the USS *Shawsheen*, by John W. Grattan (John W. Grattan Papers, Library of Congress)

opposite shore, but with the exception of the two who were picked up, they were shot and drowned; five of her officers and twenty-two men including the pilot were captured and confined in Libby Prison. [Perhaps the most notorious Confederate prison after Andersonville, Libby Prison was situated on the James River in Richmond in a warehouse formerly owned by Libby and Sons, ship chandlers. Officers only were imprisoned there.] A few days after this disaster the body of Captain Ringot was found floating in the water with a bullet wound in his head, and he was buried on shore near the scene of his death with military honors.[1]

Heavy firing was heard in the direction of Petersburg on the morning following the loss of the *Shawsheen*, and it was reported that General Smith had met with serious opposition and was engaged in burning bridges and destroying railroads.

In order to keep our communications open the vessels were stationed at the most exposed points and the trees and shrubbery on the river banks were cleared away. The iron clad *Canonicus* was ordered down to Turkey Island Bend to take the place of the *Shawsheen*. On the ninth of May a large number of float-

Monitor USS *Canonicus* receiving coal from a schooner with tug USS *Zeta* in foreground, James River, summer 1864 (Courtesy of Robert M. Browning, Jr.)

ing torpedoes were discovered in her vicinity, and a number of persons were seen skulking in the bushes a short distance from the shore, evidently watching the result of their experiment. Without a moments warning the iron clad opened fire with her immense guns and a large body of rebels with their glistening rifles were seen scattering in every direction.[2]

The flagship went down the river to inquire into the cause of the firing and from her mast head we could see a detachment of rebel infantry moving down a road about a mile distant. A few shell from our howitzers sent them flying in great confusion.

The admiral desiring a consultation with General Butler directed the *Malvern* to continue down river to City Point. The crew were piped to supper and no one remained on deck except the watch and a few officers who took advantage of the delightful weather to observe the beautiful scenery. The top of the wheel houses from their clear and elevated position were always occupied by an officer or his men who had been assigned to the flagship as an army signal station, and it was the usual lounging place for our officers when they had nothing else to do. On this occasion several of us were laughing and joking at the comical appearance the rebels made when they tried to escape our fire. We were approaching a high bluff and were in the best of humor, when suddenly we heard a volley of musketry and bullets whizzed and hissed past us and struck all around. The ladder from the top of the wheel house to the hurricane deck was very narrow and when we realized our danger, a rush was made for it; but Mr. Olcott was the only one who secured it, and he gracefully descended in a sitting position, bouncing from step to step. The others reached the deck with wonderful agility; but it was done so quickly as to leave no impression on our minds how we got there. When we had recovered our presence of mind, the muskets of the marines were taken from their racks and about a dozen shots fired at the enemy who could then be plainly seen on the bluff. [Grattan omitted a significant detail that he had recorded in his diary: "I grabbed a musket & seeing one of the rebs running along the hill in plain sight I took dead aim at him & saw him throw the gun down, throw his arms up & drop. Several shots were fired at me but only one came near me striking the wheel house about 6 inches from my leg. . . . I have the satisfaction of knowing that I shot one of the rebs as dead as he could be."[3]]

The river here makes a sharp turn and it was impossible to bring our howitzers to bear. Our tender, the tug *Poppy*, was about two hundred yards astern of us and as soon as she discovered the enemy, opened a rapid fire and drove them away. It was a matter of surprise that no one was struck as the ship was marked in over fifty places by the bullets; the rope leading to the whistle from the wheel house was cut in half, and several bullets entered the small cabin on the quarter deck which was occasionally occupied by the admiral.

Arriving at City Point the admiral had learned that General Butler had made preparations for battle and as the movements of the navy depended in a great measure upon the result of the engagement, we remained all night at Bermuda Hundred. Early on the following morning, May 12, heavy firing was heard in the direction of Drewry's Bluff. In a few hours long lines of ambulances began to arrive filled with wounded soldiers from the front, when it was reported that General Butler had met the enemy; but after a sharp battle was compelled to retire to his original line of intrenchments. When the information was verified the flagship proceeded up the river and anchored near Deep Bottom.

While the army were recovering from their repulse, the admiral went ashore and in company with a few officers called upon General Butler and inspected the line of fortifications. A consultation was had and the result was orders for the monitors and larger gunboats to move up the river on the following morning.

The *Malvern* being a very light built iron vessel unsuitable and incapable of engaging the heavy batteries it was expected to encounter, and for the additional reason that all the archives of the squadron and paymaster's funds were on board, it was deemed advisable for the present to keep her where she was.

Double-turreted monitor USS *Onondaga*, the most powerful vessel in the James River, circa 1864–1865 (Courtesy of Robert M. Browning, Jr.)

The double-ender *Agawam*, under the command of Commander Alexander C. Rhind, had lately arrived and having a battery of ten heavy guns, the admiral temporarily transferred his flag leaving the larger portion of his staff on board the *Malvern*. [The *Agawam* was commissioned on 9 March 1864.]

At daylight the vessels ordered to advance were promptly underway, and arrived as far as Trent's Reach where the monitors came to anchor. This was as far as the depth of water would permit them to go, and any further movement up the river would have to be made by the wooden vessels. General Butler's advance line of intrenchments were directly abreast of the iron clads and extended from the James River to the Appomattox.

A few hours after the arrival of the monitors the enemy was discovered at work on a formidable earthwork situated on a high bluff commanding Trent's Reach. It was subsequently known as Howlett's Battery. Under directions of the admiral the iron clads opened fire; but owing to the extreme elevation required it was some time before the range was obtained. Under the cover of darkness the battery was completed and several heavy guns mounted, one of them a 200-pounder rifle as we learned from several deserters. Three rebel iron clads had been lying for several days near Drewry's Bluff waiting for Howlett's Battery to open fire.[4]

11

Fort Powhatan attacked by the enemy and repulsed ✦ Assault
on the colored troops at Wilson's Wharf ✦ The gunboat *Dawn*
opens a terrific fire ✦ The enemy retire with great loss ✦ General
Butler engaged with the rebels ✦ Naval picket stations ✦
A scouting party from the *Malvern* ✦ Rebel cavalry charge and
repulse by the bluejackets ✦ General Butler requests obstructions
be sunk in the channel at Trent's Reach ✦ The admiral's protest ✦
General Grant arrives at City Point ✦ He requests the
obstructions be sunk to guard against a descent of the Rebel
rams and fire rafts ✦ The Army of the Potomac crossing the
James on pontoons ✦ Howlett's and a masked battery ready for a
fight ✦ The monitors and gunboats open fire ✦ The rebel rams
and gunboats descend the river and with the batteries open the
engagement ✦ The flagship under fire ✦ Result of the contest ✦
[May–June 1864]

UP TO THE TIME the monitors had anchored in Trent's Reach, the troops in occupation of Fort Powhatan and Wilson's Wharf had been left in undisputed possession of those important points, and taking advantage of the opportunity both places were strongly fortified.

On the 21st of May the enemy suddenly appeared before Fort Powhatan and made a gallant but unsuccessful assault. The iron clad *Atlanta* and gunboat *Dawn* assisted the garrison and after a short engagement the rebels were repulsed.[1]

Two days after this affair the admiral ordered the *Pequot*, then stationed at Turkey Island Bend, to proceed down to Wilson's Wharf and warn Brigadier General Edward Augustus Wild, who was in command, to strengthen his means of defence as a late Richmond paper captured by our navy pickets commented with great bitterness on the presence of the colored troops stationed there. The *Pequot* was stationed above Fort Powhatan; the *Dawn* below Wilson's Wharf and the *Atlanta* and *Young America* between the two.

[Brigadier General Edward Augustus Wild, USV, a rabid Massachusetts abolitionist, commanded the First Brigade (nicknamed "Wild's African Brigade"), Third Division, United States Colored Troops. Shortly after the brigade's arrival at Wilson's Wharf, a foraging party captured William H. Clopton, a wealthy planter renowned for his brutality. Wild ordered William Harris of Company E, who had been one of Clopton's slaves, to whip his former master. The Richmond *Daily Examiner* reported the Yankees were "committing the most atrocious outrage on the people."]

At 1.30 P.M. of the following day, the 24th, the enemy made a very sudden attack on Wilson's Wharf. The rebels consisted of a brigade of cavalry under the command of Major General Fitzhugh Lee. [Nephew of Robert E. Lee, Fitzhugh Lee distinguished himself as a Confederate cavalry leader throughout the Civil War. In the Spanish-American War he served as a major general of U.S. Volunteers.] The *Dawn* immediately opened fire and, as the troops were fully prepared, drove the enemy back; but they soon reappeared on the bank of the river above the intrenchments and fired a heavy volley of musketry into the transport *Mayflower* which was passing up the river, severely wounding her captain and pilot. Acting Ensign W. F. Chase who was on board the transport at once jumped to the wheel and brought the vessel safe through the terrible fire. The *Young America* was unable to enter into action having met with an accident to her boiler. The *Dawn* at once renewed the engagement when the fire of the enemy was directed towards the colored troops. Upon communicating with General Wild it was discovered he was nearly out of ammunition. The *Dawn* ascertained the position of the rebels, opened fire again, and drove them out of the woods in front of the intrenchments. The firing then ceased for a short time when the enemy rallied and with a yell made another desperate assault; but the *Dawn* was in an excellent position and rained shell, canister grape and shrapnel with the greatest rapidity into the close ranks of the rebels, and repulsed them in great disorder. The whole engagement occupied nearly six hours.

The force under the command of General Wild was composed of nine hundred colored troops and two 20-pounder Parrott guns, while that of the enemy was at least two-thousand strong, and it is chiefly due to the rapid firing and skillful maneuvering of the *Dawn* that the garrison was saved from capture and perhaps massacre.[2]

A few days after this gallant affair the rebels made an attempt to carry General Butler's intrenchments by assault; but were handsomely repulsed by the troops and the monitors. [No record of "an attempt to carry General Butler's intrenchments by assault" appears in the published official naval records; however, an officer on the *Delaware* wrote his wife on 30 May that his ship and the *Onondaga* silenced a "pretty sharp artillery fire on Gen Butler's lines" by the rebels that day.[3]]

It was customary for the vessels along the river to keep picket stations on shore, in order to give timely notice of the appearance of the enemy. The *Malvern* took a position near Tilghman's Wharf directly opposite the plantation of Major Allen who was in the rebel army; and a number of officers and sailors were thrown out as pickets. Almost every night there would be an alarm and the howitzers for a time would sweep the country in all directions; but our bluejackets soon got accustomed to the novel duty, and with a few uninteresting exceptions they were unmolested.

A scouting party was organized one day to visit some dwelling houses and barns which could be seen about a mile back from the river near the old battlefield at Malvern Hill. As we cautiously approached not a sound was heard nor could anyone be seen in the deserted village. Some barns were filled with grain; but owing to the positive orders of the admiral that we were not to destroy private property we did not apply the torch. The dwelling houses contained nothing of value; but bore indications of a hasty departure by their former occupants. A rebel telegraph wire was discovered and destroyed. Having fully satisfied our curiosity we returned towards the river; but had only proceeded a short distance when a troop of cavalry dashed out from the woods and charged upon us. We were all armed with rifles and revolvers and taking advantage of several hollows in the ground we prepared to resist. When within range orders were given to take deliberate aim and fire. At the first volley the saddles of two of them were emptied of riders, which checked the others from advancing any further, and after securing the two horses and their dead or wounded comrades, beat a retreat. Upon arriving on board ship several shell were sent in the direction where the enemy went, and they were seen to leave the vicinity with remarkable quickness.

After several days of inactivity it became known that for the present no further advance would be made by our fleet towards Richmond, as General Grant after terrible fighting had determined to change his base of operations to our vicinity, and the principal object now was to strengthen and hold our position. General Butler having been taught a severe lesson by the loss of Plymouth and the destruction and loss of life caused by his neglect to place obstructions so as to prevent the ram *Albemarle* coming down the Roanoke had the effect of making him over anxious concerning the rebel rams up the James, and he notified the admiral that a barque and five schooners would be furnished for the purpose of obstructing the channel above the monitors. But the situation was different in the James from what it was in Roanoke River; at the latter place there were nothing but wooden vessels to oppose the enemy, while at the former locality the monitors would have been able to conquer and destroy all the rebel iron clads had they appeared.

The admiral was not in favor of the general's naval tactics and informed him that the first consideration with him was the necessity of holding the river beyond a peradventure for the great military purposes of General Grant and General Butler; but in consulting his own wishes he said he would do everything to induce and nothing to prevent the enemy from trying to assert their strength in a pure naval contest, which in his opinion would give us a naval victory. The only contingency of such a battle was the unknown effect of the enemy's torpedo vessels, which, as the attacking party, would give them perhaps an advantage which might possibly balance our certain superiority in all other fighting material.[4]

City Point, Virginia (Courtesy of Robert M. Browning, Jr.)

After the arrival of the schooners the admiral wrote to General Butler as follows:- "I desire to keep the schooners ready for sinking when I am advised that a controlling military necessity requires that it be done."[5] On the evening of the 15th of June the admiral had a long consultation with General Grant at City Point and was then informed that it was his request that the obstructions should be sunk, as no further advance up the river would be made for several months. The obstructions were then placed in the channel and on the same day a pontoon bridge had been thrown across the river at Wilcox's Wharf near Fort Powhatan, and near midnight the grand Army of the Potomac commenced crossing over, and for nearly three days the troops were occupied in the movement.[6]

After the sinking of the obstructions the *Malvern* was ordered to Trent's Reach and anchored near the rebel shore in rear of the monitors when the admiral re-occupied his quarters. The heavy wooden vessels were stationed in the rear of the *Malvern* with their guns trained on Howlett's battery and the bend in the river above. On Sunday the 19th of June General Grant and General Butler came on board and a long consultation was had with the admiral, the result of which was orders issued to the fleet to maintain the greatest vigilance as the enemy was gathering in great numbers near the river, and efforts would be made to cut or interrupt our communications.

For several weeks we had been expecting to exchange shots with Howlett's battery, and were at loss to account for the silence of the enemy; but the reason

Pontoon bridge across the James, circa 1864 (National Archives B-451)

for their supposed inactivity was soon explained. At daylight on the 21st of June to our astonishment the trees for a considerable distance had been cleared away and a very strong heavily armed earthwork was plain in sight. The monitors were soon at work; but received no reply until noon, when four white puffs of smoke were seen and the whistling and screaming of heavy solid shot told us the engagement had commenced. The monitor *Tecumseh* under the command of the gallant Commander Tunis A. M. Craven sent five XV-inch shell in rapid succession into the battery, and destroyed a platform, throwing the earth and timber in every direction. The *Canonicus* and *Saugus* also made some very fine shots. Shortly after the beginning of the conflict, the rebel rams made their appearance on the upper side of Dutch Gap within a mile of our position and opened a cross fire. The enemy at Howlett's then fired with great rapidity and deliberation; shot after shot striking the monitors. The two-turreted monitor *Onondaga* with her XV-inch guns and the *Agawam* with her heavy Parrots and Dahlgrens opened fire on the rebel fleet, which lay concealed behind the trees. By the aid of our glasses we could see the effects produced by the monitors. At times a lull would occur when the enemy taking advantage of the opportunity would load train and fire their guns and retire to the bomb proofs.

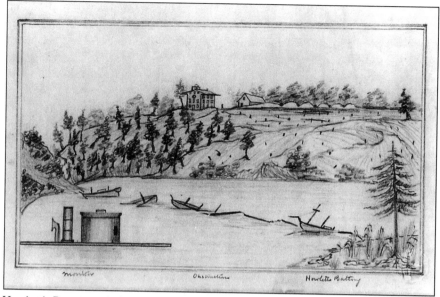

Howlett's Battery and obstructions across the James, by John W. Grattan (John W. Grattan Papers, Library of Congress)

The *Malvern* was directly in the line of fire of the rams, and during the whole afternoon their shot and shell were screaming and exploding over and around us, most of their guns were too much elevated to do any damage. Well knowing that one shot well aimed would completely destroy the flagship it is with great satisfaction I can testify as to the bravery, fearlessness, and courage of her officers and crew who unable to reply to the enemy with our light battery were compelled to listen to the roar of their guns. [Grattan recorded the event in his diary even as the battle raged around him: "At 1 P.M. the enemy sent their rams and iron clads down the river, and a general engagement ensued. Shell & shot fell within a few feet of our vessel and bursted over our heads. At 2 P.M. the fight is kept up, over 100 guns have been fired. The whole fleet is under the enemies guns and the firing is very rapid. The shell are now whistling and bursting over our heads. This is the first regular engagement with the enemy and will be a hard fight. 3 P.M. over 50 shot & shell have been fired at us up to this time great many bursting within 100 feet of us. 3,15 a shell from the rebel iron clad struck within 10 feet of the ship and threw mud over our deck in great quantity. They have now got the range and can rake us fore & aft. 6 P.M. The fight still continues nearly 100 shot & shell have been fired nearly a dozen have fell within 20 yards of the ship. One burst right ahead and threw some fragments on deck." The battle ended at 6:30.[7]]

The enemy ceased fire about sunset after expending over three hundred shot and shell. The monitor *Saugus* was struck a great number of times, one shot striking her iron deck rebounded against the turret breaking six heavy bolts; but otherwise was not much injured. The *Canonicus, Tecumseh,* and *Onondaga* were not damaged. It was estimated the battery was distant about 2,200 yards and at an elevation of one-hundred feet. From a rebel deserter it was learned that Howlett's Battery had been badly injured by the fire of our vessels, one gun was dismounted and a number of men killed and wounded. The rams had the assistance of several small gunboats; but their firing was all guess work.[8]

12

The monitor *Tecumseh* detached from the squadron and ordered
to Mobile Bay • Her subsequent destruction by a torpedo •
Arrival of President Lincoln on the flagship • A visit to the
fortifications • Army movements at Deep Bottom • Another
battery opens fire on vessels passing up and down the river •
Loss of life • Sharp engagement by the gunboats • The army
building fortifications • Celebration of the 4th of July •
No immediate advance in contemplation the admiral turns his
attention to the Wilmington blockade • The flagship preparing
for sea • Rumors that the enemy were threatening Washington •
Telegraphic communication cut • The *Malvern* proceeds to the
capital • Hasty evacuation of Willard's Hotel by the officers of
the flagship • Off for Hampton Roads • Exciting news from
the James River fleet • [June–July 1864]

A FEW DAYS AFTER THE ENGAGEMENT with Howlett's Battery orders were
received from the Navy Department detaching the *Tecumseh* and with her brave
commander and several gunboats from the Squadron with instructions to proceed off Mobile Bay and report to Admiral Farragut for duty. This reduction
greatly weakened the naval force in the James River; but we were yet able to
keep our communications open. Commander Craven parted with the admiral
with regret; but he was soon underway and safely arrived at his destination.
During the attack upon the rebel batteries in Mobile Bay the *Tecumseh* when
nearly abreast of Fort Morgan and about one hundred and fifty yards from the
beach was sunk by a torpedo. A few of the officers and men were saved; but
the majority including the brave commander were drowned.

[After striking the torpedo the *Tecumseh* capsized and went down in seconds. In the confusion as the men struggled to escape, Craven and John Collins,
the pilot, arrived at the foot of the ladder leading to the main deck at the same
time. Craven stepped back and said, "After you, pilot." Collins escaped. Craven's gallantry brought him immortal fame at the cost of his life.]

As it was necessary to have possession of both banks of the river where our
advance vessels were stationed an important military movement was successfully and quietly accomplished for that purpose a few days before the naval
conflict with Howlett's. A pontoon bridge was thrown across the river at Deep
Bottom and a division of troops under the command of Brigadier General

Robert S. Foster crossed over and threw up a line of intrenchments. [Foster commanded the First Division, X Corps. Later he served on the military commission that tried Lincoln's assassins.]

On the 29th of June a rebel battery was discovered about two thousand yards from his line of works and about the same distance from the river. An army tug passed by the battery not knowing of its presence and was fired into, losing one man killed and several wounded. When the admiral heard of it he sent two double enders down from Trent's Reach; but receiving no reply to their guns returned to their stations leaving the *Hunchback* with her heavy battery to attend to the rebels in that vicinity.

For several hours the battery remained silent when it suddenly opened fire with five guns. Lieutenant Fyffe who was in command of the *Hunchback* opened fire with his IX-Dahlgrens and the engagement continued with great vigor for two hours. Hearing the heavy guns at Trent's Reach the admiral ordered the *Saugus* to go down and assist if necessary.

Upon her arrival the enemy were discovered busily at work repairing damages and placing their guns in position; several of which had been knocked over by the splendid firing of the *Hunchback*. The *Saugus* fired a few shots but from the elevated position of the battery it was almost impossible to dislodge the enemy.

Notwithstanding the presence of the monitor and gunboat, when any vessels passed up and down the river the battery would open fire. As this threatened to stop communication on the James, the *Mendota* and *Agawam* were ordered down and taken positions as to bring a cross fire to bear; but their intentions were anticipated and the enemy evacuated their strong position.[1]

On the morning following the engagement with Howlett's we were honored with a visit from President Lincoln who was accompanied by Assistant Secretary of the Navy Gustavus Vasa Fox. After resting himself and taking refreshments on board the flagship a visit was made to General Butler who showed the presidential party the fortifications.

Lieutenant General Grant, after executing his grand flank movement and throwing up heavy intrenchments from the Appomattox to a considerable distance below Petersburg, expressed his determination to "fight it out on that line if it took all summer"; but after waiting for some time for the fighting to take place, the dull monotony of the situation became almost unendurable. The admiral called very often upon General Grant at his headquarters at City Point; but the state of affairs still remained unchanged, and as the exigencies of the service demanded a strict blockade being enforced at Wilmington, Captain Melancton Smith of the *Onondaga* was directed to assume command of the James River fleet so as to allow the admiral to devote his whole attention to that service, and on the 3d of July the *Malvern* bade adieu to her consorts and proceeded down the river and for the night anchored off City Point.

The following day being the anniversary of the Declaration of Independence orders were given to the several vessels in the river to celebrate the occasion by firing a national salute.

Double-ended gunboat USS *Mendota* in the James, 1864 (Courtesy of Robert M. Browning, Jr.)

The flagship was dressed in her gayest and handsomest colors and at noon the salute was commenced by the *Malvern* firing thirty-five guns, which was re-echoed by the other vessels and the fortifications, and for about half an hour there was one continuous roar of artillery. At the close of the celebration the flagship steamed rapidly down the James.

Being in need of repairs the *Malvern* proceeded to the Norfolk Navy Yard and after a thorough overhauling we anchored in Hampton Roads.

Receiving information to the effect that the enemy were in the vicinity of Washington and the capitol in danger of being captured the admiral telegraphed to the Navy Department to know whether any assistance was required from his squadron. Not receiving any reply and learning that the telegraphic communication had been cut, the flagship got underway and proceeded to Washington where we arrived on the morning of July 14th. [On 5 July, Major General Jubal A. Early led 14,000 Confederates into Maryland for a raid on Washington. In response to information that communications between Washington and Annapolis had been cut, Admiral Lee took the *Malvern* to Washington under full steam and reported to the Navy Department. Secretary Welles curtly rebuked him for doing so without orders.[2]]

Nothing could be seen or heard of the presence of the enemy; but to satisfy ourselves that the ruthless invader was not in full and quiet possession of the city a party of daring officers volunteered to go ashore and find out the situation of affairs. Meeting with no opposition we marched bravely through the streets and safely arrived at Willard's, where we made a few inquiries of the bar-keeper. [Willard's Hotel was and is an elegant and opulent establishment located near the White House.] Not feeling quite satisfied although much refreshed we entered a billiard room, and each one seizing a cue we commenced a furious engagement; the balls were rolling in every direction and several very fine ricochet shots were made. We were just about turning the string of points, and as it was very warm work had given another order for more ammunition, having during the action kept several waiters on a constant run to and from the magazine in the bar room, when an officer came in with a message from the admiral to cease firing and come on board immediately. Leaving the battle undecided we retreated in good order. The *Malvern* was soon underway and moving rapidly down the Potomac every revolution of the wheels increasing our distance from the terrible indignation of the Secretary of the Navy who wanted to know how we dared to come to Washington without orders.

Upon our arrival at Hampton Roads we received some interesting information from our vessels in the James River. Lieutenant Commander Stephen P. Quackenbush, captain of the *Pequot*, while stationed at Turkey Island Bend, discovered a number of the enemy preparing to set afloat some torpedoes. His pickets one night marched quietly towards them, and after a sharp fight, completely routed them. [On 15 January 1865, Quackenbush was in command of the monitor *Patapsco* when she struck a torpedo in Charleston harbor and went down with more than half of her men.]

A few days after a larger detachment appeared, and the *Pequot* opened fire, a 150-pound shell exploded in the midst of a force numbering at least one hundred, and a great many were killed or wounded. The enemy then retired to Malvern Hill where they opened fire with artillery. The first shot took a sailor's leg off and another splintered the main top mast of the *Pequot*. The *Commodore Morris* coming up the river at the time joined that vessel and soon silenced the rebel battery. The *Commodore Morris* narrowly escaped destruction during the engagement; one shot passed through her magazine splintering two barrels of gun powder.[3]

From Deep Bottom we heard that large bodies of troops supposed to be Longstreet's and Hill's Corps [respectively, I Corps and III Corps, Army of Northern Virginia] were discovered throwing up earthworks and on the 28th of July made an assault on General Foster's position; but through the aid of the *Agawam* and *Mendota* were repulsed with great loss.[4] On the same night all of General Foster's command were engaged in strengthening their position while the reinforcements which had been sent him were moved across the pontoons and rapidly marched to General Grant's lines in front of Petersburg.

The enemy made desperate efforts to interrupt river communication; but upon the approach of our gunboats were compelled to retire.

13

The headquarters of the squadron transferred to Beaufort N.C. ◆
Description of the dangers and difficulties of the blockade of
Wilmington ◆ New vessels ordered to the squadron ◆ Destruction
of the blockade runner *Wild Dayrell* ◆ The Anglo-Rebel steamer
Nutfield beached and burned ◆ A new danger to the fleet ◆
Rebel ram *North Carolina* attacks the vessels at sea ◆ A sharp
engagement ◆ She returns uninjured and is saluted by the
fortifications ◆ Increased vigilance of the blockading vessels ◆
[February–May 1864]

In ORDER TO ACCOMPLISH a more rigid enforcement of the blockade, the headquarters of the squadron were transferred to Beaufort, North Carolina, to which locality the flagship sailed on the twenty-eighth day of July.

To form a better idea of the difficulties attending the Wilmington blockade a brief description of the location becomes necessary. Cape Fear River from various natural causes was the most dangerous and embarrassing to close of any port on the Atlantic coast. The two main entrances, New Inlet and Western Bar, were forty miles apart by ocean communication, being divided by Frying Pan Shoals, which were always dangerous to navigation. Along the coast numerous batteries and fortifications had been erected, so that blockade runners were not compelled to run directly for the entrance, but by using the lead line, could run close under the land, protected by the enemy's guns, and pass in over the bar unmolested. [A "lead line" or "sounding lead" consisted of a marked line with a weight attached used for gauging the depth of the water.]

When running out the vessel would select her own time at night or in foggy weather and pass either up or down the coast before making an offing, or would proceed directly out to sea running the risk of discovery and capture or destruction by the blockading fleet.

The vessels engaged in this dangerous service were in nearly every instance constructed in England, and particular attention was paid to their speed. No expense was spared in fitting them out as two or three successful trips paid the cost of the vessels and handsomely reimbursed their owners. Among the many disadvantages under which our navy labored was the want of fast steamers. As far as fighting material was concerned we were well supplied; but were unable to compete or equal the blockade runners in speed.

Blockading fleet off Old Inlet. Fort Caswell stands to the left, Fort Holmes on the right, with a blockade runner inside. (Courtesy of Robert M. Browning, Jr.)

To remedy this difficulty the Navy Department had vessels constructed with special reference to this important object, and the *Eutaw* and *Sassacus* after a successful trial trip and having accomplished a speed of eighteen knots were accepted by the government and ordered to the North Atlantic Squadron. The *Sassacus*, previous to her encounter with the *Albemarle*, reported for duty and was placed on the line between Bermuda and New Inlet in the meridian of 75 degrees west longitude, a station which would test her speed and one in which a fast cruiser would prove a great obstacle to the blockade runners. She had not been long on the station when black smoke was discovered on the horizon, and the exciting chase began [2 February 1864]. After a few hours engaged in the pursuit the blockade runner was headed for the beach, finding it impossible to escape. She was soon aground and the crew on shore. Lieutenant Commander Francis A. Roe, captain of the *Sassacus*, boarded her with his boats and found her in perfect order and loaded with assorted cargo. She proved to be the steamer *Wild Dayrell*. Several attempts were made to haul her off, but failed and the beautiful vessel was destroyed. Her cargo alone was valued at about $200,000.[1] [A fast 215-foot iron-hulled paddlewheeler inbound from Nassau, the *Wild Dayrell* carried a cargo of small arms and nautical instruments.]

Three days after, another blockade runner was discovered and ran ashore by the *Sassacus*. Her officers and crew escaped in their boats; one boat load, however with the exception of the purser, was capsized and the crew drowned. The boats of the *Sassacus* were soon alongside and rescued a Mr. Null, the purser, from whom it was learned the vessel was the *Nutfield* from Bermuda bound for Wilmington. Her cargo had consisted of munitions of war; a battery of eight Whitworth guns and pig lead were thrown overboard during the chase. Finding it impossible to get her afloat, she was destroyed after rescuing about seven hundred rifles and cavalry sabers. She was valued at about half a million dollars with her cargo.[2]

On the day following another blockade runner was run ashore by the *Cambridge* and was destroyed. She proved to be the *Dee* from Bermuda. Her cargo consisted of lead, bacon, and coffee. Seven of her crew were captured while trying to escape.[3]

On the 10th of February, five days after the loss of the *Dee*, the *Florida* beached and destroyed two handsome blockade running steamers, the first being the *Fanny and Jenny*, commanded by a Captain Coxetter, who, with the purser, was drowned in endeavoring to reach the shore. The remainder of her crew, twenty-five in number were captured; the other vessel was the *Emily* which was discovered about half a mile distant on the beach. The *Wild Dayrell* had made one successful voyage and the *Dee* was an old blockade runner; but the *Fanny and Jenny*, *Emily*, and *Nutfield* were entirely new vessels and were destroyed upon their first attempt to violate the blockade.[4]

Up to the time the headquarters of the squadron was changed to Beaufort, forty-three steamers had been captured or destroyed by the vessels on the Wilmington blockade, and as the amount involved was several millions of dollars the loss could not have been otherwise than very disastrous to the enemy and their sympathizers.

But success was not always in favor of our vessels. Shortly after 8:00 P.M. on the sixth of May the blockading fleet were treated to a sensation of a dangerous character. The flashes of two guns and a rocket being seen, the *Nansemond* proceeded in pursuit, and discovered the blockader *Britannia* running off shore. Returning to her station the *Nansemond* remained quiet until near midnight when she discovered a vessel moving slowly towards her. The stranger was challenged but answered with wrong signals, when the *Nansemond* opened fire, which was immediately returned. After exchanging several shots the strange craft retired; at daybreak she was seen inside the harbor and to the astonishment of the fleet proved to be the rebel iron clad ram *Raleigh*. When it became lighter she again crossed the bar and stood out for the vessels accompanied by one armed steamer and two tug boats. The *Howquah* being the nearest vessel was the first one attacked; but she gallantly contested every foot of the water. The ram continued to approach and steamed out as far as the day station for the blockading fleet when she was engaged by the *Kansas*, *Mount Vernon*, *Nansemond*, *Britannia* and *Howquah*, and after striking the smoke stack of the latter vessel with a rifled shot, she hauled off and went over the bar apparently uninjured. Upon her return she was saluted with nine guns from the rebel batteries. The *Tuscarora* being the senior officer's vessel was too far off to participate in the engagement with her powerful guns; but made preparations for a furious encounter should the ram again appear. The *Raleigh* was flying the English red ensign forward and rebel flag aft during the fight, and carried a battery of eight guns. In addition to her ram she had a torpedo on her bow. This was the first and last appearance of the iron clad; but the effect was very beneficial on the fleet as it only served to increase their vigilance.[5] [The C.S.S. *Raleigh* ran aground while returning to port and broke her back.]

14

Lieutenant William B. Cushing ◆ His daring attempt to capture
the commanding officer of the defenses of the Cape Fear River ◆
His visit to the Rebel headquarters at Smithfield ◆ The general
absent but his chief engineer made prisoner ◆ Cushing returns to
his ship unharmed ◆ He organizes an expedition to proceed up
the Cape Fear River ◆ His arrival near Wilmington ◆ Captures
boats, prisoners, and a mail carrier with his horse ◆ Returns
down the river ◆ Chased by the guard boats ◆ A narrow escape ◆
Cushing receives the thanks of the Navy Department ◆
[February–March 1864]

IF THERE WAS ONE OFFICER in the squadron whose name should be handed
down to posterity and take equal rank with all those naval heroes whose lives
are perpetuated in the pages of history, that gallant officer should be Lieutenant
Commander William B. Cushing. Entering the service at a very early age, he participated in and commanded several daring expeditions in the sounds of North
Carolina, in the Nansemond River, and other waters of Virginia. Wherever there
was danger he was the first to lead, and it was not long before his bravery, coolness, and competency attracted the attention of the admiral and the secretary
of the navy. Promotion followed promotion in quick succession and he was not
quite of age when he received his commission as lieutenant, and ordered to
assume command of the U.S. steamer *Monticello*, which at that time was considered to be one of the fastest vessels in the squadron. [The screw-propelled
gunboat *Monticello* could make 11.5 knots.] After several month's service in capturing and destroying blockade runners he conceived the idea that he would
capture the commanding general of the defenses of the Cape Fear River, whose
headquarters were stationed at Smithville, a small town situated on the river
inside of Western Bar Inlet and directly in the rear of Fort Caswell.

Revealing the plan to his officers they pronounced it a wild, foolish, and
impracticable scheme; but Cushing was determined to make the attempt. On
the night of the twenty-ninth of February 1864 he started with twenty men and
two boats with muffled oars, and crossing the bar passed the fort and batteries
unobserved. After a long pull they arrived at Smithville, and concealed the
boats under a wharf. Capturing a negro, Cushing learned the location of the
troops and where the sentries were posted, and at once walked up the main
street accompanied by Acting Ensign J. E. Jones, Acting Master's Mate W. L.

John W. Grattan's personal copy of a photograph of Lieutenant William Barker Cushing. Note the steely glint in Cushing's eyes. (John W. Grattan Papers, Library of Congress)

Howorth, and one sailor. Arriving at Brigadier General Louis Hébert's head-quarters, which were directly opposite the barracks containing 1,200 troops, Cushing boldly entered the courtyard and knocked at the door, which upon being opened, he walked into the house and inquired for the general, and to his chagrin was told he had left for Wilmington the day previous. Not wishing to return empty handed he then inquired who was there in the dwelling and was informed the chief engineer of the defenses and the adjutant of the rebel troops stationed in the barracks were then in. Just as the conversation with the servant had ceased Captain Kelly, the engineer, entered the room and was ordered to surrender, which he quietly did after recovering from his astonishment. The adjutant must have overheard the command as the last seen of him was a pair of bare legs running for the woods in the rear of the house, and in his haste forgetting to alarm the garrison. Cushing secured his prisoner and unmolested reached the boats, when the men were ordered to pull swiftly but quietly for the bar. Arriving near Fort Caswell signal lights were seen flashing at Smithville and were answered by the fort. The alarm had been given, in a few seconds the long roll sounded and the guns trained; but before they could be fired the boats were over the bar and safely alongside the *Monticello*. The rebel engineer was sent to the admiral with a letter in which Cushing expressed his regrets that the general was not at home when he called or he would have sent both.[1]

After the rebel ram *Raleigh* had made her appearance among the blockading fleet, Cushing requested and obtained permission to enter the river and reconnoiter and if possible destroy the iron clad; he did not know that she had broken her back. On the night of the twenty-third of June he left his vessel with two officers and fifteen picked men in the first cutter, which was provided with sails and muffled oars, and unobserved passed Fort Caswell and Smithville but narrowly escaped being run down by a blockade runner.

The night was very dark and the greatest caution was necessary to keep on the right course; but as the men were quietly rowing the moon burst forth from a bank of clouds and revealed their presence to the sentinels in the Brunswick Batteries, subsequently known as Fort Anderson. The boat was challenged, but receiving no reply, muskets were discharged and the garrison aroused.

In this trying moment Cushing was cool and gave his orders in a quiet tone of voice for the boat to make for the opposite shore towards the rear of Fort Fisher; his object being to cause it to be believed he was going down stream. The moon was again obscured and under the cover of darkness the boat was headed up the river and without accident arrived within seven miles of the city of Wilmington. It being near day break Cushing directed the cutter to run into a swamp and the day was occupied in rest after the long pull, and watching the movement of the enemy's vessels. Three blockade runners and the flagship of Commodore William F. Lynch of the rebel navy passed within two hundred yards of Cushing and his men. [Flag Officer William F. Lynch had commanded the Confederate "mosquito fleet" destroyed by the Union navy in the sounds of North Carolina in February 1862, and remained in command of Confederate naval forces in North Carolina throughout the war.]

After dusk Cushing moved out into the river, when suddenly two boats rounded the bend; knowing it would be impossible to retreat unobserved he done the next best thing and captured them, and as the prisoners were unarmed he pressed them into his service as guides. Continuing on he arrived at the obstructions, which were about three miles from Wilmington, and as it was getting late the boat entered a creek and was concealed in a swamp near the road leading from Fort Fisher to the city. Cushing then divided his party. One half remained to guard the boat and prisoners and the other marched about two miles down the road and took cover in the bushes. About eleven o'clock on the following morning a mounted rebel soldier appeared with a mail bag. He was halted and ordered to surrender. Keeping the horse and prisoner from being seen they waited for the return mail to arrive and they were soon favored with the sounds of his horse's hoofs striking the road. He was near the ambuscade when a bluejacket accidentally exposed himself, and the courier at once suspecting danger wheeled and galloped back and down the road. Springing into the saddle Cushing started in pursuit but the mail carrier had too far a lead to be overtaken.

During the day several more prisoners were captured; but no important information was obtained. As the men were getting very hungry and exhausted Mr. Howorth, as the sun was setting, dressed himself in the courier's coat and hat and, mounting his horse, started out for supplies. He found a country store not far away and soon returned with milk, chickens and eggs. After destroying the telegraph wire the party returned to the boat and enjoyed a hearty supper. Among the prisoners was an old pilot who informed Cushing that the ram *North Carolina*, a second iron clad, was then at anchor off the city, under the command of Captain William Muse and well manned.

[The C.S.S. *North Carolina* spent most of her service as a floating battery because she was so unwieldy. "She is but little relied upon," noted Cushing in his report to Lee, "and would not stand long against a monitor." The *North Carolina* foundered off Smithville on 27 September 1864 as a result of damage from teredo worms (no doubt with Union sympathies).]

Cushing, having secured the mail bag and obtained considerable information, desired to return to his ship, and as there were more prisoners than he could accommodate, he put the civilians ashore and was soon floating down the river. Approaching the lower fortifications a boat was discovered pulling for the shore. Cushing went after it and after an exciting chase overhauled it and captured six men, four of whom were soldiers. He transferred them to the cutter then set their boat adrift. Cushing then had twenty-six prisoners on board and the boat was very deep in the water. As they were nearing the narrow channel between Zeke's Island and Federal Point one of the prisoners informed Cushing that a large guard boat containing seventy-five riflemen was afloat. The information had no sooner been communicated when she was discovered. Cushing directed his men to pull for her when his attention was called to three boats which were seen coming towards him from Federal Point, and five more from the island, completely blocking up the channel. The sailors showed no signs of excitement knowing that if anyone could save them it was their brave commander. The helm was put hard down, when a large sail boat was discovered to the windward filled with troops. The moon was bright enough to render all these objects very distinct; but the gallant lieutenant was equal to the emergency and determined to outwit the enemy or fight in spite of the heavy odds against him. Suddenly turning the prow of the cutter, he dashed off as if for the western bar, and by throwing the dark side of the boat to the rebels, was soon lost to view. The maneuver was successful and the enemy dashed away to intercept him.

By the powerful and steady pulling of his men the cutter's course was altered and Cushing gained the passage of the island before the enemy could prevent it and the heavily laden boat rushed through the breakers, every second being in danger of being dashed to pieces. The rebels did not try to follow, and before they could recover from their astonishment and signal to Fort Fisher the cutter was clear of the shoals and out of danger.

About daybreak Cushing arrived among the vessels with all his crew and prisoners, and when it was known how narrowly he had escaped, he was compelled to receive the warm congratulations of the officers. When the report of his adventures were heard in Washington he received the thanks of the Secretary of the Navy.[2]

15

Beaufort and its inhabitants ◆ Union refugees ◆
Increased activity of the blockade runners ◆ The flagship
nearly wrecked on Frying Pan Shoals ◆ Inspection of the
blockade at night ◆ The enemy at work on the fortifications ◆
Instructions to commanding officers of the fleet ◆ The blockade
runners to be run ashore or sunk and destroyed ◆ Signals
on the bar ◆ A blockade runner is heading up the coast ◆
The vessels in chase ◆ The fleet illuminated by the enemy with a
calcium light ◆ The batteries open fire ◆ Sudden darkness follows ◆
A blockade runner enters the river ◆ The flagship returns to
Beaufort ◆ The prize steamer *Elsie* ◆ [July–September 1864]

T HE FLAGSHIP ANCHORED in the harbor of Beaufort on the thirtieth of July. The town previous to the war had been noted as quite a fashionable resort for the people of that surrounding country during the summer months; but after the capture of Fort Macon which protected the mouth of the harbor it fell into the possession of poor whites and negroes. The population then was about 2,400 inhabitants, who chiefly subsisted in supplying the blockading vessels with fresh provisions, fruit, fish, and vegetables. About a mile from the town was located a camp for Union refugees, and was under the protection and support of the military authorities.

The *Malvern* had been but a few days at Beaufort when, hearing that blockade running was on the increase, the admiral proceeded to sea. The Navy Department was requested to send all the fast vessels it could spare; but was made in vain. [Admiral Lee made several requests for more ships during the period covered in this chapter. It is not clear to which one Grattan is referring.[1]] Farragut at Mobile and Dahlgren at Charleston had over sixty vessels each while the whole fleet engaged in blockading New Inlet and Western Bar rarely exceeded twenty in number, and of those not one out of five could overhaul a blockade runner on a chase.

On one occasion when the admiral visited his vessels off Western Bar, seven fine steamers were seen inside ready to run out. [A report by Captain Benjamin F. Sands dated 14 August 1864 indicates that one "single pipe" and seven "double pipe" steamers lay near Smithville.[2]] Among them was the rebel privateer *Tallahassee* which had crossed the bar a few nights previous after exchanging shots with the *Monticello*. [The *Monticello* fired at the *Tallahassee* on the night of 25–26 August as the Rebel raider ran into Wilmington. There was no report of return fire.[3]]

A vigilant watch was kept and at night the fleet moved in towards the entrance as close as the water would allow them to go. Nothing unusual was seen or heard until midnight when a simultaneous rush was made by the blockade runners; but upon discovering the close proximity of our vessels and receiving a few shot and shell they returned to the harbor and on the following morning they were all there and at anchor. [I found no mention of this "rush" of blockade runners in either the published official records, the Samuel Phillips Lee papers in the Library of Congress, or in Grattan's diary.]

As before stated it was about forty miles by water between the vessels stationed off New Inlet and Western Bar, which were separated by Frying Pan Shoals, and as the flagship during one of her many cruises to the blockade came very near being wrecked upon them the incident may prove of interest. We left the fleet at Western Bar about eleven o'clock at night on the first of September and put out to sea. The water was very smooth and sky clear overhead. All hands except those on watch had retired. Not feeling very sleepy I joined Acting Master Henry Arey who was officer of the deck and entered into a general conversation. Nothing but the paddle wheels striking the water and the monotonous voice of the man at the lead line disturbed the deep solitude of the night. Taking the soundings as reported and examining the chart we discovered we were clear of the shoals much sooner than it was possible to be expected. The water began to have a rough and broken appearance, although there was no wind. The man at the lead solemnly warbled "by the deep fifteen," and as we would have been perfectly safe in eight or ten fathoms, the captain directed the vessel's course to be changed and the bluejacket continued to sing out the depth of the water. About 4:00 A.M. we were in a rough sea, and imagining I could see white capped breakers ahead, directed Mr. Arey's attention to the same. He had no sooner discovered them when he rushed forward, seized the lead line, and sounded five fathoms; heaving it again it struck less than five, and sang out to stop the engines. Springing to the bell wire I not only pulled to stop; but also to back. The lead was hove again and touched bottom in three fathoms of water with the breakers right ahead. The headway of the vessel had ceased and we were slowly backing out, but after striking deep water the vessel's course was changed in the proper direction and at daylight turned the point of the shoals. Not a soul on board knew of the narrow escape except those on deck, and as no report was made to the admiral, I do not think he was ever aware how near he was being wrecked on Frying Pan Shoals. The man who was stationed at the lead line proved to be a new disciple of Neptune, having exchanged a needle for a marlin spike, a tailor shop for a life on the ocean wave. He was perfectly ignorant of his duties and could not explain the marks on a lead line; but after a little practice after hearing the sailors sing out the different depths he tried to imitate them, and as his efforts came near throwing us on the shoals he was placed in irons.

Arriving among the vessels at New Inlet we had the pleasure of seeing a magnificent large blockade runner inside the bar blowing off steam, having run in during the night unobserved by the fleet; but then we consoled ourselves with the fact that she would be more valuable when she tried to run out. [The "magnificent blockade runner" might have been the *Lynx*, which probably arrived in Wilmington on 2 September.[4]]

The admiral desiring to feel satisfied that his vessels were doing their duty determined to make a personal reconnaissance the following night. The fleet as usual took their stations and waiting until near 3:00 A.M. on the fourth of September the flagship stood in for the bar. We were soon challenged, and answered just in time to prevent a broadside being fired into us. It was quite a surprise to see the admiral inspecting the blockade at that hour of the night; but they had no reason to complain as everyone were found on their station.

Later that morning, signal was made for all the commanding officers to come on board the flagship, and among other instructions were cautioned not to be particular about capturing the blockade runners; but must in future endeavor to *sink* and *destroy* them, and if possible obstruct the channel of the river and bar with their wrecks. This plan of operations would have the effect of decreasing the amount of prize money; but on the other hand would render blockade running very dangerous, and the admiral was fully determined to break it up as far as it was possible.

[On 26 August Secretary Welles had rebuked Admiral Lee because one of his ships engaged in a chase had stopped to pick up cotton thrown overboard from a fleeing outbound blockade runner. Proceeds from the sale of such captured enemy goods were divided among the blockader's crew after the government took its cut. While the blockader retrieved the booty, the runner slipped away. "The Department has noticed other similar instances of neglect," wrote Welles, "and considers it necessary that officers should be cautioned not to allow their pecuniary interests to stand in the way of duty."[5] Lee's admonition to sink and destroy blockade runners was probably given orally rather than in writing.]

At sunset the vessels were moving slowly in to their night stations, and all was quiet until near eight o'clock when a rocket and the flash of a gun was seen near the bar. Another rocket was fired, and then it became known that a runner had passed out and was heading up the coast. Several vessels started in pursuit and opened fire but she was lost in the darkness. The outside cruisers *Santiago de Cuba* and *Quaker City* being near the scene started after the chase and was soon following the luminous wake of the stranger. The flagship stood in towards the bar to occupy the station of any vessel which might be absent, when it was learned that the *Britannia* had discovered the blockade runner and had fired six shots into her at close quarters.

The *Malvern* cruised slowly along the line until two o'clock in the morning of September 5 when signal lights were seen flashing along the coast from the northward, and were answered at different intervals until they reached Fort Fisher. All lights were extinguished on the fort and Mound Battery and in a few moments a large calcium light of great power was turned on the fleet, exposing them to the enemy. [A "calcium light" was a searchlight powered by acetylene gas generated by adding water to calcium carbide.]

Immediately after, the fort and batteries opened fire and as every vessel including the flagship was within range we were compelled to haul out of danger. The firing continued for about an hour when it suddenly ceased, the light was extinguished, and at daylight a large steamer with the rebel flag at the fore and English ensign at the main was seen inside the bar blowing off steam, having run in after the firing. [The steamer in question might have been either the *Helen* or the *Will of the Wisp*, both of which probably arrived in Wilmington on 5 September.[6]] The use of the calcium light was a new plan adopted by the rebels for the purpose of bringing the vessels on blockade under the guns of the fortifications, and at the same time guiding the runners to the entrance of the harbor.

After doing duty as a blockading vessel for several nights the flagship was ordered to Beaufort and upon our arrival [6 September] saw the prize steamer *Elsie* coming in. She was the same vessel that had escaped the *Britannia* the night the batteries opened fire, and after a long chase was captured by the *Quaker City*. She was shot in five places, one shell exploding among her cotton setting it on fire. She was a beautiful side wheel steamer and very fast, and would no doubt have escaped had the crew not been engaged in throwing the burning cotton overboard, eighty bales of which were destroyed.[7]

At no time during the history of the blockade were such efforts made by the enemy to run in supplies for their armies. Hardly a night passed but that one or more vessels were captured, destroyed, or escaped, and after the admiral had established his headquarters at Beaufort, he ordered all the seaworthy vessels that could be spared from the James River to report for duty on the blockading line. The Navy Department at last saw the necessity of increasing the squadron and the admiral had the satisfaction in a few weeks of having a force that would almost close the port of Wilmington.

16

General Butler's great engineering feat ◆ Work and death on the
Dutch Gap Canal ◆ The Rebel rams and batteries assist in
excavating with shell ◆ The gunboats and the batteries along
the river ◆ An important military movement ◆ The army line
within seven miles of Richmond ◆ Vessels ordered in the
Wilmington blockade ◆ The USS *Daylight* on the shoals
off Beaufort ◆ A storm rising ◆ She is saved from shipwreck ◆
Chase and destruction of the *Lynx* ◆ Extracts from the
Wilmington press ◆ The *Lynx* struck eight times and
driven ashore ◆ The *Night Hawk* chased and destroyed ◆
Capture of the *Bat* ◆ Admiral Lee detached from the squadron
and ordered to the command of the Mississippi Squadron ◆
[August–October 1864]

THE FLEET STATIONED IN THE JAMES RIVER had for a number of weeks
been lying quietly at anchor, and as the weather was very warm, even the guerrillas were forced to keep cool and for a time navigation of the stream was not
interrupted.

The same state of affairs existed in the army and it was the universal opinion that it was too hot to fight; but General Butler soon became tired of the
inactivity, and if he could not proceed to Richmond, he would bring that city
nearer the scene of operations by digging a canal through the Dutch Gap. If it
proved a success it would enable the gunboats to pass up the river unmolested
by Howlett's Battery and obviate the necessity of passing over the flats and
shoals in Trent's Reach.

["Dutch Gap" was the name for the narrow neck of land connecting Farrar's "Island" to the mainland. "Trent's Reach" was the name for the east-west
oriented straight stretch of the James south of Farrar's Island. Several Confederate batteries covered the obstructions in Trent's Reach and the bend of the
James around the western half of Farrar's Island.]

The great work was soon commenced, and a large number of soldiers were
provided with shovels and picks. The enemy were puzzled at first; but quickly
comprehended the general's intentions, and then opened their batteries upon
the unarmed troops in the excavation, killing and wounding a large number.
On the 13th of August two rebel rams came down the river and assisted the
batteries in trying to drive the soldiers from the gap; but were unsuccessful
although the brave fellows lost over thirty in killed and wounded.

Construction of the Dutch Gap Canal (National Archives B-451)

On the same day the enemy paid their attention to the fleet, the *Agawam* and *Hunchback* had a lively engagement with a rebel battery and both vessels were slightly damaged, the former also lost two killed, one mortally and three severely wounded. The *Saugus* went to their assistance and the enemy soon retired in disgust.[1] [Actually three Confederate ironclads, the *Virginia II*, *Richmond*, and *Fredericksburg*, along with three gunboats made the attack.]

Three days after this affair General Butler requested naval co-operation from Captain Smith in a movement of the troops at Dutch Gap and a force from Deep Bottom whose object was to reconnoiter from a point known as Aiken's Landing, which was situated between the two former places, and take any advantage that might offer for a further advance. The gunboats were expected to cover the troops at Dutch Gap and at Aiken's Landing. The supply steamer *Mount Washington* was directed to transport the soldiers from Dutch Gap to the landing, and to be ready to re-embark them if necessary. The gunboats *Delaware* and *Mackinaw* and the monitor *Canonicus* were stationed so as to cover the advance and shell the rebel lines. The *Onondaga* was held ready for operations upon the rebel rams should they appear.

At the appointed time the *Mount Washington* received the detachment and landed them at Aiken's. At 5:00 P.M. the advance was commenced and the vessels opened fire, which was continued with great vigor until 7:00 P.M. The enemy made several attempts to drive the troops back; but were compelled to

Union vessels in the James near Dutch Gap (Courtesy of Robert M. Browning, Jr.)

retire out of range of the guns. The movement of our soldiers was a complete success, and resulted in the capture and occupation of Signal Hill Battery (an earthwork which had created a great amount of annoyance), Cox's farm, and the rebel lines towards Aiken's Landing. The army intrenchments by this advance were then about seven miles from Richmond.[2]

The day following this movement the rebel rams came down and with Howlett's Battery opened a heavy fire upon the troops, and numerous other attempts were made to dislodge them; but always proved unsuccessful.

General Butler continued his work upon the Dutch Gap Canal with great persistence but in the end it proved a miserable failure.

Knowing that the administration of affairs in the James River was in competent hands when Captain Smith was in command the admiral turned his whole attention to increasing the efficiency of the Wilmington blockade. Vessels were arriving almost every day from the north and after receiving instructions proceeded at once to the stations assigned them.

The weather for nearly two months had been very favorable for blockading service; but we knew it would not continue so, much longer. We had just returned from another visit to the fleet when dark clouds began looming up in the eastward, and the barometer gave indications of the approach of one of those storms which makes navigation along the Atlantic coast so full of danger. As evening approached the air became very close and after supper the officers went on deck and watched the gathering storm. About 9:00 P.M. the wind was slowly rising in fitful puffs and the dull roar of the surf and breakers could be heard, when a flash followed by the report of a gun was heard at sea just outside of the harbor. Signals were made, and we soon learned the steamer *Daylight* had run aground. She had arrived from the north and being a very poor sea boat, tried to cross the bar before the storm set in. Owing to the impossibility of navigating a vessel through the winding channel and breakers at night time, nothing could be done to save the *Daylight* until we saw daylight. In the meantime the storm had been slowly, but surely rising. Gun after gun was fired by the unfortunate ship and signal lights were burned all the remainder of the night. Several tugs were directed to go to her assistance as soon as they could see.

The greatest anxiety was manifested, and everyone was watching the tugs as they plunged and rolled in the heavy swell. Fortunately the tide was rising and at first effort the vessel was hauled off the shoals and piloted safely in the harbor. She had no sooner anchored when the storm burst upon us with great violence, and the breakers roared and dashed with terrific force on the shoals along the beach.

After the gale had moderated the admiral received information of the exciting chase and total destruction of the blockade runner *Lynx*. She was a long double-smoke-stack steamer and was discovered by the *Niphon*, Acting Master Edmund Kemble commanding, off New Inlet on the evening of September twenty-fifth coming over the bar at full speed. The *Niphon* was on the alert and giving chase was soon within range and fired several broadsides into her, nearly every shot taking effect. The *Howquah*, Acting Volunteer Lieutenant J. W. Balch, and *Governor Buckingham*, Acting Volunteer Lieutenant John MacDiarmid, then came up and joined in the exciting chase. The shore batteries opened fire and one shot struck the *Howquah*, cutting through the main rail, killing one man and wounding four others. The *Buckingham* tried to board the *Lynx*; but failed owing to the great speed the vessel was making. She was close enough however to fire musketry and revolvers into her crowded decks. The *Niphon* by a dexterous movement headed her off, and being then completely hemmed in the runner headed for the beach, hotly pursued by the blockaders. Striking the coast near Half Moon Battery she was quickly abandoned and set on fire and totally destroyed. At daylight on the following morning the *Buckingham* picked up twenty bales of cotton which had been thrown overboard by the *Lynx* in her endeavors to escape.[3]

The following extract from the *Wilmington Daily Journal* of September 26, 1864 speaks for itself:

> Last night the fine blockade running steamer *Lynx*, belonging to John Fraser & Co, and commanded by Capt. Reid, crossed New Inlet Bar and put to sea, bound to Bermuda with a cargo consisting mainly of over six hundred bales of cotton, one half on government account. She had also $50,000 in gold on freight for the government. She had some few passengers. Just as she got out

USS *Eolus* capturing the blockade runner *Lady Stirling* (Courtesy of Robert M. Browning, Jr.)

she was pursued by the blockading fleet, by which she was completely hemmed in. She was struck eight times, six at or below the water line. Finding the ship in a sinking condition, the captain beached her about six miles above Fort Fisher. The crew and passengers escaped with a portion of their effects and the vessel was burned to prevent if from falling into the hands of the enemy. The gold belonging to the government was saved. The enemy got as close as to fire a volley of musketry at the *Lynx*, by which one of the crew was wounded.

An editorial in the same paper remarked: *"There is a thundering blockade off here now,* that's pretty certain, whether the man with the queer name [Rear Admiral Lee] has got anything to do with it or not." No better evidence as to the severity and vigilance of the blockade could be required, coming as it did direct from the enemy.

Two days after the loss of the *Lynx*, the *Niphon* destroyed another blockade runner. About 11:00 P.M., she discovered a steamer standing in towards New Inlet, and immediately gave chase. Coming within range the *Niphon* opened fire when the runner struck the shoals near Federal Point. A boat was armed and manned and put in charge of Acting Ensign E. N. Semon and Second Assistant Engineer Thomas L. Churchill, with orders to board her, and try to float her off. Shortly after midnight the boat ran alongside through a heavy surf and boarded her without opposition. Mr. Churchill immediately went to the engine room and started the engines but she remained firm and immovable. As the steamer lay right under the guns of Fort Fisher it was not considered advisable to waste too much time and it was determined to destroy her. All the combustible material that could be found was collected together in the cabin and ignited, and several shovels full of live coal were thrown in the bunkers. When the fire was progressing favorably all hands were ordered into the cutter; but being too small to hold all, one of the boats of the steamer was lowered and manned. As the boats were leaving the burning vessel the fort and batteries opened fire on her and the *Niphon*. Without accident the boats reached the *Niphon* with twenty-three prisoners, the balance of the blockade runner's officers and crew to the number of nineteen having escaped. She was the English steamer *Night Hawk* with a general cargo, and had cleared from Bermuda. She was a long low sidewheel vessel, double smoke stacks and cost £30,000 sterling, equal at that time to about $240,000 dollars in our national currency.[4]

The *Night Hawk* made the fiftieth blockade running steamer captured and destroyed off Wilmington while the squadron was under the command of Admiral Lee, and the aggregate loss to the enemy and their friends could not fall short of twelve millions of dollars ($12,000,000).

On the tenth of October the *Montgomery* discovered a blockade runner and after a long chase captured her. She proved to be the *Bat*, a splendid side wheel steamer with a valuable cargo of machinery.[5]

Two days after her capture and after two years of hard labor, faithful service, and many sleepless nights Admiral Lee was relieved from command of the North Atlantic Blockading Squadron and directed to assume command of the Mississippi Squadron.

With the limited facilities under his control Admiral Lee well merited the thanks and approbation of his country.

17

A FEW WEEKS BEFORE the detachment of Admiral Lee, I received a short leave of absence from the Navy Department, and as the *Britannia* after many months service on the blockade was ordered to Norfolk for extensive repairs, I took passage on her for Hampton Roads. The weather looked very stormy, but fortunately did not come on to blow until we arrived at our destination. The sea was very smooth at 8:00 P.M. we passed Cape Hatteras. All was quiet on board until about day break when the alarming information was communicated that the ship had sprung a leak. Her bow was very deep in the water and the slightest swell would have plunged her to the bottom. The pumps were promptly manned and all the buckets brought in use. As the engine room was yet free of water, the vessel's course was changed towards the beach, but before reaching it the crew had gained on the leak and after a few hours hard work the ship was pumped dry and the cause of the trouble temporarily repaired. We were relieved from all further anxiety when we anchored in Hampton Roads a few hours before the storm broke upon us. [Grattan departed Beaufort for Hampton Roads on 20 September 1864 and arrived home two days later. He left New York on 10 October.[1]]

After a few days rest from active service I returned to duty. On October 11, 1864, I reported to Rear Admiral David D. Porter who had assumed command of the squadron. The *Malvern* continued to be the flagship and was anchored

Rear Admiral David Dixon
Porter (Courtesy of Robert
M. Browning, Jr.)

in Hampton Roads. Having been assigned to service on the admiral's staff as
special aid I at once resumed my duties, and as nearly all his officers had served
with him in the Mississippi it became necessary to instruct them as to the location and personnel of the vessels and officers of the squadron.

In a few days after the admiral took control a large number of frigates,
sloops of war and gunboats began arriving and assembling off Fortress Monroe,
and it was evident to all that hot work was contemplated. Fort Fisher and
Wilmington were the objective points, and the greatest activity prevailed night
and day in placing the fleet in a sea worthy and fighting condition.

As many of the staff were killed in action or rendered invaluable aid to the
service, I will insert their names and rank:

> Lieutenant Commander K. Randolph Breese, Fleet Captain.
> Lieutenant Commander Henry A. Adams, Jr., Ordnance Officer.
> Chief Engineer Theodore Zeller, Fleet Engineer.
> Surgeon John L. Fox, Fleet Surgeon.
> Paymaster Horace M. Hieskill, Fleet Paymaster.
> Lieutenant Morton W. Saunders, Flag Lieutenant.
> Lieutenant Silas W. Terry, Detailing Officer.

John W. Grattan with Rear Admiral David Dixon Porter (center) and his staff on board the USS *Malvern* at Hampton Roads, December 1864. William B. Cushing stands at the far left; Lieutenant Commander Kidder R. Breese, the fleet captain, fifth from left (with arms folded); Lieutenant Commander Thomas O. Selfridge, Jr., to Porter's right; Lieutenant Samuel W. Preston, second from right; Grattan, far right. (Naval Historical Center NH 61924)

Acting Ensign James M. Alden, Aid de Camp.
Acting Ensign John W. Grattan, Aid de camp.
Mr. Charles F. Guild, Admiral's Secretary
Mr. Carlisle P. Porter, Admiral's Clerk

The following officers were subsequently added to the staff:

Lieutenant Samuel W. Preston, Special aide de camp.
Acting Ensign Harry Woodruff, Assistant Detailing Officer.
Acting Ensign Aaron Vanderbilt, Assistant Signal Officer.
Acting Ensign Frank W. Grafton, Assistant Aide de Camp.
Second Lieutenant William W. Clemens, Army Signal Officer.

The command of the *Malvern* was given to Lieutenant Benjamin H. Porter who with Lieutenant Samuel W. Preston reported to the admiral for duty in the squadron. Both of these gallant officers had highly distinguished themselves for

Lieutenant Benjamin H. Porter
(Naval Historical Center NH
47380)

bravery. They were almost inseparable companions and, during the disastrous boat attack on Fort Sumter in Charleston harbor, were captured and confined together in several rebel prisons and, after a number of months of great suffering, were exchanged. As they were quite broken down in health the Navy Department granted them an unlimited leave of absence; but hearing of the contemplated movement against Wilmington, they sacrificed all the comforts and pleasures of home in which they stood in so much need, and reported to the secretary of the navy for active service.

For more than a month the admiral and staff were busily engaged in preparing the vessels as they arrived for action, and when the commanding officers reported they were ready for sea, the admiral notified General Grant and requested him to send the troops necessary to cooperate in a combined attack against Fort Fisher.

While the busy preparations were going forward, the flagship made several visits to City Point, and consultations were had between the general and the admiral as to the proper mode of conducting the great expedition.

Lieutenant Samuel W. Preston
(Naval Historical Center NH
47236)

During one of our trips to General Grant's headquarters a circumstance occurred which for a time created the greatest excitement and anxiety. The *Malvern* was moving rapidly up the James River, when the beautiful army steamer *Greyhound* was seen coming down with General Butler on board. The admiral went on board of her and directed the flagship to continue on and anchor at Dutch Gap.

Towards evening a dispatch was received from Hampton Roads directing the vessel to return immediately, and informed us that the *Greyhound* had been destroyed by fire, and the admiral and General Butler had barely escaped with their lives. We were soon moving rapidly down the river and in a few hours passed the wreck, which was still burning, and had the pleasure of receiving the admiral on board uninjured.

At midnight on the thirtieth of November a dispatch was received from General Grant informing the admiral he had 12,000 troops ready to cooperate with the navy.[2] The monitors *Saugus*, *Canonicus*, and *Mahopac* which were then stationed up the river were ordered to Hampton Roads, and the vessels there assembled were directed to hold themselves in readiness to sail at an hour's notice. When it became known that the long looked for departure was near at hand, cheer after cheer resounded throughout the fleet.

But contrary to our expectations the troops did not arrive at the time specified, and it subsequently appeared the delay was caused by General Butler, who wished to try an experiment with gunpowder and confidently imagined he could paralyze and destroy the garrison in Fort Fisher by the explosion of a powder boat. General Grant had given his consent and although the admiral had no faith or confidence in this novel mode of warfare he cheerfully commenced carrying out the suggestions of the hero of New Orleans. [On the contrary, at the time Porter expected the powder boat to work as intended. Only afterward, in the context of his feud with Ben Butler, did he denounce the idea.]

The gunboat *Louisiana* being old and unseaworthy was ordered from the sounds of North Carolina, and after a tedious delay was sent to the Navy Yard and everything of value except her machinery was taken out of her. She was then housed over from stem to stern and partially filled with gunpowder, the balance to be put on board and connected with a Gomez fuse upon her arrival at Beaufort, making in all 215 tons of powder. [Invented by New York City native Edwin Gomez, the "Gomez fuse" was a long, ropelike detonator, not a burning fuse, designed to set off all of the powder simultaneously.] Commander A. C. Rhind at his own request was temporarily detached from the *Agawam* and placed in charge of the powder boat.

A circular was then issued to the fleet calling for volunteers and the result was a very large number of officers and sailors offered their services to the admiral who would have been more than necessary to man a hundred *Louisiana*s. It was very gratifying to the admiral to witness such an outburst of enthusiasm and with such men to command he felt confident he would achieve a glorious victory.

Lieutenants Preston and Porter having just arrived, the latter as before stated was appointed Flag Captain of the *Malvern*, and the former at his special request was directed to assist Commander Rhind and accompany the powder ship on her dangerous mission.

There was one gentleman who deserves more than a passing observation. Mr. John S. Bradford of the United States Coast Survey service had been of invaluable assistance to Admiral Lee, and furnished a number of charts of the James River, the sounds of North Carolina, and the coast and shoals for the Wilmington blockade. His familiarity with the locality was of the greatest benefit to Admiral Porter in forming his vessels in line of battle. Every fighting ship had a battle chart showing the soundings, coast line, fortifications and the position of each vessel in the line during the engagement.

Mr. Bradford a few weeks previous to the departure of the fleet made his appearance on the blockade, and under the cover of darkness took soundings close in shore near the batteries. After selecting a favorable spot he marked it with a buoy which was subsequently found by the *Louisiana*. He reported to the admiral and offered to pilot the powder boat, and his services were accepted with many thanks for his bravery.

While the busy preparations for battle were in progress, the ladies of Norfolk possessing Union proclivities were vying with each other in giving receptions and sociable entertainments to the officers who were not otherwise engaged, and almost every evening the wardroom of the flagship presented a scene of confusion, caused by the officers who were going on shore trying to appear as fascinating and glittering as their uniforms would allow. The gallant and handsome Terry would yell out from his state room, "Here, boy. Moses, John Brice, Cornelius, come here you black rascals and shine my boots," and immediately one of the rascals would appear. From another state room a half naked ensign would emerge boiling with indignation, "Come, you black lumps of India rubber, every one of you, come here or I will slay thee, tell me who has confiscated my razor." The servants are always on a jump; but on these festive occasions it may be said that they were everywhere at once. In another state room far away the feeble voice of the gay, dashing Saunders could be heard singing out "Boy, boy, I say boy, come here and get me a pair of socks." The summons would be quickly obeyed and about ten inches from the elbow of the brave but lazy and good natured mate the articles would be produced. The same voice would again be heard "Terry my dear fellow lend me a handkerchief." Terry replied, "No, I'll be darned if I will. You have not returned the pair of drawers you borrowed last week when you went to Miss Blank's reception." This answer would not please the gay lieutenant, who would advance with overwhelming force on Terry's room, secure all he wanted, and beat a rapid retreat followed by a pillow.

But the merry scenes were not destined to continue much longer. Lieutenants Preston and Porter did not join in many of the festivities on shore, as the duty of superintending the preparation of the powder ship kept the former almost constantly engaged and the latter being in command of the *Malvern* determined to bring the crew into a high state of discipline.

18

A daring but unsuccessful attempt to destroy the rebel ram
Albemarle ♦ Lieutenant Cushing determines to sink her ♦
Steam launches and torpedoes constructed ♦ His arrival at and
mysterious disappearance from Hampton Roads ♦ Completes his
preparations in the sounds ♦ He ascends the river ♦ Rebel pickets
captured ♦ The *Albemarle* at Plymouth ♦ The launch advances
and is discovered ♦ New dangers and difficulties ♦ The launch
under full steam ♦ The torpedo exploded under the ram ♦
Sinking of the launch ♦ A swim for life ♦ In the swamps ♦
"The rebel ironclad at the bottom of the river" ♦ Cushing returns
to the fleet ♦ The result of the daring undertaking ♦ Cushing is
promoted to the grade of Lieutenant Commander ♦ He is placed
in command of the *Malvern* ♦ [May–October 1864]

AFTER THE GALLANT but unsatisfactory engagement of the gunboats with
the rebel ram *Albemarle* in the sounds of North Carolina, a daring attempt to
destroy her with torpedoes was made by five volunteers from the steamer *Wyalusing* on the night of May 25, 1864. The party left the vessel at two o'clock in
the afternoon and ascended the river in a small boat with two torpedoes, each
containing one-hundred pounds of powder, and transported them on a stretcher
across the swamps. Charles Baldwin, coal heaver, and John W. Lloyd, coxswain,
then swam the Roanoke River with a line, and hauled the torpedoes over to
the Plymouth shore, above the town. The torpedoes were then connected by a
bridle, floated down with the current, and guided by Baldwin, who intended to
place them across the bow of the iron clad, one on each side, and Alexander
Crawford, second-class fireman, who was stationed on the opposite side of the
river, in the swamp, was to explode them when he received the signal.

Everything had worked favorably until the torpedoes were within a few
yards of the ram, when Baldwin was discovered and hailed by a sentry on the
wharf. Two shots were then fired, which were quickly followed by a volley of
musketry. Upon hearing the challenge and reports of fire arms, Lloyd cut the
guiding line, threw away the coil, and swam the river again to join John Laverty,
first-class fireman, who was left in charge of his clothes and arms. After an
absence of thirty-eight hours in the swamps, these two men with the boat
keeper Benjamin Loyd, second-class fireman, returned to their vessel. Two days
later Baldwin and Crawford made their appearance, very much exhausted by

travel and loss of rest and food. Although unsuccessful in their attempt to destroy the ram, the gallant fellows were rewarded with "medals of honor" for their courage and zeal.[1]

It remained for Lieutenant Cushing to accomplish one of the most daring and successful feats of the war. He had communicated his wishes to destroy the *Albemarle* to the secretary of the navy and Admiral Lee and every facility was given him to carry out his design. He was directed to report to the commandant of the Brooklyn Navy Yard and confer with the chief engineer. Launches with steam engines and propellers were at once constructed and each one was armed with a howitzer and a torpedo boom, made so as to be run in or out at a moment's notice, and accommodations provided for about fifteen men.

The torpedo to be used was an invention of Chief Engineer William W. W. Wood and numerous experiments were made by Cushing who expressed himself as well pleased with their destructive power. Several weeks were occupied in maturing his plan of operation, and it was after the detachment of Admiral Lee before Lieutenant Cushing was ready.

While the vessels were preparing for sea, Cushing arrived at Hampton Roads and reported to Admiral Porter. As it was absolutely necessary that his intentions should be kept a profound secret no one except the admiral and a few intimate friends were entrusted with it. Up to a late hour at night he was laughing and joking with the officers, who feeling rather tired and sleepy, bade him good night. Many of them expected to see him at the breakfast table in the morning.

When all was quiet he jumped into one of his launches and silently but rapidly was moving through the canal bound for New Bern. Arriving without being discovered, he reported to Commander William H. Macomb, the senior naval officer in the sounds, who supplied him with a small boat and five volunteers to be taken in tow.

Everything being ready for the desperate attempt, Cushing with thirteen men on the night of the twenty-seventh of October 1864, started on his mission of death and destruction. The rebel ram lay at anchor about eight miles from the mouth of the Roanoke, and the shores on both sides of the river were guarded by the enemy's pickets. Approaching the wreck of the *Southfield*, which could be faintly seen in the darkness, the small boat cast off and boarded her, capturing four rebels who were discovered sound asleep. A short distance above could be seen the ram alongside the wharf, illuminated by the light of the camp fires on shore.

As the launch drew near the unconscious monster, the torpedo boom was placed in position, when suddenly the boat was discovered and challenged. Now was the moment for action. Cushing directed the launch to go ahead under full speed. The enemy saw her coming and called the crew to quarters, rang the alarm bell, and opened fire with musketry. When within a few yards of the iron clad an unexpected obstacle was revealed by the camp fires. Around the ram within twenty feet of her sides a pen of logs for protection against torpedoes were discovered; but it was too late to retreat and Cushing directed the launch to strike the logs and force them in. Volley after volley of musketry poured into the boat; but Cushing stood there undismayed with his hand grasping the lock string of the torpedo. In a few seconds the launch struck the logs with great force and drove them towards the *Albemarle*. The deck of the ram was crowded with her officers and men and the launch's howitzer was discharged with terrible effect upon the enemy. Cushing lowered the torpedo under the overhang of the ram and exploded it just as a heavy shot plunged through the bottom of the launch. As Cushing's boat was rapidly filling with water, he directed his men to swim for their lives; but many of them being badly wounded and unable to save themselves were drowned or captured. Only one of the crew besides Cushing was able to escape.

After swimming about two miles and feeling his strength rapidly leaving him, the brave officer put for the shore; but was unable to drag himself out of the water until daylight.

Concealing himself in a swamp near a foot path he lay down to rest; but was soon aware that some persons were approaching. Watching the path he saw two of the *Albemarle*'s officers pass but could not hear their conversation. When they were out of sight Cushing started through the swamp. After a few hours traveling through mud, cane brake, and briars, he came across a negro and persuaded him to go to Plymouth and gain all the information he could. While waiting for the return of his messenger Cushing occupied the time in resting himself. The faithful scout came back with the gratifying intelligence that the ram was on the bottom of the Roanoke River.

Collecting all his energies, Cushing dashed through the swamp and after terrible sufferings discovered a rebel picket boat in a small creek. He sprang into the boat and shoved out in the river, and by eleven o'clock the following night, the gallant hero safely arrived on board the steamer *Valley City*. He was very much exhausted and his feet, face, and hands badly cut and lacerated by the briars in the swamps. The surgeon who attended to him recommended quiet and rest; but when it became known that the *Albemarle* was destroyed the crew appeared to be wild with joy and at midnight awakened the whole fleet with loud cheering. The news soon spread and for a time the waters of the sounds were illuminated in honor of the victory and the cheers of the bluejackets could be heard for miles.

As soon as he was able to move, although still suffering greatly, Cushing proceeded to Hampton Roads; but the news had arrived before him, and when he appeared on the flagship he received a perfect ovation; but his honors had only commenced.

The secretary of the navy upon receiving information of the gallant exploit, presented his name to the President and Congress for a vote of thanks, in order

Destruction of the CSS *Albemarle* (National Archives 79-CWC-3F-31)

that he might be promoted to the grade of Lieutenant Commander in the navy, and the request was no sooner asked than granted.[2]

Lieutenant Commander Cushing obtained an unlimited leave of absence to recuperate his energies; but he did not remain long unemployed. After visiting several northern cities and receiving honors and thanks from his delighted countrymen and innumerable friends he returned to Hampton Roads in time to sail with the fleet. Being senior to Lieutenant Porter, Cushing was placed in temporary command of the *Malvern* and Porter became his first lieutenant.

Cushing was a strict disciplinarian; but in spite of his strong will and apparent harshness the sailors fairly worshipped him. His smooth beardless face always wore a smile except when annoyed or engaged on dangerous service, when it would change into a settled frown. His blue eyes always had a determined and fearless look and his coolness and self possession was the subject of many remarks.

When not on duty and in the privacy of our wardroom he was as jolly and free as a schoolboy; could sing a few sailor songs and ballads and tell a good yarn or laugh heartily at a good joke. One of his principal characteristics was his extreme modesty in the presence of strangers and he very rarely spoke of his daring achievements and never in a spirit of braggadocio.

19

The signal gun ♦ "Prepare to get underway" ♦ Departure of
the Army transports ♦ The naval vessels engaged in the
grand expedition ♦ Instructions to the commanding officers ♦
A magnificent spectacle ♦ The flagship follows the squadron ♦
Arrival at Beaufort and final preparations ♦ Underway for
the rendezvous ♦ At anchor out of sight of land ♦ General Butler
on the *Malvern* ♦ A storm arising ♦ The squadron exercised in
naval tactics ♦ The gale increases ♦ Apprehensions for the safety
of the iron clads ♦ General Butler and his troops proceed
to Beaufort ♦ A terrible storm ♦ Clear weather at last ♦
The admiral reconnoiters the fortifications ♦ Astonishment
at the strange conduct of General Butler ♦ [December 1864]

AT DAYBREAK ON THE THIRTEENTH OF DECEMBER 1864, the flagship fired a
gun and hoisted the general signal "prepare to get underway." It was answered
by every vessel and in a few moments the fleet began to move.

The transports loaded with troops had arrived and when the signal had
been given were the first to leave Hampton Roads. The powder boat soon followed and at 8:00 A.M. the monitors with their convoys and the frigates, sloops
of war, and gunboats started for sea. As the vessels fell into line the sight was
magnificent and cheer after cheer greeted their departure by the great throng
of spectators who lined the shores and filled the wharf at Fortress Monroe.

At noon all the vessels ordered to participate in the coming conflict, with
the exception of the flagship, had left the vicinity of Hampton Roads, and at
5:00 P.M. the admiral ordered the *Malvern* to get underway and follow the fleet.
As we were rapidly passing the fortress the cheering on shore was heartily
resumed. The naval portion of the squadron in this expedition numbered
seventy-three vessels, and was composed of the best wooden and iron men-of-
war in the service, with an armament of over 650 guns. The following is a list
of the vessels and the divisional commanding officers:

1st Division: Commodore Henry K. Thatcher
2nd Division: Commodore Joseph Lanman
3rd Division: Commodore James F. Schenk
4th Division: Commodore Sylvanus W. Godon
5th Division: Commodore William Radford

145

Ships of the North Atlantic Blockading Squadron departing Hampton Roads for Fort Fisher, December 1864 (Naval Historical Center NH 1557)

Iron Clads

New Ironsides, Monadnock, Mahopac, Canonicus, and *Saugus*

Frigates and Sloops of War

Minnesota, Colorado, Wabash, Brooklyn, Mohican, Tuscarora, Juniata, Susquehana, Shenandoah, Powhatan, Ticonderoga

Double-Ender Side-Wheel Gunboats

Sassacus, Iosco, Maratanza, Mackinaw, Tacony, Osceola, Pawtucket

Screw Gunboats

Chippewa, Maumee, Kansas, Seneca, Yantic, Nyack, Unadilla, Huron, Pequot, Vicksburg

Ocean Steamers Transformed into Gunboats

Vanderbilt, Quaker City, R. R. Cuyler, Nereus, Eolus, Montgomery, Mount Vernon, Monticello, Rhode Island, Santiago de Cuba, Fort Jackson, Alabama, Howquah, Wilderness, State of Georgia, Keystone State, Nansemond, and *Governor Buckingham*

Reformed Blockade Runners

Aries, A. D. Vance, Britannia, Banshee, Cherokee, Dumbarton, Emma, Fort Donelson, Gettysburg, Lilian, Little Ada, Tristam Shandy

Tugs, Tenders, and Dispatch Boats

Anemone, Bignonia, Clematis, Clinton, Unit, Moccasin, Heliotrope, and a few others.

Previous to sailing each commanding officer was furnished with a battle chart with the position his vessel was to take plainly marked upon it, and a printed general order, in which the naval vessels were directed to keep out of sight of the enemy and remain at anchor about twenty-five miles off New Inlet until after the explosion of the powder boat.[1] But before assembling at the rendezvous, they were ordered to take in a full supply of coal and ammunition at Beaufort.

It was near evening before the flagship passed Cape Henry. In the distance could be faintly seen the last vessels in the squadron. The weather was all that could be desired; the moon was shining brightly and the ocean as quiet and smooth as a mill pond. On the following evening we had passed all the vessels and sighted Cape Lookout; but owing to the great danger of entering the crooked harbor at night, we were compelled to wait until daylight. When the *Malvern* crossed the bar she was followed by the monitors, powder boat, and light draught vessels. On account of their size the frigates, sloops of war, and *New Ironsides* were compelled to anchor outside, and were supplied by tugs and schooners with coal and ammunition. [The *New Ironsides* carried two 150-pounder Parrott rifles, two 60-pounder Parrott rifles, fourteen XI-inch Dahlgren smoothbores, and two Dahlgren boat guns. One of the first three experimental armored vessels ordered by the Union navy in 1861, she proved almost invulnerable to gunfire. The Confederates feared her more than any other Union ironclad because of the rapid-fire capability of her heavy battery.]

The greatest activity prevailed and in two days the squadron was ready for action, when the signal was made to proceed to the rendezvous, and by sunset on the eighteenth of December they were at anchor on the station.

Shortly after dark General Butler and his chief engineer Major General Godfrey Weitzel came on board the flagship and held a council of war with the admiral and several commanding officers. [Major General Godfrey Weitzel, USV, was brevetted a major general on 29 August 1864, then commanded successively the XVIII and XXV Corps. Weitzel had been Butler's second-in-command at New Orleans, and he resumed that role in the first Fort Fisher expedition. During the final operations of the war, Weitzel commanded all Union troops north of the Appomattox River. On 3 April 1865, he electrified the North with a laconic telegram: "We entered Richmond at eight o'clock this morning."]

It was decided to send the *Louisiana* in that night, and she was directed to execute her dangerous mission, but before she had proceeded far the weather bore indications of a rising storm, and as it would have been impossible to go into action with a rough sea, a vessel was dispatched after the powder boat and she was directed to return and anchor with the fleet.

The clouds began gathering and the wind increased throughout the night and by daylight the sea was quite rough. Not wishing to waste any time the admiral occupied the entire day in exercising the vessels in squadron tactics and maneuvers. All the movements were directed by signal, and in forming a line of battle the fleet occupied a distance of over five miles in length; the last ship in the line being just visible on the horizon from the head of the column. A number of intricate orders were executed with a surprising degree of proficiency; being the first time our naval vessels were exercised on such a large scale. Admiral Porter was greatly pleased and no doubt was very proud to command such a magnificent squadron. The vessels anchored at night about twelve miles from Fort Fisher; but still out of sight of land.

The gale of wind which had been blowing all day increased in force after dark, and during the night shifted to the northward and eastward which caused a very heavy sea. At daylight several vessels were discovered dragging their anchors and a few were in close and dangerous proximity to each other. The monitors were swinging at their cables; but at times they would be almost invisible as the waves and spray dashed over them.

The *Louisiana* with her brave crew of volunteers rolled and pitched in a fearful manner; but she stood the gale much better than was anticipated. During the afternoon the wind changed to the southward and westward and for a time appeared to be moderating when shortly after sunset the gale suddenly increased, and howled and roared all night with the greatest fury. With the approach of day break the wind blew from the northward and westward and as it appeared to be its intention to box the compass, we had nothing to do but submit with philosophical dignity, although I regret to say a few damned the weather all in heaps, and many eyes were blasted metaphorically.

The sea was very rough and apprehensions were felt for the safety of the iron clads. The admiral directed several of the larger and more steady vessels to go as near them as it was safe to anchor and render any assistance that might be required; but fortunately their services were not called into requisition. It was without doubt one of the severest storms that ever visited our coast and at times the wind blew with the violence of a hurricane. The vessels being heavily laden with coal and ammunition rolled and pitched in a very dangerous manner; but all weathered the gale.

When the storm first commenced General Butler ordered his transports to proceed to Beaufort and remain until it was over; but his intentions were not communicated to the admiral, and it was supposed his vessels had put further out to sea to avoid being blown on shore or running afoul of our men-of-war, and when the gale had gone down would appear.

The monitors had been fairly tested for the first time and their sea worthy capacity demonstrated to the satisfaction of every one who witnessed their actions during the height of the tempest.

The twenty-third of December dawned upon the fleet with a clear cloudless sky and in a few hours the sea became quite calm. The gale had occupied nearly five days; but none of the vessels were seriously damaged, and the admiral directed the powder boat to be exploded that night and on the following morning the fleet were ordered to go into action.

The day was spent in preparations for battle and waiting for the appearance of the transports. In the afternoon the *Malvern* stood in for the blockading fleet and upon our arrival the admiral was informed that the enemy were fully aware of the presence and object of the expedition. Up to this time the admiral had supposed General Butler had taken his transports to the rendezvous which had been agreed upon; but instead of doing so, sailed along the coast in full view of Fort Fisher and the batteries, with his colors flying, troops exposed and bands playing. It was a very injudicious movement and about as ludicrous as the Chinese mode of warfare.[2] [Chinese military technology, administration, and professionalism lagged so far behind the state of the art in Europe and the United States that in ethnocentric Western eyes, the Chinese way of warfare seemed ludicrous.]

The flagship went within a mile of the beach, and the admiral made a careful reconnaissance. We were within easy range of their guns; but the enemy were too busy with their preparations for defense to notice us.

20

The powder boat beached and exploded • The scene from the fleet • The squadron forming in divisions and line of battle • Taking position off Fort Fisher • The first shot • Commencement of the engagement • The flagship under fire • Vessels disabled • Loss of life by bursting of the guns • Terrific bombardment • No appearance of General Butler • The admiral during the action • The reserve division open fire on the Mound Battery • Rebel flags shot away • Cheering by the bluejackets • At anchor for the night • General Butler and the transports arrive • Repairing damages • Christmas Eve • [24 December 1864]

The POWDER BOAT *Louisiana* started towards New Inlet at 8:00 P.M. on the twenty-third of December in company with the *Nansemond* which vessel was to receive the gallant volunteers when they abandoned her. The blockading fleet was discontinued and the vessels ordered to fall in line and take their stations among the battle ships.

About midnight two rockets were seen in the direction of Fort Fisher. This was the signal to inform the admiral that the *Louisiana* had been fired and the officers and crew were safe in their boats. It was calculated that only fifteen minutes would elapse before she exploded. In order to ensure an instantaneous explosion of such a mass of powder, a fuze was circulated in every part of the vessel where the barrels were stored away, and the end to be ignited was inserted in a sperm candle, a few inches from the flame; but in case this failed all the combustible material at hand was to be gathered in the cabin and set on fire. It subsequently appeared that all the arrangements had been carefully executed. The vessel was anchored close in shore and under the guns of Fort Fisher. Alongside were the boats to enable the crew to escape, and the candle and the material in the cabin were simultaneously ignited. Quietly entering the boats, the brave men pulled quickly for the *Nansemond* and fired the signal rockets.

As great results were expected to follow the explosion the decks and rigging of the different vessels were crowded with officers and sailors all waiting with breathless anxiety for the event to occur. Shortly after midnight a bright red fire was seen in the direction of the *Louisiana*, which continued to burn for more than an hour and a half, when suddenly a bright flash was observed and a stream of flames ascended to a great height and spread out in an immense sheet of fire, illuminating for an instant the whole horizon. In a few seconds a loud report followed by a deep booming roar told us General Butler's experiment had been tried. The concussion was not as great as we were led to expect; but the result was yet to be seen. [Grattan relied on his diary rather than any particular report for his account of the explosion.[1]]

Immediately after the explosion the admiral gave orders by signal lights to the fleet to be ready for an early start, and the final preparations for the coming conflict consumed the balance of the night.

With the exception of the army transports whose absence were unaccountable, the vessels were underway at daylight. The fleet stood in towards the coast by divisions in line of battle, and as the sunlight flashed on their numerous polished guns the scene was very grand and imposing. The flagship led the van and at 10:00 A.M. arrived within five miles of Fort Fisher when the wind suddenly freshened and the squadron came to anchor. But the wind ceased as quickly as it arose, and by noon the vessels were again underway.

While at anchor Commander Rhind, Lieutenant Preston, Mr. Bradford, and the crew belonging to the *Malvern* came on board and received the hearty congratulations of the admiral. Lieutenant Preston then assumed his duties as special aide-de-camp and Commander Rhind having destroyed his ship was made the admiral's guest.

The first line of battle consisted of the iron clad division. The *New Ironsides* with her twenty heavy guns led the monitors to their anchorage within half a mile of the coast, and commenced the engagement. The frigates then took up their positions and opened fire, followed quickly by the sloops of war and the large gunboats. This line of battle numbered twenty-seven vessels with an armament of 390 heavy guns, and was anchored about a mile from Fort Fisher. Another line comprising fourteen vessels and about 230 guns, formed an arc of a circle and directed their fire on the Mound Battery and the earth works between it and the Fort. Just outside of range, the reserve division lay at anchor; but ready to move whenever their services were most needed.

At 1:00 P.M. the whole fleet with the exception of the reserve division were fully engaged and the enemy opened fire with great vigor. The monitors' heavy guns created terrible destruction, their shot and shell striking and bursting in the traverses with great accuracy.

After the vessels had taken their positions the flagship stood in for the frigates and was soon in the thickest of the fight. The admiral's presence so near the fortifications had the effect of concentrating their fire; shot and shell could be heard screaming and bursting all around us but the *Malvern* seemed to be invincible. While the forecastle was crowded with bluejackets watching the exciting contest a shot struck the water near the bow and threw a cloud of spray over them, causing considerable amusement.

The admiral was on one of the wheel houses with his glass watching the effects of our shots. Commander Rhind was walking the quarter deck and appeared to be about as happy as a chained tiger. While moving along the line the *Mackinaw* signaled that she was in a disabled and defenseless condition having received a shot in her boiler. Upon receiving this information the admiral in his laconic style signaled, "Remain where you are and fight." As we ran alongside of the frigate *Wabash* the admiral communicated with her captain who reported several of his crew killed and wounded, and while doing so a solid shot struck her mainmast, throwing the splinters in every direction. Other shots had previously cut her rigging in several places.

After leaving the *Wabash* the flagship approached within speaking distance of the *Juniata* when we were startled by a deafening report, much louder than the roar of the guns. It soon became known that she had burst a 100-pound Parrott rifle which had killed and wounded eighteen of her officers and crew, among whom was Lieutenant David D. Wemple, a young, brave, and estimable officer who was literally blown to pieces; and Second Lieutenant Jonas Pile of the Marine Corps who was blow overboard, and his mangled and mutilated body was picked up as it was floating by the *Malvern*.

This mournful event had no sooner been reported when signals were seen on the *Ticonderoga* and the *Yantic* informing the admiral that they had each burst a Parrott rifle. As we had lost more men from the bursting of these guns than we did from the enemy's fire, the vessels which had them on board were directed to discontinue using them.

The bombardment of the fortifications continued until nearly 4:00 P.M., when a general signal was made for the entire fleet, including the reserve division, to move in closer and engage the enemy with deliberation. While the vessels were occupied in changing their positions the fort and the batteries opened a very rapid and destructive fire. With the exception of a piece of shell which struck the wheel house near the admiral the *Malvern* passed through the ordeal unscathed. The reserve division paid attention to the batteries on Zeke's Island which had proved very troublesome.

Shortly after four o'clock the entire fleet renewed the engagement, and the magnificent and rapid firing superseded all previous efforts. A continual sheet of flames leaped from the muzzles of the guns and the booming roar rivaled the artillery of heaven. [In his diary Grattan described the noise as "one continuous roar."[2]]

The spectacle was most grand and exciting. Not a cloud could be seen in the bright blue sky. The immense volumes of smoke were wafted seaward by a gentle breeze, and the ocean was without a ripple. All day long the admiral had been expecting the arrival of the transports, but as evening approached no signs of them could be seen.

In order to obtain a better view of the fort and the effects produced by our guns the admiral directed the *Malvern* to go alongside the *New Ironsides*, which lay within half a mile of the beach. While passing the *Brooklyn*, Captain James Alden ordered his crew to cheer the flagship, which were heartily given and as vigorously acknowledged. [At the battle of Mobile Bay (5 August 1864), the *Brooklyn* was leading Farragut's ships past Fort Morgan, when Alden suddenly stopped her and began backing to clear "a row of suspicious-looking buoys" at about the time the *Tecumseh* struck the torpedo. For a moment the whole line lay motionless under the guns of Fort Morgan, allegedly prompting Farragut to shout "Damn the torpedoes! Full speed ahead!" Whether Farragut actually uttered those immortal words or not, he led his ships past the *Brooklyn* and on to victory.]

In the thickest of the fight the admiral still remained on the wheel house giving orders through his flag lieutenant and aides to the different vessels by signals. Some were directed to move in closer, others to fire more deliberately, and give their guns more elevation, while a few whose crews were nearly exhausted were ordered to fire more rapidly. Then a few complimentary signals would be made: "Excellent." "Do it again." "A beautiful shot," and other encouraging terms. Every ship was under his sharp flashing eye, and every order was clear and practicable. Whenever the fire slackened the enemy would bring every one of their available guns into action and throw shot and shell into, over, and around the vessels with great rapidity until they were driven to their bomb proofs by our terrible broadsides.

Shortly after the resumption of the bombardment the rebel flags on Fort Fisher and the Mound were shot away, which was no sooner discovered when loud cheers broke out among the fleet. Every vessel took up the cry, and for a few moments the voices of over 12,000 bluejackets could be heard above the roar of their guns.

At half past four o'clock the *Shenandoah* hauled out of line, and signaled that she was badly damaged. A number of other vessels sustained serious injuries but still maintained their stations. Up to this time the fleet had fired about six thousand shot and shell.

At sunset, 5:15 P.M., the vessels were signaled to withdraw from action and anchor for the night. The engagement had been hotly contested for nearly five hours, and as the fleet were anchoring out of range, General Butler with his transports made his appearance. A consultation was held on the *Malvern*, and preparations were made to land the troops on the following morning.

This was Christmas eve, and after supper the officers and men were assembled to discuss the scenes and incidents of the day. Poor Wemple had been a great favorite with many of our mess, and it was with the deepest regret we heard of his terrible death. For many months he had been attached to the floating prison *Roanoke* in the James River with no chance to earn distinction, or even prize money, and now on the first day of his entry into real warfare was destroyed by his own gun. [On 24 and 25 December Grattan paused periodically to record the progress of the bombardment in his diary. His account of the first Fort Fisher expedition is based on these entries, Grattan's memory, a wide variety of official correspondence, and the log of the *Malvern*.[3]]

21

The iron clads renew the engagement ♦ The reserve division
convoy the transports to the beach ♦ The sailors land and
capture Half Moon Battery and a hundred prisoners ♦
The troops commencing to land ♦ Lieutenant Cushing dragging
for torpedoes near Fort Fisher ♦ Burning of the barracks in the
fort ♦ Destroyed by the monitors' shell ♦ A soldier captures a
rebel flag and a mule ♦ General Weitzel makes a reconnaissance ♦
The frigates move into action ♦ The *Powhatan* in a sinking
condition ♦ Slow movements of the troops ♦ General Butler
remains on his transport ♦ The effects of the enemy's shots on
the iron clads ♦ The bombardment at night ♦ [25 December 1864]

THE SUN ROSE WITH GREAT SPLENDOR on Christmas day, and the water was
very smooth. Early preparations were commenced to renew the engagement.
The ramparts of Fort Fisher were covered with men repairing the damages sustained by our tremendous fire, and above them waved a new rebel flag.

The iron clad division steamed in and took their stations. While they were
occupied, the reserve division got underway and convoyed the transports to a
favorable locality near Half Moon Battery where the troops could be safely
landed. Although this battery had been of great service to the blockade runners,
it was harmless to prevent the soldiers' disembarkation. [So named by Union
forces because of its crescent shape (the Confederates called it Battery Gatlin),
Half Moon Battery consisted of several field pieces behind a wall of loose sand
located near the beach about 5 miles up from Fort Fisher. The guns had fired
upon blockaders whenever they drew within range after chasing blockade runners inshore.]

While the troops were manning their boats the reserves opened a vigorous
fire, shelling the woods and the battery. About noon the landing was commenced; a boat load of sailors from the *Santiago de Cuba* preceded the soldiers,
and as they struck the beach made a charge with a yell upon Half Moon Battery and captured it with about one hundred demoralized rebels and one gun.
The prisoners were turned over to the army authorities who were then landing,
and forming into companies and regiments. A strong skirmish line was thrown
out and their position under the protection of our guns was impregnable.

While the debarkation was progressing, Captain Cushing volunteered to
sound the channel and drag for torpedoes under the guns of Fort Fisher and

Union troops landing above Fort Fisher (Courtesy of Robert M. Browning, Jr.)

the Mound. Receiving the admiral's permission and in company with Acting Masters Mate William F. Horton and twelve men of the *Malvern*, he started on his dangerous mission in the first cutter, which had been provided with grappling irons, lead lines, and buoys.

The daring adventurers approached to within a quarter of a mile of the batteries and commenced operations. For a time the rebels were astonished and nonplused at Cushing's impudence, but upon discovering his object, they opened fire.

A few boats from the other vessels had started to assist, and while under a heavy fire succeeded in discovering a number of heavy torpedoes and placed buoys in their vicinity. One of the boats was struck by a solid shot and sunk, but her crew were saved by the cutters. After Cushing had accomplished his purpose, he returned to the flagship and from his report the admiral was convinced the vessels could move in closer to the beach without danger of running aground.

While the boats were slowly landing, the *New Ironsides* and the monitors had been keeping up a deliberate fire on the fort, every shell doing considerable damage. The admiral was watching the effects produced by their shots when an immense volume of smoke was seen rising from the interior of the great earthwork. It soon became known the rebel barracks, capable of accommodating two thousand men, were burning; the fire being caused by the bursting of one of our shell. The conflagration raged fiercely for over an hour, completely destroying the barracks, and nothing but the dark gloomy bomb proofs available to shelter the unfortunate confederate soldiers.

The debarkation was still progressing when the skirmish line had advanced to within half a mile of the fort, and one of the soldiers more daring than his general captured a rebel flag which was found unprotected and a mule.

After a portion of the troops had been landed General Weitzel went ashore and made a bird's eye reconnaissance of the enemy's works; reporting the results of his observations to General Butler who continued to remain on board his ship. [Weitzel made his "bird's eye reconnaissance" from high ground near the beach at some 600 yards from the fort.]

At two o'clock the frigates and gunboats were signaled to move in and engage the enemy. A rapid fire was opened to which the rebels replied; but were soon forced to take cover in the bomb proofs. The fleet then had it all their own way, and at very short range struck and dismounted several of the heaviest guns in the fort, and made several large breaks in the wooden stockade which ran from the river to the beach. [In fact, Union naval gunfire disabled only three rebel guns during the two-day bombardment.]

Not wishing to expend too much ammunition before the army was ready to make the assault, the vessels were directed to slacken their fire; but this had no sooner been done when the enemy manned the remaining guns and opened a furious attack, almost every shot taking effect on the wooden vessels. The admiral seeing the serious effects of the fire, signaled to the fleet to open their batteries with all the vigor they possessed. In a few moments their heavy guns began to tell on the rebels; broadside followed broadside in quick succession, and in and over the fort and batteries clouds of dust, smoke and fragments of bursting shell were flying and scattering in all directions. Several more guns were broken and dismounted and for a time the enemy was silenced.

Many of our vessels had been struck at or below the water line; but with one exception the damages were quickly repaired. The *Powhatan* made a signal that she was in a sinking condition, a shot below the water line had splintered the planking. She was hauled out of range and after great exertions by pumping and bailing, the damage was temporarily repaired and she returned to the scene of action. The *Colorado* that afternoon was struck about twenty-five times and the *Wabash* received several shots in her hull; but they still remained on their stations.

The slow tedious movements of the troops began to attract considerable attention and as it was getting rather late in the day, the flagship ran alongside of General Butler's transport and the admiral passed a few pleasant words with him, but nothing was said about the troops. While we were passing the transports the soldiers who were still on board heartily cheered the admiral, and it could be easily seen they were impatient to get on shore. The last we saw of the general was his right eye resting upon his troops who were on the beach and the left one glaring at right angles on Fort Fisher.

The rapid firing of our vessels still continued, and the admiral wishing to see the effects produced directed the flagship to run along shore near the monitors. The rebels in spite of the heavy bombardment showed great bravery and continued to keep up an irregular fire.

While the *Malvern* lay alongside the *Mahopac* a solid shot struck her turret, glanced off and just grazed our bow. Many of our vessels having exhausted their supply of ammunition and others including the frigate *Wabash* being badly injured were compelled to retire from action. The balance of the fleet were directed to continue the bombardment throughout the night to prevent the enemy from repairing damages.

Shortly after dark the tugs and tenders began supplying the vessels with ammunition from ordnance schooners which had arrived from Beaufort and the greater part of the night was occupied in preparation for renewing the hostilities on the following day when it was hoped the grand assault by the army would be made. [Grattan used Porter's initial after-action report, possibly the *Malvern*'s log, his own diary and memory, and other unidentified sources for this chapter.[1]]

22

Only a portion of the troops on shore ◆ Their camp fires ◆
Fort Fisher dark and gloomy ◆ Message to the admiral ◆
"General Butler embarking his troops" ◆ Astonishment
and indignation ◆ The admiral requests General Grant to send
him a fighting general ◆ General Butler and his chief engineer
abandon their troops ◆ Saved by the navy from capture and
starvation ◆ The blockade re-established ◆ The admiral directs
the squadron to rendezvous at Beaufort ◆ The admiral applies
to his old friend General Sherman at Savannah for troops ◆
Preparations for another expedition ◆ Waiting for the arrival
of the transports ◆ Festivities on the flagship ◆
[25–31 December 1864]

THE FLAGSHIP ANCHORED NEAR THE BEACH abreast of the troops whose camp fires were brightly burning throughout the night. In the direction and vicinity of Fort Fisher all was dark and gloomy. With the exception of an occasional flash of a gun and shell bursting in the air not a light could be seen. Those who were not on duty were trying to catch a few hours sleep when it became known that a singular movement was in progress on shore and on board the transports. About 9:00 P.M. lights were seen moving along the beach and boats were rapidly passing to and fro from the army vessels.

The admiral's attention had been called to the strange scene, and as he was about going on deck a boat came alongside with a message from Captain Alden of the *Brooklyn*, stating that General Butler had just hailed him from his ship and asked naval protection as he had just heard that a division of the enemy under Major General Robert Frederick Hoke had arrived from Wilmington and was about to attack his troops. [Major General Robert F. Hoke, CSA, received promotion to that rank for his brilliant action in capturing Plymouth, North Carolina, in the joint operation with the *Albemarle* on 20 April 1864. Hoke subsequently distinguished himself at Bermuda Hundred, Cold Harbor, and Petersburg. Near the end of the war he fought at Bentonville and surrendered with General Joseph E. Johnston in North Carolina. His principal flaw, an inability to cooperate with others, often canceled out his virtues.]

In addition to this General Butler stated that he had commenced re-embarking his men, having been advised to do so by General Weitzel, his engineer, who had pronounced the fort impregnable and uninjured by the naval bombardment.

The feelings of the admiral, his officers, and sailors when this astonishing intelligence became known can be better imagined than described, and it was well that General Butler did not call upon the flag ship and bid the admiral a gentlemanly farewell. Had the general attempted the assault and been defeated there would have been some excuse for his retreat; but to run away without firing a shot or making the slightest effort to capture the fort; it was stigmatized as a most cowardly, humiliating and dishonorable proceeding. [At the time, Grattan wrote in his diary: "The news to us of Butler's intention was astonishing, and the Admiral was exceedingly angry. To think that the army should do so mean a thing as retreating." [1] Porter noted in his after action report that he had hoped "to present to the nation Fort Fisher and surrounding works as a Christmas offering." [2] Several days later Grattan wrote his parents: "It may be for the best that Butler did not have the honor of capturing Wilmington, as he has killed himself beyond all remedy and knocked all his plans for the next presidency. He allowed personal motives to influence him, to the cost of his country. We all believe Butler to be a rank traitor and a coward and everything but a gentleman." [3]]

All our hard fighting and the loss of many valuable lives were thrown away; but the admiral determined not to abandon the object of the expedition, and a vessel was at once sent to Hampton Roads with dispatches and a request to General Grant to send him a fighting general. [On 27 December Porter wrote Welles that Fort Fisher "can be taken at any moment; in one hour's time, if the right man is sent with the troops." Welles gave this dispatch to Grant, who wrote back to Porter that he intended to send another force "without the former commander." [4]]

Towards midnight the wind began rising and heavy clouds spread over the water and land like a pall, and we all felt that it was an appropriate tableau for such a disgraceful act; abandoning victory when it was within our grasp. It is but just to say that the soldiers on shore and on the transports felt keenly the humiliating position in which they were placed; but there was no help for them as long as they were under the command of such a general and his chief engineer. Throughout the remainder of the night boats were passing to and from the beach and the troop ships. Toward daylight a heavy surf broke on the shore, and several boats were swamped and capsized and their occupants drowned.

General Butler did not wait to see his troops safe on board the transports; but proceeded at once for Hampton Roads, leaving his men under the protection of the admiral who had as much as he could do to look after his squadron. The rain was falling heavily and many of the vessels were too badly injured to risk a severe storm; but the admiral was too much of a man to desert the poor soldiers who stood shivering on the beach, without rations or shelter and unable to get off.

Shod in slippers, his tent mounted on a wooden platform, Ben Butler was not what you would call a "soldier's general." (Library of Congress B-8184-B-28)

The reserve division shelled the woods to the rear of the troops and had their boats ready to land as soon as the heavy surf would permit. The rain continued all day and night and the same state of affairs on shore still existed. The soldiers were half starved and their clothing saturated with the cold water.

On the following day the storm moderated and after much labor the remnants of Butler's army to the number of about two thousand [actually Porter picked up 700 soldiers[5]] were rescued by the naval vessels, and the transports sailed for Fortress Monroe; but those officers who were on the blockade and saw the troops passing in review before Fort Fisher quietly observed that their departure for the north was not as cheerful and enthusiastic as their grand advent on the scene of their general's subsequent cowardly retreat.

When the transports had departed the admiral ordered the vessels requiring temporary repairs to proceed to Beaufort which place was made the headquarters and rendezvous of the squadron. The blockade was again established with a larger number of vessels, and when the admiral had thoroughly inspected the fleet directed the *Malvern* to get underway for Beaufort.

Upon our arrival information was received of the capture of Savannah by General Sherman. The admiral and the general being old friends, having fought and won victories together in the Mississippi, determined to communicate with him and if he could spare any troops to send them at once. Fleet Captain Kidder R. Breese was the admiral's messenger, and taking the steamer *A. D. Vance* made a very rapid trip to Savannah and back, and reported that General Sherman had yet considerable fighting to do and advised the admiral to hold on a while when he hoped to be able to spare a few soldiers to co-operate and *fight* with the navy.[6]

Nothing was left for the admiral to do but patiently wait for the arrival of troops either from General Grant or General Sherman. Meanwhile the vessels were undergoing repairs; loading with provisions, coal and ammunition, and everything that could be done to make the next expedition a success was carried out in every particular. No more time would be wasted in Chinese experiments with powder boats; if any result followed the destruction of the *Louisiana* and three hundred barrels of gunpowder the enemy reaped the benefit of it. Instead of destroying or paralyzing the garrison it had the effect of awakening them up, infusing new life in their ranks, and made them look down with pitying contempt upon the author of such a silly invention.

Lieutenant Commander Cushing at his own request was placed in command of his former vessel the *Monticello*, and Lieutenant Benjamin H. Porter resumed the command of the *Malvern*.

While waiting for the arrival of intelligence from General Grant, the admiral would often walk the quarter-deck in deep thought, and his eyes would sparkle when they rested upon the magnificent fleet inside and outside the harbor. He was well pleased with their splendid behavior during the late engagements; but he determined to make them fight harder and go in closer to the beach during the next struggle.

Cushing's vessel lay but a short distance from the flagship and almost every hour of the day he was on board the *Malvern*, and with Captain Benjamin Porter, Preston, Terry, Saunders, and a few others would assemble in the cozy cabin on deck, where the admiral would not be disturbed, and for hours they would gather around the table singing songs, telling yarns, cracking jokes, and occasionally cracking a few bottles of wine if the jokes were too dry.

23

Arrival of dispatches from General Grant • The transports are on the way • General A. H. Terry in command of the troops with orders to fight • Great enthusiasm in the squadron • A severe storm delays the arrival of the soldiers • A hearty welcome • All ready for sea • The departure for the battleground • General orders to the commanding officers • The sailors to assist in storming Fort Fisher • The flagship leads the van • Appearance of the vessels • At anchor off the fort • Landing of the troops • Capture of a drove of cattle • General Terry with his soldiers • The fleet engaged with the enemy • The scene at sunset • The bombardment at night • The troops throwing a line of intrenchments • Landing of stores, artillery, mules and ammunition • A rebel gunboat opens fire • Damage to the fleet • General Terry on the flagship • The hour appointed to storm Fort Fisher • [1–14 January 1865]

On the first day of the new year 1865, an army steamer was discovered outside the bar signaling for a pilot. A tug was immediately sent out to communicate with her and returned with Lieutenant Essex Porter, aide-de-camp on the staff of General Grant, who brought dispatches for his father, the admiral. It then became known that the troops brought away from Fort Fisher would be returned and under the command of Major General Alfred Howe Terry, who was directed to co-operate and *fight* with the navy. They were expected to arrive on the 4th of January.[1]

[Major General Alfred H. Terry, USA, had fought in the siege of Charleston and at Petersburg before taking command of the army forces assigned to the second Fort Fisher expedition, dubbed "Terry's Provisional Corps." He received the thanks of Congress for his actions at Fort Fisher. After the war, he was George Armstrong Custer's superior officer during the debacle at Little Big Horn. During the Civil War Terry earned a reputation as a top-notch commander able to cooperate equally well with superiors, peers, or subordinates.]

The day following the reception of General Grant's New Year's present the flagship went outside the bar and the dispatch was read to the divisional officers and the good news was soon communicated to the whole fleet, and created the greatest enthusiasm. ["All is again life & enthusiasm," Grattan wrote in his diary, "and the coming fight will eclipse our last."[2]]

About this time a severe storm set in, and continued for several days, and it was the eighth of January before the transports began to arrive. As they entered the harbor heavily laden with troops their appearance was hailed with loud cheers from the fleet, and the soldiers, many of whom had been rescued by the navy, returned the salute with great vehemence.

General Terry was soon clasping the admiral by the hand, and at first sight both appeared to be pleased with each other; and although the general was a very modest man we could all see he was a brave soldier. Pomposity, arrogance, cowardice and self conceit seemed to be elements foreign to his character.

The vessels were all ready to sail, but another storm delayed the departure until the twelfth of January. At day's dawn the flagship fired a gun and signaled the fleet to weigh anchor and proceed direct to their stations off Fort Fisher.

Before leaving Beaufort each commanding officer was directed to detail as many of his men as he could spare from the guns as a landing party. The boats were to be lowered on the off side of the vessels and the sailors were to be armed with revolvers and cutlasses. When the signal was made the boats were to be manned and pull around the stern of the iron clads and board the fort on a run. The marines accompanying the bluejackets were to form on shore in the rear of the sailors and cover them with their muskets during the assault. The admiral expected that two thousand men could be mustered from the different vessels and not prevent a proper working of the guns. [Porter's General Order 81 of 4 January 1865 directed the sailors to "board the fort on the run in a seaman-like way."[3]]

Another printed general order was also issued in which the details for the coming engagement were set forth in very plain language and special instructions given as to the range, elevation, and ammunition for the guns. [Actually Porter issued several general orders for the second Fort Fisher expedition.[4]]

At 10:00 A.M. every vessel was underway and the flagship soon took the lead. In the former expedition no system of organization was observed by the transports, but General Terry in the short space of time in which he was in command had brought his vessels in a state of order and discipline which would have done credit to any naval officer. [For example, Terry issued detailed sailing orders to the transports.[5]]

The ocean was very calm and the sun was brightly shining. In addition to the distinguishing pennants every vessel—both army and navy—carried a large national flag, which fluttered and waved in a gentle breeze. A more animated and beautiful sight as the vessels glided rapidly over the water cannot be imagined.

At 4:00 P.M. we arrived within sight of Fort Fisher and the fleet moved in towards the coast taking their position for the night. On the following morning the reserve division shelled the woods and at 9:00 A.M. the troops began to land. The iron clads in the meantime had occupied their original stations and opened fire on the enemy. By 1:00 P.M. the soldiers were all on shore, with the exception of a few colored volunteers who were intended to protect the rear when the white soldiers advanced on the fort. [Porter's after-action report of 17 January indicates that the troops began landing operations at 8:30 A.M. and by 2:00 P.M. 8,000 men had gotten ashore.[6]]

For the space of two miles the beach was occupied by our troops. [In his diary Grattan wrote: "It was a splendid sight to see the troops land and take their positions. . . . The beach was black with men with their bayonets glittering in the sunshine and their regimental flags fluttering in the breeze. The weather is lovely."[7]] Regiments were forming and a line of skirmishers were slowly advancing. General Terry was on shore with his men and personally superintended every movement. The first boat load that landed had the good fortune to capture a drove of cattle belonging to the rebels. There was a slight surf in the beach; but no accidents occurred, and immense quantities of ammunition, artillery and hard tack and pork were piled up on the sand. It was very evident that the troops had come to stay this time. Camp fires were burning and about 2:00 P.M. the soldiers were cooking their breakfast. A few bluejackets who were on shore, afterwards informed their messmates that beef steaks were very common articles of diet throughout the camp.

Finding that the army was being organized in an intelligent and satisfactory manner the admiral directed the vessels to take their stations and engage the fortifications, his object being to get them all in thorough working order so as to be fully prepared when the grand assault took place, and at the same time inflict as much damage on the enemy as possible.

At about 4:00 P.M. the fleet were in position and commenced a very heavy bombardment. The *Mohican* attracted considerable attention by having a large evergreen tree fastened at her bow. It was the same she had in the fight on Christmas Day.

The enemy occasionally replied to our guns but during most of the time were compelled to retire to the bomb proofs. General Terry and the troops were watching the bombardment when the admiral directed the fleet to do their best. The reserve division had taken up their former position and opened fire on the Mound and Zeke's Island Batteries, and at sunset the firing was at its greatest fury. The scene from the *Malvern* was one of the wildest, the most exciting and at the same time most awful and sublime that the human imagination can possibly conceive. Immense furrows were plowed through the traverses by the monitors' shell; guns were dismounted and the platforms and carriages knocked into splinters, and dark clouds of smoke and dust inside the fort showed where the bursting fragments were scattering. As the shades of evening began gathering the wooden vessels hauled out of action and began filling up with ammunition. The iron clads continued a steady and deliberate fire throughout the night. General Terry's forces were at work throwing up entrenchments and by daylight he had a line of earthworks extending from the coast to the Cape Fear River, and a short distance up the peninsula a strong rear guard was posted. The transports were moved as near as they could go to the beach and the whole day was occupied in landing mules, artillery and ammunition.

At 11:00 A.M. on the fourteenth the admiral again turned his attention to Fort Fisher. The iron clads had been reserving their ammunition; but upon receiving the signal to fire more rapidly they again made the welkin ring with their tremendous guns. [The word "welkin" appears frequently in Old English poetry. It means "the apparent arch or vault of heaven overhead; the sky, the firmament."[8]] About two o'clock in the afternoon the light draughts *Huron, Maumee,* and *Unadilla* were sent inside the monitors, close up to the beach and opened a rapid fire with their heavy guns. While thus engaged several shots were noticed coming over from the river in the rear of the fort, and upon investigation they were found to proceed from a gunboat. Captain Cushing with the *Monticello* at once started in for the shore and obtaining the range from aloft, opened fire and succeeded in driving the rebel vessel up the river. [Cushing reported driving the Confederate gunboat *Chickamauga* and three transport steamers upriver on the fifteenth.[9] The CSS *Chickamauga* supported Fort Fisher's defenders on 14–15 January by firing on Union troops ashore. It is possible that she encountered the *Monticello* on both days. The Confederates scuttled her on 25 February 1865.]

The enemy deeming it useless to waste so many shots on the iron clads, paid particular attention to the wooden vessels when they approached so close to the beach. The *Huron* soon had her mainmast shot away and a shot put in her hull near the water line; several other vessels were slightly injured and the *Vicksburg* burst her 30-pound Parrott rifle.

At 4:00 P.M. the *Shenandoah, Brooklyn,* and *Pequot* were sent in to draw the enemy's fire and relieve the damaged gunboats, and with the frigates were directed to keep up the bombardment throughout the night to prevent the rebels from repairing damages. During the day the *Saugus* and *Mahopac* reported they had burst their XV-inch guns and the *Ironsides* informed the admiral they had been struck twenty-five times, and one solid shot had loosened some of her iron plates. Many solid shot struck the decks and turrets of the monitors but no serious injury was done.

The evening was ushered in with a clear full moon, which brought out the fortifications and fleet in full view. Thousands of camp fires were burning on shore surrounded by our troops; but nothing of the character could be seen in Fort Fisher; with the exception of an occasional flash and report of a gun, all was dark, gloomy and silent there.

General Terry came on board the flagship and after a consultation named the hour for the assault to commence on the following day. If everything worked satisfactory the soldiers would charge on Fort Fisher at three o'clock in the afternoon.[10]

We had now been engaged four days in all with the enemy and hopes were entertained that the morrow would bring victory. [Like his account of the first attack on Fort Fisher, Grattan based his account of the second expedition on his diary and memory as well as a variety of official reports and correspondence.[11]]

24

Sunday January 15th 1865, a day long to be remembered ◆
The fleet renews the engagement ◆ Landing of the sailors
and marines ◆ Fleet Captain Breese in command of the
bluejackets ◆ Lieutenants Preston and Porter on shore ◆
The sailors organizing and advancing near the fort ◆ The troops
rapidly forming ◆ Death of Lieutenant Preston ◆ The fleet moves
closer to the beach and opens a furious bombardment ◆ General
Terry gives the signal "change fire" ◆ The exciting moment
arrived ◆ The flagship blows her whistle and it is repeated by the
squadron ◆ The enemy swarm on the ramparts ◆ The sailors on
the beach ◆ The charge, the assault, and repulse ◆ The scene
from the flagship ◆ Death of Lieutenant Porter ◆ The sailors join
the soldiers who have entered the fort ◆ Hand to hand fighting ◆
A lull and signal from General Terry ◆ "Fort Fisher Ours" ◆
Wild enthusiasm ◆ The fleet celebrating the victory ◆ The dead
heroes on the sands brought off ◆ [15 January 1865]

SUNDAY, JANUARY 15, 1865 will be a day ever memorable by those who participated in and survived the army and navy expedition against Fort Fisher.

Early in the morning on that calm and beautiful Sabbath day the men-of-war were busy preparing their quota of sailors and marines to assist in the grand assault. The vessels took their stations and at 9:00 A.M. twenty-eight of them were engaged with the enemy. Soon after a rebel steamer came down the river filled with troops, and reinforced the garrison in the fort. [Late on the fourteenth, the Confederate steam transports *Sampson*, *Petteway*, and *Harlee* departed for Battery Buchanan with 1,000 troops. The *Petteway* and *Harlee* grounded soon after leaving the dock, leaving only the *Sampson* able to deliver reinforcements. Only 350 of the troops reached Fort Fisher.]

At ten o'clock the signal was made to man the boats and land the sailors and marines. In a few moments hundreds of boats covered the water and before landing came up under the stern of the flagship and saluted the admiral. The *Malvern* sent two boats. The first one contained many of the best sailors in the ship and Fleet Captain Breese, who was placed in command of the naval detachment and represented the admiral. He was accompanied by the admiral's son Carlisle who acted as aide-de-camp.

The other boat contained Lieutenant Preston, Lieutenant Benjamin H. Porter, Acting Master James A. Hamilton, Acting Masters Mate William F.

Bombardment of Fort Fisher before the assault of the Naval Brigade, 15 January 1865, by John W. Grattan. The USS *Malvern* steams in the right foreground, flying the blue pennant from her mainmast. (Naval Historical Center NH 50468-KN)

Horton, and a few bluejackets and marines. Many more would have gone, but their services were required on board the flagship.

As the flotilla struck the beach the iron clad division opened fire and the enemy were forced to retire to the bomb proofs. While the sailors were mustering, a few grape shot from the Mound Battery fell among them, which was no sooner communicated to the reserve division when a rapid bombardment commenced and the rebels were driven from their guns; but before this was accomplished the *Santiago de Cuba* was struck three times in her hull.

The bluejackets were organized into three divisions and placed under the command of Lieutenant Commander Charles H. Cushman, Lieutenant Commander Thomas O. Selfridge, and Lieutenant Commander James Parker. The marines were commanded by Captain Lucien L. Dawson. The gallant Cushing was placed in command of himself and anyone who dared to follow him. It was useless to try to give orders to that dare-devil and the admiral gave him a roving commission.

When the organization was completed the sailors advanced to within a mile and a half of the fort and commenced throwing up earthworks and digging trenches to protect them from the enemy's shell and grape. Lieutenant Preston was in command of an advance battalion, and although within close range of the rebel guns, gave his orders in a cool, encouraging, and cheerful manner.

The bluejackets had advanced to within four hundred yards of the fort, and while waiting for the signal to assault, a fragment of a bursting shell struck the gallant Preston and he fell mortally wounded. His men immediately carried him to the rear but owing to the terrible nature of the wound and loss of blood he died before seeing his brother officers. [A bullet struck Preston in the left thigh or groin, severing his femoral artery. A sailor stooped to assist, was shot, and fell on top of him. Another sailor pulled the man off of Preston, who rolled over on his back and quickly bled to death.[1]]

The troops under General Terry were rapidly forming; and the line of skirmishers had arrived near the heavy stockade. In a short time the glistening bayonets and regimental colors were seen through the trees and the column halted. The last orders and instructions were being given for the assault. While the army was preparing, every vessel was moved as close to the beach as they could go and a furious bombardment was commenced. The frigates were firing whole broadsides of twenty-seven guns at one discharge, and the iron clads kept up a running fire into the fort and surrounding works. The enemy possessing a degree of courage not generally given to human beings, bravely maintained their position and at intervals would reply with their remaining guns, every shot taking effect.

The tremendous bombardment was continued with great vigor until 2:40 P.M.,[2] when the admiral received General Terry's signal informing him he was about to commence the assault and requested the squadron to change fire, and pay attention to the Mound Battery and the batteries in the rear of Fort Fisher. [Porter's after-action report of 17 January states that he received Terry's signal at 3:00 P.M. Grattan's diary says that Porter received the signal at 2:40 P.M.]

In a few seconds the flagship signaled to the fleet to change fire and commenced blowing her steam whistle. Every vessel answered the signal and blew their powerful whistles. The *Malvern* then started for the beach and accompanied the bluejackets in their gallant charge. The noise of the guns, whistles, cheers, and yells of the sailors and marines was terrific and made the most exciting and indescribable event during the whole engagement.

When the assault commenced by the sailors; which was several moments before the army was in motion, the enemy came out of their bomb proofs and swarmed on the ramparts facing the sea, in great numbers. Supposing it to be the main attack the rebels concentrated their whole force to oppose them, and as the bluejackets reached the palisades a murderous fire of musketry was opened on them. It was impossible to scale this obstruction and the sailors had to rush in the water to get on the other side. Upon reaching the moat they dashed forward and amid cheers and groans and yells charged up the steep face of the fort, but a very few arrived at the top, and those who did fell back and rolled down into the ditch riddled with bullets.

Conventional rendering of the bombardment of Fort Fisher from the Confederate perspective at the Mound Battery (Naval Historical Center KN 3310)

During the whole charge the enemy had been firing volley after volley into the bluejackets, and the ground was soon covered with the dead and wounded. The marines did very little if any service to protect their comrades and in consequence of their demoralization the slaughter was terrible.

Captain Breese, the admiral's chief of staff, and Lieutenant Commander Cushing were at the head of the line and made several gallant efforts to get the men on top the ramparts but the enemy were in too great force to accomplish it. A sailor boy attached to one of the divisions managed to reach the parapet and planting the ensign which he carried, fired his boarding pistol into the face of the enemy, fell backwards and rolled down into the ditch, and when his body was afterwards found it was pierced with nine bullets. Finding it impossible to storm the fort the sailors retreated. Many found protection under the palisades, and remained there until after dark before they could escape.

The troops under General Terry in the meantime had made an assault on the opposite end of the fort facing the river, and when the sailors were repulsed had effected an entrance and were charging over the traverses in great numbers. Brevet Brigadier General Newton Martin Curtis' brigade were the first troops to enter the fort and plant their battle flags.

THE NAVY AT FORT FISHER.

ASSAULT OF THE NAVAL COLUMN ON THE NORTH-EAST SALIENT OF FORT FISHER.

Sailors attempting to "board" Fort Fisher (Naval Historical Center NH 42756)

The rebels threw their whole force on the brigade; but were compelled to retire behind the traverses. General Curtis was soon joined by the 2nd Division of the 24th Corps and a secure foothold was obtained.

The enemy fought with great valor and desperation; but were gradually forced back. There were fifteen large traverses or mounds separating the guns from each other on this side of the fort, over which our troops were obliged to climb; each one of the mounds in itself a fort. When the rebels were driven out of one traverse they would rally behind the next one and we could plainly see them cautiously crawl up the sides of the mound with our soldiers doing the same thing on the other side, and when near the top would bring their muskets into position and the one who could fire first generally had the best of the position. It was throughout a hand to hand or rather musket to musket encounter, and the enemy contested every inch of the ground.

Immediately after the repulse of the sailors, the iron clads opened fire on the sea face wall of the fort, and the traverses occupied by the rebels; but while so engaged the Mound Battery imitated them by firing grape and canister into the traverses occupied by our troops.

As the assault was favorably progressing General Curtis and General Galusha Pennypacker fell seriously wounded, and Colonel Louis Bell, Colonel John W. Moore, and Lieutenant Colonel Jonas W. Lyman were killed while gallantly leading their soldiers, who lost very heavy in killed and wounded.

High-water mark of the Naval Brigade, by John W. Grattan. The USS *Malvern*, second from left, flies the blue pennant from her maninmast. To the right are three monitors and the USS *New Ironsides*. (Naval Historical Center NH 50467-KN)

[Galusha Pennypacker had been "the only officer in the history of the U.S. Army who was not old enough to vote for or against the President who appointed him."[3] He was born on 1 June 1844. Twenty-seven-year-old attorney Louis Bell, the son of Samuel Bell, former governor of New Hampshire and two-time senator, had seemed destined to follow in his father's footsteps in a political career. Pennsylvania native John W. Moore was only twenty-five when he was killed. Jonas W. Lyman had been shot dead leading a charge.]

At sunset the fighting was at its height, and as the sun was sinking behind the fort every object was rendered very distinct. Nine traverses were in possession of General Terry. The roar of musketry was incessant, and after dark we could judge by the flashes how the terrible struggle was progressing.

Shortly after 7:00 P.M. the admiral received a signal message from General Terry informing him that the enemy were being reinforced, and requested the fleet to shell the river and shore in the rear of Fort Fisher and the Mound, which was at once ordered to be done.

While the army were engaged in driving the enemy from the traverses, an officer came on board the flagship and reported the losses sustained by the sailors in the assault. Lieutenant Benjamin H. Porter was killed while leading his men at the parapet of the fort, a musket ball having entered his breast.

Among the volunteers was Assistant Surgeon William Longshaw, Jr. of the *Minnesota* who was killed by a grape shot while engaged in dressing the wounds of a sailor. The naval loss in the terrible assault was about two hundred and fifty men. Lieutenants George M. Bache and Roswell H. Lamson, Lieutenant Commander Charles H. Cushman, Acting Ensigns James Birtwistle and Frederick A. O'Connor, the two last from the *Minnesota*, were among the wounded. [Longshaw, Birtwistle, and O'Connor had been shipmates of Grattan on board the *Minnesota*. Lamson and Preston had been friends since their days together at the Naval Academy. Grattan must have known Bache, Cushman, and Lamson. Porter recommended Bache, Cushman, and Lamson for promotion for their conspicuous gallantry.[4]]

After their bloody repulse the officers, sailors, and marines who were not wounded followed the soldiers into the fort and assisted them during their last struggles with the desperate foe.

Owing to the danger of injuring our troops the fleet ceased firing about 9:00 P.M. and with the exception of an occasional volley and a desultory discharge of musketry in the farther end of the fortifications all was quiet.

The admiral was calmly smoking his pipe in the cabin waiting for signals from the general. His incessant labors and anxiety had made him quite ill; but he would take no rest until the result was known.

The army signal officer was with us in the wardroom, and all were engaged in quiet conversation and lamenting the deaths of our gallant mess mates when the ships bells proclaimed the hour of ten. The echoes had scarcely died away when Lieutenant Clemens was on deck to answer an army signal. The signal torch was waving its secret message on the ramparts where the bluejackets were repulsed. In a moment the meaning of the signal was conveyed to the admiral, who jumped on deck, called all hands aft to the quarter deck. Every man and boy was soon around him, and in a loud, thrilling voice he directed them to give three cheers for the capture of Fort Fisher. The admiral never before gave an order which was so heartily obeyed. Everyone appeared to be wild with joy, all discipline was relaxed and the cheers of the officers and the sailors could be heard far and wide over the smooth water. Loud cheering could be heard in the fort and lights began to flash in all directions. The flagship signaled the fleet and repeated the admiral's order, and in a few seconds thousands of voices united in tremendous cheering. All the vessels were quickly illuminated, rockets and signal lights were flashing in the air, bells were rung and steam whistles were screaming forth the glad tidings.

The admiral when he saw the effect the victory produced on his officers and men went below completely exhausted and overcome and had to be assisted into his cabin.

During the progress of the celebration the dead heroes on shore were not forgotten. Boats were sent for the dead and wounded. After a long search the

The fleet celebrating the fall of Fort Fisher (Courtesy of Robert M. Browning, Jr.)

bodies of poor Preston and Porter were found and brought on board the flagship. The gallant flag captain was in full uniform, his coat glittering with gold lace; a bullet wound was discovered in his breast. A calm peaceful smile played around his mouth; but Preston wore a look of agony as his sufferings must have been terrible.

On the following morning Lieutenant Saunders was sent north, on board of a dispatch boat with the remains of his old mess mates and the admiral's dispatch announcing the fall of Fort Fisher.

25

ON THE MORNING AFTER THE VICTORY the national flag could be seen proudly waving over the blood stained fortifications. After a most desperate resistance the enemy to the number of two thousand surrendered to General Terry. [Actually 1,400 to 1,500 garrison troops surrendered.] Major General William Henry Chase Whiting and Colonel William Lamb who were in command were badly wounded. [Whiting, who was second in command under Major General Braxton Bragg, head of the Confederate Department of North Carolina, died of his wounds on 10 March 1865. Lamb, commander of the Confederate garrison at Fort Fisher, was wounded in the hip but survived to reminisce about the battle thirty-eight years later at a reunion with some of the Union naval officers against whom he had fought on 15 January 1865.]

All the earthworks on Federal Point, mounting over seventy-two heavy guns—one of which a magnificent Armstrong on a handsome mahogany and other hardwood carriage upon which was a silver plate bearing the name of President Jefferson Davis, to whom it was presented, fell into the possession of our troops. The enemy lost about five hundred in killed and wounded, but General Terry's dead and dying and wounded numbered over nine hundred men, among whom were many valuable officers.

[The Armstrong gun was Fort Fisher's most famous cannon. It was a state-of-the-art English-made muzzle-loading banded or "built-up" rifled cannon with an 8-inch bore that fired a 150-pound projectile. Sir William Armstrong had sent it through the blockade in 1864 as a gift to the Confederacy. The rebels mounted the piece in Purdie Battery at about the mid-point of Fort

Fisher's sea face. Its beautiful mahogany and rosewood carriage and brass hardware made it look more like a piece of parlor furniture than ordnance, according to one Confederate soldier. The gun crew supposedly took great pride in the gun and worked hard to keep it bright and shiny.[1]]

For a time we hoped the slaughter had ceased, and after breakfast many officers were preparing to go on shore. The soldiers were resting from their labors and everything bore a calm and peaceful appearance; when suddenly without a second's warning an immense quantity of earth, timbers and smoke rose to a great height inside the fort and fell with crushing weight in every direction. A loud booming report informed us the rebel magazine had exploded. About four hundred soldiers were buried alive or crushed by the falling debris. It was a terrible accident and with the losses already suffered a feeling of melancholy and gloom was cast over the army and navy. Two naval officers belonging to the *Gettysburg* were walking on the ramparts at the time and were killed by the explosion. [The explosion occurred just after sunrise moments after three to four marines carrying lit torches entered the magazine. Some 13,000 pounds of gunpowder blew up, killing about 200 Union and Confederate soldiers by most estimates.]

Shortly after this sad event several officers of the flagship and fleet went ashore to visit the battle ground, and the boat crews were directed to gather and bury their dead comrades. With some difficulty we managed to ascend the steep side of the fort nearest the sea, and stood upon the parapet from which a clear and uninterrupted view could be obtained of the interior and exterior of the immense earthworks. All around us in every conceivable attitude lay the dead and mangled bodies of both rebel and union soldiers. Fragments of our shell lay thick and scattered in every direction, and the only thing that saved the garrison from annihilation during the bombardment was their bomb-proofs.

A deep blackened cavity in the centre of the fort marked the place where the magazine had been, around which a large number of soldiers were engaged in exhuming the bodies of their dead comrades. The bomb proofs were filled with wounded rebels, many of them had been there several days, horribly mangled by the fragments of our shell and now beyond a surgeon's aid; but the largest number were wounded by the troops during the assault.

Entering into a conversation with a wounded rebel officer, we learned that he was on duty in the naval battery known as Fort Buchanan, situated in the rear of Fort Fisher on Federal Point, during the first attack made by the squadron in December. At that time there were only six hundred men in the fort and surrounding batteries, and no troops in Wilmington or its vicinity to re-inforce them. [Numbers vary from one account to the next. According to the best estimates, on Christmas Day 1864 the Confederates had roughly 1,370 men inside Fort Fisher. On 21 December, Robert E. Lee had detached Major General Robert F. Hoke's division of 6,155 men from the Army of Northern Virginia and dispatched it to Wilmington. Elements of Hoke's division arrived piecemeal on Federal Point over the next several days. Above Butler's landing site on 25 December the Confederates mustered a ragtag force of approximately 1,200 North Carolina militia, consisting of teen-age boys and men aged forty-five to sixty, and leading elements of Hoke's division. By the end of 26 December, the Confederate force above the remaining Union soldiers on Federal Point numbered nearly 3,400 men. In all, Butler's command numbered approximately 6,500 troops.] The rebel officer also informed us the fleet caused a great deal of damage, and during the bombardment they were compelled to remain nearly all the time in the bomb proofs; those who did man the guns suffered terribly for their bravery.

A large number of guns were dismounted and their carriages shattered and destroyed and over fifty men were killed and wounded. The rapid bombardment of our vessels at sunset on Christmas Day was as terrific as to completely demoralize the rebel garrison, and if General Butler had made an assault with about one-tenth of his command, the enemy would have surrendered without resistance. The subsequent withdrawal of his forces caused greater surprise to the enemy than the loss of the fortifications would have occasioned. A few days after Major General Braxton Bragg arrived from Wilmington with six thousand troops; but finding their services not required they were sent to Charleston to re-inforce Major General William Joseph Hardee. When the fleet made its second appearance the Fort and batteries were reinforced and about the time the assault was made the rebels mustered nearly three thousand men.

[Hardee had tried in vain to stop Sherman's march through Georgia. He left Charleston in January 1865 to join Joseph E. Johnston in North Carolina. During the second Fort Fisher expedition Terry's 9,600 men faced some 1,900 Confederates in the fort and Hoke's full division to the north on Federal Point. During neither expedition did Hoke try to interfere with the landing, nor did he attack the Union beachhead.]

Bidding the wounded officer a kind adieu, we continued on our tour of inspection and approached the formidable Mound Battery. It mounted two heavy guns which were in good order, the enemy having neglected to spike them before the surrender. The ground was thickly covered with the iron fragments of our shell, and one of the guns was splattered with blood and brains of a rebel gunner who must have been engaged in training the gun—which was loaded—on our soldiers in the traverses, when a fragment of a shell from the reserve division struck him down. The Mound was a very elevated earth work and contained bomb proofs and a large magazine. It commanded the channel to Cape Fear river, and on its summit reflectors and signal lights were used to guide the blockade runners in and out of the harbor. It was connected with Fort Fisher by a chain of batteries and redoubts, which were composed of cotton bales covered with sand. In several of the bomb proofs galvanic batteries were discovered with wires attached leading to a large number of torpedoes in the channel. Gangs of sailors were soon engaged underrunning these wires and in a few hours several were hauled ashore. A number of boats were dragging the bar and placing buoys for the guidance of the fleet. It was very fortunate for our soldiers and sailors that they did not charge directly on the land face of Fort Fisher; after the surrender a line of torpedoes placed a short distance apart and connected by wires to galvanic batteries in the bomb proofs were discovered to extend from a short distance near the beach over the land to the river, and of sufficient power to blow up and destroy an entire brigade.

The valuable services of the frigates, iron clads, and other vessels drawing over ten feet of water could not be made available for operations in Cape Fear river, and with the exception of light draught vessels the fleet was disbanded. The vessels requiring repairs were sent north and the remaining few were ordered to Charleston and other points along the coast.

About four o'clock in the afternoon the steamer *Spaulding*, with the secretary of war, Edwin M. Stanton, on board, was discovered coming in. Upon her arrival the flagship fired a salute, and the admiral went on board; but had no sooner stepped on her deck when he was almost overwhelmed with congratulations. It was a genuine surprise for the secretary to see our flag waving over Fort Fisher after what he had heard in regard to its great strength and impregnability, and he hastened to tender his thanks to General Terry who had been signalled to come on board. When the general appeared a very interesting incident occurred. He presented the secretary with the rebel flag captured during the assault, who in acknowledgement gave the admiral and the general a complimentary letter, thanking the officers and men of the army and navy on behalf of the President of the United States for the gallantry and prowess displayed in capturing the strongest earthwork on the Atlantic coast, and closed by saying a powerful nation would not forget the poor fellows who fell in the bloody engagement. [Grattan interjected his own thoughts into the letter, which actually read: "The Secretary of War has the honor to acknowledge the receipt of the rebel flag of Fort Fisher, and in the name of the President congratulates you and the gallant officers and soldiers, sailors, and marines of your commands, and tenders you thanks for the valor and skill displayed in your respective parts of the great achievement in the operations against Fort Fisher and in its assault and capture. The combined operations of the squadron and land forces of your commands deserve and will receive the thanks of the nation, and will be held in admiration throughout the world as a proof of the naval and military prowess of the United States."[2] After a very pleasant interview and renewed congratulations on the part of the secretary of war the *Spaulding* got underway and under full speed started for Washington.

Soon after dark several bright flashes and heavy explosions were seen and heard in the direction of Fort Caswell and the batteries at the entrance of Western Bar. The presumption was that the enemy were evacuating and destroying their works which were rendered useless after the fall of Fort Fisher. Captain Cushing was ordered to proceed with his vessel and ascertain if the forts were abandoned, and if they were he was directed to notify the admiral of the fact by hoisting the national flag on Fort Caswell.

Leaving a few gunboats to protect our troops on the sea coast the light draughts were ordered to cross the bar and anchor in the river. When this was safely accomplished the *Malvern* soon joined them and anchored in the rear of Fort Fisher where a number of transports were engaged in taking on board the rebel prisoners.

On the following morning our flag could be seen on Fort Caswell. It was a very busy day for everybody. The gunboats occupied in repairing damages and filling up with coal and ammunition. General Terry was engaged in strengthening his advance line of entrenchments, and towards evening his whole force, with the exception of a small garrison in Fort Fisher, were in position to oppose any attack the enemy might feel disposed to make. The gunboats on the coast were of great assistance in keeping the rebels at a safe distance, and on the slightest suspicion their guns would rake the country.

26

Cushing occupies Smithville and raises the flag ◆ The admiral
puzzled ◆ Cushing and his headquarters ◆ The flagship arrives at
the town ◆ General Terry dines with the admiral ◆ An attempt to
decoy and capture blockade runners ◆ The rebel signal lights
in order ◆ Midnight ◆ A runner coming in ◆ Falls in the trap ◆
Capture of the steamer *Stag* ◆ Another vessel discovered ◆
She anchors near the *Stag* ◆ English lords disgusted ◆
The blockade runner *Charlotte* from Bermuda ◆ Scenes of
debauchery ◆ Drunken and fighting sailors ◆ An attempt to excite
a mutiny and its result ◆ The blockade runner *Blenheim* captured
near the Mound ◆ List of guns and fortification in possession
of our troops ◆ [19–25 January 1865]

O N THE MORNING OF JANUARY NINETEENTH the admiral was informed that
our flag could be seen in the direction of Smithville. Orders were at once given
for the *Malvern* to proceed there and investigate this un-looked for capture, as
it was well known that this town was fortified by a very strong battery. Upon
our arrival the mystery was soon solved. Cushing and a few bluejackets were in
full possession and had his pickets thrown out.

It appeared that after raising the flag on Fort Caswell, Cushing determined
to make a reconnaissance towards Smithville. Owing to her draught of water the
Monticello was unable to enter the harbor and Cushing started in a small boat
with four men under a flag of truce. When within a short distance of town, a
boat filled with Negroes approached and he was informed the enemy had
spiked their guns and evacuated the place. Substituting the stars and stripes in
place of the white flag, Cushing pushed boldly for the town, and as he landed
was met by the civil authorities and a number of citizens who formally surrendered.

In the name of the admiral Cushing modestly accepted the capitulation,
and at once hoisted the national flag over the abandoned fort. The boat was
sent back to the *Monticello* with orders for all the men who could be spared to
report for duty at Smithville. When they arrived they were armed, and martial
or rather naval law declared. In Cushing's headquarters all the liquor and
firearms that could be found were stored. With the exception of two hospitals
filled with wounded not a rebel soldier could be found. When Cushing had
made his report, the admiral said nothing but went down into his cabin and had

a hearty laugh at his impudence and audacity. [Cushing apparently made this report in person. He later filed an official report.[1]]

In the afternoon we were joined by the *Maratanza, Wilderness* and *Nansemond*, and shortly after they had anchored General Terry came on board the flagship and dined with the admiral. It may be here remarked that Cushing had one large room in his headquarters set apart for livestock; but so far his scouts had only captured about a hundred head of poultry, and when he had made his statement, presented the admiral with some very fine young fowl. When General Terry was informed how the town was occupied and in possession of the bluejackets it created a great deal of merriment.

As it was yet too early for the news of the downfall of Fort Fisher to reach Bermuda, the admiral thought a blockade runner might be captured that night if the lights were kept burning as usual at the entrance of the harbor. Cushing was accordingly sent to execute the experiment, and after dark the lights could be seen brightly shining. Cushing was stationed at Fort Caswell with a few men and everybody was watching the bar. Shortly after midnight a large blockade runner was discovered coming in and upon arriving within hail of the fort stopped her engines and began signaling. For a moment Cushing was at a loss what to do; but soon recovering himself sang out, "Aye, aye. It's all right. Signal Corps drunk. Great victory. It's all right. Go ahead." After a little further delay the steamer started ahead for Smithville; her captain no doubt greatly surprised to hear that the signal corps was intoxicated, but then that might result after a victory over the "bloody yanks."

All was still as death on board our vessels, and as the runner approached the admiral was training a gun on her, to prevent any attempt to escape should she discover the trap in which she had fallen. In a moment she passed the *Maratanza*, which greatly resembled a blockade runner, and anchored within a few yards of the *Malvern*.

As the chain was running through her hawse-hole, the *Maratanza* hailed her in the usual nautical style and was answered "Confederate steamer *Stag* from Bermuda." She then hailed our consort and received in reply "United States man-of-war *Maratanza*." It was too late for her to escape, and the flagship sent a boat's crew on board and claimed her as a prize to the navy. Her captain and a few passengers were struck dumb with astonishment. The hatchways and engine room were placed under guard and absolute silence maintained.

The capture had no sooner been accomplished when signal lights were again seen flashing on the bar. After a little delay another steamer came up the harbor in splendid style. In the meantime the *Stag* had commenced blowing off steam, and as it drowned our voices it had the effect of allaying any apprehensions the stranger might have, who took for granted everything was safe when another runner had preceded her. When within a short distance of our vessels she hoisted her lights and commenced blowing her steam whistle, followed by a rousing English hurrah in honor of their success in running the blockade.

Without the slightest suspicion she passed closely by the flagship and anchored astern of the *Stag*. A boat was quickly dispatched to board her, and as the officers and sailors jumped on her deck not a soul could be found to welcome them. Guards were placed over the hatches and our officers descended to the cabin, where they found the captain and a number of jolly English passengers around a long table drinking to each other's health and happiness. All were laughing and talking in a loud manner when the door opened and the naval officers entered. Had a shell exploded in their midst no greater excitement or consternation would have been created. They were informed of the trap into which they had fallen and the surrender of the vessel demanded.

She proved to be the Anglo-rebel steamer *Charlotte*, and in addition to a valuable cargo she had brought over six full-blooded English noblemen who had come to America for a "lark" as they expressed it. At first they were very indignant and said it was a "blarsted shame" to serve such an "outrageous trick on British subjects," but they soon regained their good temper, as they had nothing valuable to lose, and invited our officers to join them in a champagne supper which they were about discussing when they were so unexpectedly interrupted, but their invitation was politely declined. Many of the officers, passengers, and crew passed the balance of the night in wild revelry and dissipation and by daybreak were beastly intoxicated. [Cushing's official report states that it was actually Acting Ensign Thomas B. Huntington of the *Monticello* who had signaled the blockade runners.[2]]

Nearly every bluejacket who was placed on board the prizes I regret to say forgot themselves and their duty. They had not been on board but a short time when they found the liquor casks and began drinking; towards daylight they were very noisy and began fighting among themselves. As quickly as possible other sailors were sent on board to maintain order and fill their places; but they were soon in the same condition. With the exception of a few reliable men and the marines, the whole drunken gang were then brought off with much trouble and the most noisy and turbulent ones were put in double irons.

The *Stag* and *Charlotte* were both side wheel steamers of about seven-hundred tons burden each, beautifully and gracefully modeled and reported to be very fast. Their cargoes consisted principally of wines, liquors, provisions, preserved meats and vegetables and fancy goods which, with the vessels, cost about half a million dollars in gold.

At ten o'clock on the morning after the capture the *Malvern* with the prize steamers got underway and proceeded up the river to where our vessels had advanced and anchored off Battery Lamb, another abandoned earthwork.

Lieutenant S. W. Terry took a boat's crew and went on board the *Charlotte*, and as a few of the men were yet under the influence of liquor they were ordered to remain in the boat. While Mr. Terry was engaged in the cabin of the prize one of the men came on board for the purpose of getting more liquor. He was ordered into his boat; but would not obey, and became quite insolent; as

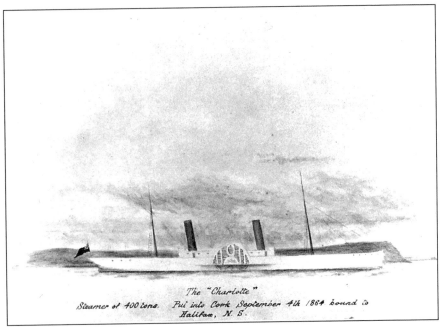

The "Charlotte"

Steamer of 400 tons. Put into Cork September 4th 1864 bound to Halifax, N. S.

Blockade runner *Charlotte* (St. George's Historical Society, St. George's, Bermuda)

several others showed signs of mutiny, to make an example Mr. Terry struck the stubborn rascal over the head with his sword, cutting a deep gash. When the boat returned to the flagship the half drunken sailor showed his wound to his messmates, the majority of whom were intoxicated, having smuggled some of the liquor on board, and tried to raise a mutiny. Soon after fighting was heard among the sailors, and as we were aware we had a few very hard characters on board, the officers armed themselves with cutlasses and revolvers and rushed among them on the berth deck, and many were knocked down and the most disorderly secured. Some of the best sailors we had were the worse for liquor; but in a few hours they came to their senses and a finer ship's crew could not be found in the service.

One morning a few days after the capture of the *Stag* and *Charlotte* the fleet were astonished to see a strange craft quietly at anchor in the harbor near the Mound. She proved to be the Anglo-rebel blockade runner *Blenheim* from Bermuda with supplies for the rebel army. A prize crew was placed on board and she was sent north with the two other prizes to be condemned and sold for the benefit of the government of their captors.[3]

With the fall of Fort Fisher the enemy evacuated all their defenses at the two entrances of Cape Fear River, and our victory was much greater than we at first anticipated.

27

Operations in the Cape Fear River ✦ Fort Anderson and
the obstructions ✦ Generals Grant and Schofield arrive ✦
General Terry promoted for gallantry and bravery ✦ Arrival of
the light draught monitor *Montauk* ✦ The vessels in the river ✦
Cushing makes a reconnaissance ✦ An attempt to repeat it and
the consequences ✦ Discovered by the enemy ✦ The long roll ✦
Under fire and escape ✦ Movements of the troops ✦ Engagement
of the gunboats with Fort Anderson ✦ Loss of life ✦ A "dummy"
monitor set afloat ✦ The troops advance and find the fort
evacuated ✦ Dragging for torpedoes and advance of the fleet ✦
Passing the obstructions ✦ Within five miles of Wilmington ✦
Checked by the enemy at Fort St. Phillip ✦ The fleet at anchor ✦
[26 January–19 February 1865]

B EFORE A FURTHER ADVANCE could be made on Wilmington, it became necessary to capture Fort Anderson. [Fort Anderson lay 15 miles by road below
Wilmington on the west bank of the Cape Fear.] It was a very strong earth work
and mounted a number of heavy guns. Directly in front of this formidable
obstacle was a row of obstructions extending across the river with a narrow passage way in the channel near the fort. In this channel a number of large torpedoes with their wires leading inside the fort had been placed, and it would have
been madness to have tried to run the gauntlet. The troops under the command
of General Terry were able to hold their lines and Fort Fisher, but were not
strong enough to advance or assist in the attack on Fort Anderson.

General Grant shortly arrived with General Schofield and his entire corps
and in company with General Terry called upon the admiral. After a council
of war [on 28 January 1865], immediate preparations were made to continue
the hostilities. General Schofield being senior in rank was placed in full command of the military forces; but General Terry was ordered to retain his original command, and at the same time received his promotion to the grade of
Major General.

While the vessels were preparing for the unknown dangers before them,
we were pleased to see the light draught monitor *Montauk*—the only iron clad
we had that could cross the bar—coming in the harbor. In a few hours, she was
followed by the new gunboat *Shawmut* from the north. The *Montauk* was under
the command of Lieutenant Commander Edward E. Stone, formerly of the *Iron*

Age. He had just come from Charleston where his vessel had a very rough experience. She had been struck repeatedly by enemy gunfire, and on one occasion was nearly destroyed by a torpedo; but was still able to fight.

The fleet operating in Cape Fear River at this time was composed of twenty light draught but heavily armed vessels and was stationed in line just below Fort Anderson. Every night a strong picket force was sent ahead of the fleet and every precaution taken to guard against torpedo boats, fire rafts or any other possible danger.

General Schofield soon after his arrival commenced landing a portion of his troops at Smithville for the purpose of marching on Fort Anderson and it was decided he and General Terry would advance simultaneously on the morning of the ninth of February; but owing to the obstacles the soldiers encountered the fort was not reached in time to make an attack. In the meantime however, General Terry had advanced and had an engagement with a division of the enemy under the command of General Hoke and captured a number of prisoners.

Cushing having been relieved of his duties as military governor of Smithville his bluejackets returned to their ship, and their gallant commander made the flagship his temporary home. But Cushing could not remain long unemployed and two days after he came on board, he obtained the admiral's consent to organize a reconnoitering expedition. Three boats were manned by officers and men from the *Malvern* and about ten o'clock at night on the tenth of February started up the river. Without being observed the forts and obstructions were quietly passed and the adventurers arrived within three miles of Wilmington; the lights of the city being plainly seen. After examining the upper row of obstructions and the several batteries which they had passed the boats returned to the flagship without being discovered.

On the following night another attempt was made for the purpose of gaining further information. Shortly after dark the boats were manned; but unfortunately the moon was shining with great brilliancy. Cushing however determined to risk it, and at 8:00 P.M. the boats started up the river again. It was then flood tide and as the boats neared Fort Anderson the men ceased rowing, and they floated with the current. Music from a brass band was heard inside the fort. The night was very calm and the slightest noise afloat or ashore could be distinctly heard. The music soon ceased and the voice of a man could be heard engaged in a grand oratorical effort to the rebel garrison who frequently interrupted the speech with loud cheering. When the boats were nearly abreast of the fort, a relief guard was discovered making their rounds. The music again was heard amid great applause when suddenly a sentry near the wharf sang out, "Corporal of the guard number six!" Cushing knew he was seen; but coolly awaited the result. Being too much engaged the guard or garrison did not hear or notice the sentry, and the call was repeated in much louder tones. The long roll was quickly sounded, the music ceased and in a few seconds the ramparts were covered with rebel soldiers with their rifles glistening in the moonlight.

Finding it impossible to pass the fort in safety the boats were turned around and the men pulled for the fleet; but before they succeeded in getting out of range several volleys of musketry were fired into them, which were followed by canister and grape; but as usual Cushing escaped and was soon on board the *Malvern* without the loss of a man.

Preparations for renewing the conflict were going rapidly forward, and at daylight on the sixteenth of February a division of troops under the command of Major General Jacob D. Cox left Smithville with orders to attack Fort Anderson, and on the afternoon of the same day arrived within a mile of the earthwork, with his pickets on the river bank abreast of the flagship. General Schofield was with his soldiers, and during the night signal communications were going in between him and General Terry on the other side of the river.

While the army was advancing the fleet went into action, and was engaged all day with the fort. With the exception of two men killed and a few wounded on board the *Pequot*, the enemy's fire did not cause much damage.

It was expected an assault would be made on the eighteenth of February, but owing to the difficulties the troops encountered in the way of dense woods, cane brakes, briars, and almost impassable swamps, they could not get in position before darkness set in.

In the meanwhile the fleet were ordered to move up closer to the fort and open fire. The monitor took the lead and dropped anchor near the obstructions. The *Maratanza* soon followed and was joined by the *Pequot, Lenapee, Sassacus, Pontoosuc, Huron,* and *Chippewa.* A rapid fire was then commenced, and the enemy replied with great vigor; but when the vessels had obtained the exact range, they were compelled to retire to the bomb proofs where they were imprisoned the greater part of the day. Several guns had been dismounted in the fort and the fleet were having everything their own way when a rebel battery situated on a hill in front of General Terry's entrenchments opened fire; but was soon silenced by our heavier guns. As the assault could not take place that day, the vessels dropped down the river as darkness set in.

During the night [of February 18] Cushing set adrift on the flood tide a dummy monitor which he had constructed during the day out of an old flat boat, several barrels, and canvas which had been painted black. The *Mahopac* was faithfully reproduced—smoke stack and turret perfect imitations of the original. The moon was shining brightly as the dummy slowly drifted within range of the fort. Everybody was watching the effect which was expected to be produced by the enemy exploding their torpedoes; but nothing interrupted the silent course of the floating fraud. It passed the fort and continued up the river until it was out of sight. We could not understand or account for the silence of the enemy but at daylight the cause was explained.

At an early hour a reconnaissance was made by the army; but nothing could be seen of the enemy, and in a few moments the troops entered an abandoned fort. The enemy had hastily evacuated both Fort Anderson and their position

Torpedo-clearing operations in the Cape Fear, February 1865 (Naval Historical Center NH 59172)

before General Terry during the night. Having hoisted our flag over the fort and leaving a small garrison inside General Cox started in pursuit of the retreating and demoralized rebels.

The admiral went on shore and inspected the earthwork, but soon after returned, and gave orders to advance up the river. About fifty boats were manned and equipped with grappling irons and forming in line across the channel above the gunboats, started ahead dragging for torpedoes. Before reaching the obstructions several boats dropped out of line, each having secured a torpedo, which they buoyed and started ahead again.

When the boats had passed the obstructions the *Malvern* led the fleet under the directions of a rebel pilot who had deserted the enemy. He informed the admiral of the location of many of the torpedoes; and said directly in front of the fort there were a great number which floated only a few feet under the water and were intended to explode by a vessel's striking against them. He appeared to be quite nervous as we approached the dangerous locality; but upon being assured by the admiral that if we were blown up we would all go together, he said nothing but gave the admiral a peculiar look as much as if he had asked whether he was a man or a devil. Without accident we passed the fort; which upon closer examination proved to be much more formidable than we were led to expect. It had mounted twelve heavy guns and a number of Whitworth rifles and light artillery, but the latter had been withdrawn during the evacuation. General Terry's troops were nearly abreast of the flagship and marching rapidly up the peninsula.

Without meeting any accident the small boats continued ahead dragging for torpedoes, and were closely followed by the fleet with the exception of the monitor; but when we had approached to within five miles of Wilmington a rebel battery, subsequently known as Fort Strong, opened fire. As this obstacle was on General Terry's line of march, the vessels dropped anchor out of range, waiting for him to appear. [Many of the details Grattan included in this chapter do not appear in the published official records.[1]]

28

Preparing for action • The obstructions • Engaging the enemy •
A heavy bombardment • The *Sassacus* struck below the water
line • Dispatches received by special steamer from Admiral
Dahlgren • The fall of Charleston • The effects of the news on
the fleet • General Terry advancing up the peninsula • A terrible
night • An attempt to destroy the fleet by floating torpedoes •
The *Osceola* struck and damaged • A boat destroyed and loss
of life • Renewing the attack on Fort St. Phillip • A tremendous
bombardment and the enemy driven from their guns •
General Terry at work • Washington's birthday celebration •
Passing the abandoned fort and the obstructions • Wilmington
in sight • Army signals • General Terry entering the city •
The flagship arrives at the wharves and fires a salute of
thirty-five guns • The loss to the enemy by the capture •
The *Malvern* underway for Beaufort and Hampton Roads •
[20 February–5 March 1865]

AT THE FIRST DAWN OF DAY on the twentieth of February the fleet began to move in position to engage the enemy. In front of the battery and extending across the river was a row of obstructions consisting of heavy steel-pointed logs or sawyers chained together and in the channel several steamers had been scuttled only a few hours before our arrival.

When our vessels opened fire on Fort Strong no signs of the enemy could be seen, and we were congratulating ourselves that it was also evacuated; the fleet advanced quite near the line of obstructions, when suddenly the fort opened fire with ten-inch guns, and the *Sassacus* was struck three times below the water line. The vessels at once replied and a very heavy bombardment was kept up until after sunset.

During the engagement a vessel arrived up the river from Charleston with a dispatch to the admiral from Admiral Dahlgren announcing the capture of that important city. The information was at once signaled to the fleet, and amid the roar of their guns every vessel sent forth loud and prolonged cheers for the glorious victory. The news appeared to act like wine upon the officers and men, and their exertions at the guns were redoubled.

After dark the vessels dropped down the river a short distance and anchored for the night. General Terry was rapidly marching up the peninsula, and his advance skirmishers were abreast of the fleet. During the night he was reinforced by a large detachment from General Cox's division, who crossed the river in flat boats.

The camp fires of our troops could be seen on both sides of the river and the fleet had the picket boats out to warn them of any danger. There was nothing to disturb the deep silence until near midnight, when a loud explosion was heard among the vessels. Everyone rushed on deck to inquire the cause when it soon became known that a torpedo had exploded in one of the *Osceola*'s wheel houses, shattering it and blowing the wheel to splinters.

Dark objects were then discovered floating on the water, and a number of boats were manned to pick them up. As we expected, they proved to be torpedoes. The boats were ordered to seize them carefully and drag them ashore, and while so engaged another explosion was heard. The greatest excitement prevailed and every available boat was sent in search of these infernal machines. It was soon reported to the admiral that the *Shawmut*'s cutter was blown to atoms, two men being instantly killed and several others severely wounded. By daybreak the boats had towed about fifty torpedoes ashore and rendered them harmless. It was a most desperate attempt to destroy the fleet; but fortunately discovered before much damage was accomplished.[1]

At daylight the vessels again moved in position before the fort and opened a deliberate fire, every shell taking effect; but receiving no response, a boat was sent ahead near the obstructions to sound the channel. This movement brought the rebels to their guns and a rapid fire was the result. Every vessel was then directed to do its best, and an incessant shower of shot and shell fell and bursted inside the earthwork. The enemy tried to reply but were soon driven in confusion from their guns. The fleet were nearly out of ammunition and many of the vessels were firing their last rounds when the fort was silenced. The monitor had managed to pass the obstructions at Fort Anderson and arrived among the fleet off Fort Strong but there was no further use for her.

During the afternoon the army under General Terry was engaged with the enemy and heavy volleys of musketry would be heard in the rear of the fort. And in the direction of the city of Wilmington immense clouds of smoke could be seen rising. The rebels were destroying a large quantity of cotton on the wharves, and a number of steamers in the river, as we subsequently learned.

The following day was the anniversary of the birth day of Washington. General Terry advanced early in the morning; but could find no signs of the enemy. The fact was signalled to the admiral and the vessels got underway. During the night the rebels evacuated Fort Strong and were in full retreat. Captain Breese took a small boat to examine the obstructions and reported to the admiral that a shot had broken the connecting chain, leaving room enough for our vessels to pass. The flagship at once started ahead and successfully passed through wrecks and steel-pointed logs with the fleet in our wake, and upon rounding a bend in the river caught a glimpse of Wilmington. Another row of so called obstructions but slightly checked our progress. At this time it was twelve o'clock and in honor of the day a salute of thirty-five guns were fired by each vessel. When the smoke had cleared away an army signal flag was seen waving on shore, and the admiral was informed that the enemy were in full retreat and General Terry was entering the city.

In order to avoid running on wrecks, torpedoes, and obstructions of which the river was full, it was three o'clock before the *Malvern* arrived at Wilmington. We anchored off the wharf where the burning cotton was still smoking and a salute of thirty-one guns was fired in honor of the victory.

With the fall of Wilmington the last hope of the enemy to obtain foreign aid and supplies for their armies was gone, and with Sherman's army on its way to join Grant at Appomattox, the downfall of the Confederacy was assured.

Before the capture of Fort Fisher, Wilmington was considered to be the most wealthy and prosperous city within the rebel lines. Immense quantities of cotton were shipped on blockade runners and nearly all the supplies for the armies and luxuries for the people who could afford to pay for them were landed on the wharves of this city.

When the enemy were forced to evacuate they destroyed all of the government property, railroad depots, rolling stock, bridges, foundries, machine shops, cotton, rosin and turpentine, warehouses, and a number of fine steamers lying at the wharves. The loss was almost incalculable; but fell only upon the enemy and their sympathizers.

The work of the North Atlantic Blockading Squadron was finished and with the exception of keeping up a strong guard on the James River nothing further in the way of fighting remained.

Leaving a few vessels to hold the city while General Terry pushed on after the flying rebels, the flagship with the surplus gunboats and monitor weighed anchor and proceeded to New Inlet, where the vessels no longer required received their orders for Hampton Roads.

Bidding adieu to the scenes of his triumphs the gallant admiral directed the flagship to proceed to Beaufort, where we arrived with our boilers leaking badly and the engines showing indications of breaking down. A few temporary repairs were made and we managed to reach Hampton Roads on March 5.

29

Undergoing repairs at Norfolk • The flagship on fire •
Saved from destruction • Movements of the admiral and
General Grant • The *Malvern* and monitors at Dutch Gap •
A visit from Major General Meade and ladies • Baltimore belles •
The admiral in an ambulance • A brilliant cavalcade • A visit to
the fortifications, and view of the rebel entrenchments •
Ridiculous appearance of some of the naval officers on their
horses • The return to the river • Arrival of President Lincoln
and family on the flagship • General Sheridan and his cavalry at
Deep Bottom • Arrival of General Sherman and a council of
war held at City Point • General Grant in the saddle • April 1st
1865 • The monitors in Trent's Reach celebrate the day •
An awful hoax on the enemy • Movements of the army • A visit
to the battlefield • Scenes in the field hospitals • General Grant
having hot work • Rebel prisoners guarded by bluejackets •
The president and admiral at City Point • Waiting for the result •
Heavy explosions heard in vicinity of Richmond •
[5 March–2 April 1865]

T HE *MALVERN* HAD PASSED through innumerable dangers and always escaped uninjured. She had weathered some of the heaviest gales and dashed through and over dangerous shoals and breakers; she had safely passed under the fire of hundreds of guns and over numerous torpedoes and through dangerous obstructions; but there was one more ordeal to encounter before her list of hair-breadth escapes could be said to be complete. While undergoing extensive repairs at Norfolk Navy Yard she was discovered to be on fire. The bell was quickly rung and the crew called to fire quarters. Great masses of smoke began rolling up from her fore hold near the forward magazine. A few sailors who were below at the time were with difficulty rescued from suffocation, but the crew were in a good state of discipline and after considerable exertion the fire was extinguished. Upon investigation it was found to have originated in a store room adjoining the magazine, the bulk head of which was nearly burned through. It was a very narrow escape from instant destruction, but as before observed the flagship was noted for such narrow escapes, and in a few hours the circumstance was forgotten.

Previous to our arrival at Hampton Roads the admiral had gone to Washington and when the repairs on his flagship were completed he was notified, and the *Malvern* was anchored in Hampton Roads awaiting his arrival.

General Grant at this time was busily engaged in perfecting his plans for a grand movement against General Robert E. Lee, who was in command of the flower of the Confederate army. [Grant recalled: "I contemplated just what took place; that is to say, capturing Five Forks, driving the enemy from Petersburg and Richmond and terminating the contest before separating from the enemy."[1]]

The admiral after a few days rest in which he stood in so much need returned from Washington and on the nineteenth of March directed the *Malvern* to proceed to City Point, and after an interview with General Grant we continued on up the river and anchored near Dutch Gap.

A few days after our arrival we were honored with a visit from the gallant commander of the Army of the Potomac, Major General George G. Meade, who was accompanied by his staff and a number of beautiful ladies. The admiral and staff received the party in the luxurious cabin, and after a while spent in conversation and refreshments, the officers and ladies were escorted through the ship. After expressing their admiration of the polished guns, clean white decks, and comfortable quarters of the crew, several boats were manned and a visit made to the iron clads. Their immense guns and ammunition created great astonishment to those who saw them for the first time, but when they were shown into the cabin and wardroom and informed they were several feet under the level of the river, the ladies scampered on deck like so many scared deer, which of course they were with a slight exception.

The entire party then went ashore, and those who could ride were provided with horses; but as naval officers are not generally provided with straps to their pantaloons, and for want of sufficient practice, many of us made a ridiculous appearance. All were in full uniform and glittering with gold lace, but when we had proceeded a short distance the motion of the animal would cause our nether garments to work up towards and over the knee. It would not have been so annoying if we were not alongside the ladies, but to see a lot of bare legged officers trying to converse with their fair charges and steer their d——darling chargers and control their constantly rising wrath and pantaloons all at the same time is an experience we none of us wish to suffer again. The admiral was sensible enough to ride in an ambulance in which he was stowed like a herring in a box surrounded with a number of beautiful laughing damsels. It seemed to us the laughter appeared to be more hearty and louder whenever they happened to glance at the admiral's most unfortunate staff. However the cavalcade, after a lively gallop over the hills, corduroy roads and along the lines of the Army of the James, arrived at Fort Harrison from which could be plainly seen the enemy's line of intrenchments. [Fort Harrison stood on the east bank of the James at Chapin's Bluff. Looking to the north from the fort, Grattan could see the Confederate lines stretching north toward Richmond.] About sunset we were unintentionally favored with some excellent music from a rebel brass band, after which the party returned to the river much pleased with their visit afloat and ashore.

In a few days after this pleasant affair, on the twenty-sixth of March, the admiral was notified that President Lincoln was coming up the river.[2] Immediate preparations were made to receive him, and the flagship was decorated with flags. As Major General Philip Henry Sheridan's corps of cavalry were then crossing the river in pontoons at Deep Bottom a slight delay was occasioned before the steamer *River Queen* could pass.

The President and wife with little Tad were brought on board the *Malvern* and received by the admiral and staff with all the honors and respect due to his high office. General Sheridan was discovered on board the *River Queen*, having accompanied the President from the pontoons, but declined the admiral's earnest invitation to join the presidential party for the reason that he must at once return to his men who were then engaged in a very important movement. The President had a very care-worn and fatigued appearance and it was at the earnest solicitation of his friends that caused him for a short time to take a little relaxation, and away from the capital find some rest for his almost broken down constitution. After a very pleasant reception the party visited the iron clads and then went ashore to inspect the fortifications and the enemy's lines.

On the twenty-eighth of March, General Sherman arrived at City Point and the admiral was notified to appear at a council of war. The President was present and when the appointed time arrived Generals Sherman, Sheridan, Meade, Edward Otho Cresap Ord, George Armstrong Custer, and the admiral assembled at General Grant's headquarters. After the consultation General Sherman returned immediately to his army in North Carolina and the other officers at once began preparations for a vigorous prosecution of the war. [The meeting took place on board the steamer *River Queen* in the James River by Grant's headquarters at City Point. Major General Ord had replaced Butler as commander of the Department of Virginia and Army of the James.]

Large bodies of troops were soon moving towards the city of Petersburg and the entrenchments were heavily reinforced. The strong force which had occupied the lines on the left bank of the James was withdrawn, with the exception of one corps under the command of General Weitzel.

When the military preparations were completed General Grant left his headquarters at City Point, and on the twenty-ninth of March 1865 was in the saddle personally directing the movements of his magnificent army. The hostilities commenced with artillery, which continued throughout the day. General Sheridan in the meantime was moving his cavalry and a large infantry and artillery force to the south of Petersburg for the purpose of flanking the enemy. Thus far everything was working satisfactorily, but unfortunately about midnight a heavy rain storm set in and continued for two days. Owing to the mud

Meeting of Sherman, Grant, Lincoln, and Porter on board the *River Queen* at City Point (Library of Congress LC-USZ62-67405)

and impassable condition of the roads all further operations were discontinued until the 1st day of April when the conflict was immediately resumed.

The *Malvern* was stationed off City Point after the departure of General Grant and the roar of artillery of both armies could be plainly heard. It was aggravating for the admiral to listen to the music of the guns and unable to participate in the engagement; but in honor of the day he determined to play an April fool joke upon the enemy who had just about as much as they could attend to in checking the advance of General Grant's legions.

The monitors and all the other vessels stationed at or near Trent's Reach were directed to open fire at midnight and shell the enemy's lines and Howlett's Battery, and to make as much noise as possible. The bombardment was intended as a feint, to divert the attention of the rebels from the movements of General Sheridan who was then on the march for the rear of Petersburg.[3]

At the hour appointed the vessels opened a furious fire, and for an hour the report of the heavy guns could be heard all along the lines. It was afterwards learned the admiral's novel idea had the desired effect, as the enemy were greatly puzzled and bewildered to hear such a terrific noise in such an unexpected locality, and a large force was rapidly marched to reinforce their entrenchments near Howlett's.

At day light on the following morning, the second of April, General Ord made a grand assault and succeeded in capturing seven rebel redoubts and two-thousand prisoners. This was the first charge of any importance and the engagement became general along the lines.

As everything was quiet in the river several of our officers went ashore and taking passage on board of the military railroad train, arrived at Meade's Station and near the front about noon. From Fort Stedman we had a very elevated view of our army lines and the rebel intrenchments. [Fort Stedman stood 150 yards from the Confederate trenches near the right of the Union line outside Petersburg, about three quarters of a mile southeast of the Appomattox River.]

The troops were then engaged and amid the smoke and dust the long lines of infantry were firing with great rapidity, and the rattle and sharp volleys of musketry could be plainly heard. Batteries of light artillery were moving in every direction with their horses on a gallop. Long lines of ambulances filled with wounded were hastening to the field hospitals in the rear, and the greatest excitement everywhere prevailed. While viewing the exciting scene, a loud yell was heard and in a moment the enemy could be seen charging in great numbers on our lines; but after a desperate struggle they were driven back in great disorder.

At 2:00 P.M. information was received from General Sheridan to the effect that he had cut the Southside Railroad, thus depriving the rebel army of their means of communication with and stopping all further supplies. [The Southside Railroad ran west from Petersburg. Shortly after 3:00 P.M. on 2 April 1865, Robert E. Lee instructed the remnants of the Army of Northern Virginia to withdraw from Petersburg and Richmond and reassemble at Amelia Courthouse, almost halfway to Appomattox Court House. The Rebels withdrew from Petersburg that night.]

While the hostilities were progressing we paid a visit to the field hospital of the Ninth Corps. The wounded soldiers as they arrived were carefully laid on the grass in the shade of the trees and tents, and a large number of surgeons in their shirt sleeves were busily occupied at their vocation. Blood was everywhere, the surgeons and their assistants were covered with it, the grass was stained with it and the tents, stretchers, and camp stools were smeared with it. Alongside the operating tents were large mounds of quivering flesh, composed of amputated arms, hands, feet, legs, and indistinguishable fragments blackened with powder. After the poor fellows had been attended to and survived the surgeon's saw and knife they were placed on cots inside the tents and watched by careful nurses. A large number whose groans could be heard far and wide were lying there in great agony; but nothing could be done to relieve them. The quick experienced eye of the surgeon would express no hope and there they lay waiting for death. It was a horrible sight but a necessary consequence of a bloody war.

Hearing that a mysterious movement was then preparing, we returned to Fort Stedman, and from its ramparts cavalry, artillery and infantry could be seen

rapidly hurrying towards the left, and it soon became known they were reinforcements for our troops who were fighting desperately at Hatcher's Run.
[Hatcher's Run was a creek located near the extreme Union left.]

Late in the afternoon General Grant requested the admiral to send him all
the sailors and marines he could spare to take charge of about nine thousand
prisoners he had. He also requested the admiral to take control and garrison
City Point as every soldier there was ordered to proceed immediately to the
front. Shortly before dark a train of cars filled with sailors and marines left City
Point and arrived at Humphrey's Station where they took charge of the prisoners, and marched them to the transports which were waiting for them at City
Point.

The President was on board the *River Queen* receiving telegraph dispatches
from the front and waiting with anxiety the result of General Grant's last formidable movement.

In addition to the large number of transports for conveying the prisoners,
hospital boats were arriving and departing every hour with thousands of
wounded soldiers, whose terrible groans would occasionally disturb the death
like silence of City Point.

The engagement of the armies of General Grant and General Lee continued long after dark, and bright incessant flashes of the bursting shell and roar
of the artillery could be plainly seen and heard from the flagship; but about
midnight heavy explosions were heard and the glare of a large conflagration
could be seen in the direction of Richmond, where all was still throughout the
balance of the night.

30

Fall of Petersburg and evacuation of Richmond ✦ The enemy in
full retreat ✦ A visit to Petersburg by the President and admiral ✦
The flagship and gunboats ordered to Richmond ✦ Passing the
obstructions in Trent's Reach ✦ Drewry's Bluff and the obstacles
in the river ✦ The President, admiral, and staff proceed in small
boats ✦ Arrival at the city ✦ The flagship follows and fires
a national salute ✦ Arrival at the executive mansion of
Jefferson Davis ✦ The officers of the army and navy drink to
each others' health in some of the ex-president's applejack ✦
Admiral Farragut arrives and congratulates the President ✦
Richmond inspected ✦ A visit to Libby Prison and Castle
Thunder by candlelight ✦ The horrors of the places ✦
President Lincoln sleeps on the flagship ✦ A hearty breakfast
and kind farewell to the admiral and staff ✦ The vessels of the
rebel navy in the James River and their destruction and capture ✦
Excitement on shore ✦ News of the surrender of General Lee ✦
National salute fired by the flagship and gunboats at Richmond ✦
City Point and the formal celebration of victory ✦
[3–10 April 1865]

Oₙ THE EVENING OF THE THIRD OF APRIL 1865 the President and admiral
received telegraphic dispatches from General Grant informing them of the fall
of Richmond and Petersburg and that the enemy was in full retreat towards
Danville closely followed by our victorious troops. General Weitzel's corps
[XXV Corps] being nearest to Richmond was directed to occupy it, and in a few
hours the stars and stripes floated over the monument of a million lives.

Immediately after the reception of the intelligence, the President and
admiral went ashore and took the first military train for Petersburg and upon
their arrival the tremendous fortifications were examined and a short visit paid
to the several objects of interest in the city. Upon his return the admiral ordered
the flagship to proceed to Richmond in company with the *River Queen*.

Arriving at Trent's Reach a passage was cleared through the obstructions
and several gunboats were directed to follow. Passing by Howlett's silent battery we continued on until we arrived at Drewry's Bluff, where we were compelled to wait until a passage had been cleared through the strong row of
obstructions, consisting of sunken steamers, canal boats, and crates filled with
stone and a number of very large torpedoes. A large water gate which had been

constructed for the use of the rebel rams to allow them to pass up and down the river was closed and in some unknown manner securely fastened. As it would require some time to open it, the admiral determined to go to Richmond in his barge and invited the President to accompany him, having orders for the vessels to follow as soon as they could pass the obstructions. The marine guard of the flagship was directed to follow the admiral's barge, and the staff and several officers of the gunboats started after them in the cutters. [A "barge" was a spacious, elegantly furnished, smartly kept and handled, double-banked boat of state reserved for the admiral.]

It was about seven miles by water to the city and a long pull for the bluejackets; but they never murmured and in a short time we approached within sight of the famous capital of the southern Confederacy. A number of wrecks were passed on our way among which were the rebel rams. [Between 1:00 and 2:00 A.M. on 3 April, the Confederates torched the *Virginia II*, *Richmond*, and *Fredericksburg*. Her shell rooms full of loaded shells, the *Virginia II* soon exploded. "The spectacle was grand beyond description," recalled Raphael Semmes, former skipper of the famous commerce raider CSS *Alabama*, who was then in command of the James River Squadron. "The explosion of the magazine threw all these shells, with their fuses lighted into the air . . . the shells exploded by twos and threes, and by the dozens, the pyrotechnic effect was very fine."[1]]

As we arrived near Belle's Isle the *Malvern* was discovered rapidly coming up. A landing place near Libby Prison being found the President and admiral and staff stepped on shore just as the flagship commenced firing a national salute of thirty-five guns.

Under the protection of the guard of marines the party walked through the streets closely followed and surrounded with thousands of blacks and whites, who made the air ring with their cheers; we entered the headquarters of General Weitzel, which were located in the mansion just vacated by Mr. Jefferson Davis.

We soon made ourselves quite comfortable in the executive mansion of the Confederacy, and commenced examining the apartments. The furniture and all the fixtures were very elegant and luxurious, and indicated the residence of a refined gentleman. The walls of the parlors were adorned with a number of very fine paintings, and one in particular attracted great attention; being a representation of the pirate *Florida* under full sail with the rebel ensign very conspicuous; but as the original, having been captured by the *Wachusett* and accidentally sunk in the James River, was of more importance to the government than a "painted ship upon a painted sea," no objection was made for all that was left of her in remembrance should be treasured by the enemy.

But there was one thing that pleased us better than anything else in the fine old mansion, and that was some of the Confederate ex-president's prime old rye and applejack, of which his former servants politely helped us. Toasts

Lincoln visiting Richmond (Library of Congress LC-USZ62-25045)

were drunk to the health of the absent owner and everyone regretted he was not present to join in the impromptu festivities.

The applejack was very strong, and we had sense enough not to pull at it too long, but one of the army officers who did seem to love it said that no wonder the rebels fought so well when they could get such stuff to drink, and he maintained that if a man should take about a pint of it before each meal he would eat like a horse and would be courageous enough to kill his own grandmother, and we believed him.

While President Lincoln was resting himself in President Davis' easy chair we were surprised and pleased to see Admiral Farragut enter the room. He had just arrived and once more the President was heartily congratulated by the gallant bluejacket.

The presidential party then went out on the balcony and were enthusiastically greeted and cheered by an immense throng of civilians but owing to great weakness and exhaustion caused by the exciting events of the past five days, Mr. Lincoln was unable to give utterance to his feelings and simply bowed his acknowledgment for their kindness.

Lincoln visiting the Confederate executive mansion (Library of Congress LC-USZ62-6932)

Mr. Davis' family carriage having been brought to the door the President and Admiral Porter entered it and were rapidly whirled away by four handsome horses. Nearly a hundred army and navy officers followed on horseback and the city was visited in every quarter.

We entered the capitol and strolled through the deserted halls lately occupied by the rebel congress. Confusion and disorder reigned everywhere. In the treasury building Confederate bonds, coupons, and currency were scattered in all directions over the floor, and everything bore evidence of the hasty and unexpected evacuation.

The lower part of the city near the river was an immense area of smoldering and in many places burning ruins. The space covered the larger portion of the ground used for the purpose of business and the buildings were destroyed by the enemy as they were leaving the city during the evacuation.

About 9:00 P.M. while on our way to the wharf near which the flagship was at anchor, we called at Libby Prison and were shown through that horrible den. In one corner on the ground floor there was a large pile of shoes and ragged clothing taken off the bodies of those who had died while in captivity. In another corner were several tiers of common pine coffins of which a number of carpenters were constantly engaged in constructing, the demand for them being as great. A deep excavation was shown us in which it was the intention of the enemy to put a large quantity of gunpowder and blow up the prison when the city was captured; but their neglect to do so was no doubt dictated by the laws of humanity.

Our explorations were conducted by candle light; but sufficient was seen to impress upon us the horrors of the terrible place. The prison was then occupied by about seven hundred demoralized rebels who were captured as our troops entered the city. Many of them were under the influence of apple jack, and a few were worn out soldiers who were unable or unwilling to follow the fortunes of the retreating army. After making a short call at Castle Thunder, another strong and filthy prison situated a short distance from Libby, we returned to the *Malvern* near midnight.

The President and the admiral had returned from their long ride and the former remained on board all night, the *River Queen* with Mrs. Lincoln and son remaining at Drewry's Bluff. Before the President retired he sat up for several hours writing. We were all unremitting in our efforts to make the old gentleman happy and comfortable and after a pleasant breakfast he bade the admiral and his officers a gentle and kind farewell.

While waiting for further information from General Grant, the gunboats were stationed along the river from Richmond to City Point with orders to hold themselves in readiness for any emergency that might arise. In the meantime the obstructions at Drewry's Bluff were being cleared out of the channel in which was found thirty of the largest size torpedoes.

The following vessels belonging to the enemy were destroyed during the evacuation:—viz.

Virginia II	flagship of the fleet— iron clad ram	four guns
Richmond	iron clad ram	four guns
Fredericksburg	iron clad ram	four guns
Nansemond	gunboat	two guns
Hampton	gunboat	two guns
Roanoke	gunboat	one gun
Torpedo and *Shrapnel*	tenders to the flagship	
Patrick Henry	side wheel steamer school ship	

The following vessels were found uninjured and taken by the government:—viz.

Beaufort	gunboat
William Allison	steamer transport
Three tug boats	tenders to the iron clads
Texas	iron clad ram not quite finished

In a few days after our arrival the city began to have a more lively appearance, and the tradesmen being satisfied our soldiers were not thieves and robbers opened their stores and the resumption of business generally commenced. But still there was a settled gloom and anxiety apparent on every face, both the inhabitants and the troops, the former anticipating the downfall of the Confederacy and the latter waiting for the news of General Grant's victory or defeat. The admiral, his officers and men shared in the general anxiety, and we all felt like the gambler waiting for the result of the last throw of the die.

On the evening of the ninth of April the officers of the flagship assembled as usual and in the calm soft air of that beautiful night we brought our chairs on deck and in a general conversation fought our battles over again and many eloquent tributes were paid to our absent mess mates and friends whose lives had been sacrificed in this bloody war. Near midnight we bade each other good night and were about going below when an unusual commotion was discovered on shore. Loud cheering followed by a discharge of artillery was heard and lights could be seen flashing in the direction of the army headquarters.

Not knowing the cause of the excitement the crew of the *Malvern* were called to quarters and an officer sent on shore for an explanation from General Weitzel. He soon returned with the information that General Lee and his entire army had surrendered to General Grant.

There was not much sleep on board the flagship during the balance of the night and at the dawn of day the admiral directed the *Malvern, Sassacus, Maumee*, and *Commodore Perry* which were lying off the city to fire a national salute in honor of the glorious victory.

As it was the last time our guns would be heard on rebel territory the salute was handsomely given, and the roar and concussion brought thousands of the inhabitants of the city to the wharves to witness the beautiful performance of the fleet.

After the salute the flagship started down the river and the vessels as we passed were informed of the victory and directed to give thanks with all the power their guns possessed. Upon arriving at City Point a more formal celebration of the victory was ordered. There being about a dozen gunboats there, every one were dressed in flags and signal pennants and at noon opened their batteries. The large number of merchant vessels and steam transports added to the tremendous noise by ringing bells, blowing steam whistles, and hearty and prolonged cheering by the different crews hailed the dawn of peace.

With the surrender of General Lee the rebellion was virtually at an end. General Sherman shortly after received the capitulation of General Johnston, and the stars and stripes waved over every portion of the conquered Confederate states.

Appendix

Ships Mentioned in *Under the Blue Pennant*

KEY:

a.	armament	l.	length
b.	beam	pdr.	pounder
cl.	class	r.	rifle
cpl.	complement	s.	speed
dp.	displacement	sb.	smoothbore
dr.	draft	t.	tonnage
k.	knots		

NOTE: Not all categories of information are available for every ship. Since ships were often altered once or more during their lifetimes, the statistics given below might not be accurate for a given iteration of a vessel. Lengths and tonnage vary in definition in the primary materials used by the source compilers and should be regarded as indices for the sake of size comparison rather than absolute measurements. Unless otherwise stated, all screw-propelled vessels, monitors, and Confederate ironclads were driven by a single propeller. In the armament category, smoothbore guns designated by bore diameter (e.g. "8-inch") are shell guns. Shell guns designated by roman numerals (e.g. "IX-inch") are Dahlgren guns with the distinctive "soda-water bottle" shape. Rifled cannon and shot-firing smoothbores are designated by projectile weight, except for Confederate made Brooke rifles, which are designated by bore diameter. Ships are listed with their 1864 armament. "Acquired" ships were purchased from private sources for the navy. Those vessels not designated as "acquired" were built as warships in navy yards or under navy contracts.

A.D. Vance, USS	(also called *Ad Vance* or *Advance*) captured sidewheel blockade runner: dp. 1,300; l. 230′; b. 26′; dr. 12′; s. 12 k.; a. 1 20-pdr., 4 24-pdr. sb.
Agawam, USS	sidewheel double-ender: dp. 1,173; l. 205′; b. 35′; dr. 8′8″; s. 8.5 k.; cpl. 145; a. 2 100-pdr. r., 4 IX-inch sb., 2 24-pdr. sb., 1 12-pdr. r., 1 12-pdr. sb.; cl. *Sassacus*
Alabama, USS	acquired screw merchantman: t. 1,261; l. 214′4″; b. 35′2″; dr. 14′6″; s. 13 k.; cpl. 175; a. 8 32-pdr. sb., 1 20-pdr. r.
Albemarle, CSS	ironclad ram: l. 152′; b. 34′; dr. 9′; a. 2 6.4-inch r.

Anemone, USS	acquired screw tug: t. 156; l. 99′; b. 20′5″; dr. 11′; s. 11 k.; cpl. 30; a. 2 24-pdr. sb., 2 12-pdr. sb.
Aries, USS	captured screw blockade runner: t. 820; l. 201′; b.27′10″; dr. 16′; s. 12 k.; cpl. 90; a. 4 8-inch sb., 2 30-pdr. r., 1 12-pdr. r.
Atlanta, USS	captured ironclad ram: t. 1,006; l. 204′; b. 41′; s. 10 k.; cpl. 162; a. 2 150-pdr. r., 2 100-pdr. sb.
Banshee, USS	captured screw blockade runner: t. 533; l. 220′; b. 20′4″; dr. 10′; s. 15 k.; cpl. 89; a. 1 30-pdr. r., 1 12-pdr. sb.
Bat, USS	captured sidewheel blockade runner: t. 750; l. 230′; b. 26′; dp. 8′; s. 16 k.; cpl. 82; a. 1 30-pdr. r., 2 12-pdr. sb.
Beaufort, CSS	tender: t. 85; l. 85′; b. 17′5″; a. 1 32-pdr. r.
Bendigo	sidewheel blockade runner: t. 178; l. 162′; b. 20′; dp. 11′
Bignonia, USS	acquired screw tug: t. 321; l. 131′; b. 22′; dr. 10′8″; s. 10 k.; cpl. 50; a. 1 30-pdr. r., 2 12-pdr. sb.
Blenheim	sidewheel blockade runner: t. 948; l. 210′; b. 31′; dr. 16′
Bombshell, CSS	captured Erie Canal steamer: l. 90′; dr. 3′6″; cpl. 37; a. 4 boat guns
Britannia, USS	captured sidewheel blockade runner: t. 495; l. 189′; b. 26′; s. 12.5 k.; a. 1 30-pdr. r., 2 12-pdr. r., 2 24-pdr. sb.
Brooklyn, USS	screw sloop: dp. 2,532; l. 233′; b. 43′; dr. 16′3″; s. 11.5 k.; cpl. 335; a. 2 100-pdr. r., 2 60-pdr. r., 20 IX-inch sb., 2 12-pdr. sb.; cl. *Brooklyn*
Cambridge, USS	acquired screw merchantman: t. 868; l. 200′; b. 32′; dr. 13′6″; s. 10 k.; cpl. 96; a. 4 8-inch sb., 4 30-pdr. r., 2 24-pdr. sb.
Canonicus, USS	single-turret monitor: t. 1,034; l. 225′; b. 43′8″; dr. 13′6″; s. 7 k.; cpl. 85; a. 2 XV-inch sb.; cl. *Canonicus*
Ceres, USS	acquired sidewheel merchantman: t. 144; l. 108′4″; b. 22′4″; dp. 6′3″; s. 9 k.; cpl. 45; a. 2 30-pdr. r.; 2 24-pdr. sb.
Charlotte	sidewheel blockade runner: dp. 1,165; l. 226′; b. 28′; dr. 13′
Cherokee, USS	captured screw blockade runner: t. 606; l. 194′6″; b. 25′2″; dr. 11′6″; s. 13 k.; cpl. 92; a. 2 20-pdr. r., 4 24-pdr. sb.
Chickamauga, CSS	acquired twin screw blockade runner: t. 585; l. 175′; b. 25′; dr. 15′; cpl. 120; a. 1 84-pdr. r., 2 32-pdr. r., 2 24-pdr. sb.
Chippewa, USS	screw gunboat: dp. 691; l. 158′; b. 28′; dr. 9′6″; s. 10 k.; cpl. 114; a. 1 XI-inch sb., 1 20-pdr. r., 2 24-pdr. sb.; cl. *Unadilla*
Clematis, USS	acquired screw tug: t. 297; l. 127′; b. 22′; dr. 10′; s. 12 k.; cpl. 46; a. 1 30-pdr. r., 2 12-pdr. sb.
Clinton, USS	acquired screw tug: t. 50; l. 58′8″; b. 15′10″; dr. 7′; s. 11 k.; cpl. 16
Cohasset, USS	acquired screw tug: t. 100; l. 82′; b. 18′10″; dr. 9′; s. 8 k.; cpl. 12; a. 1 20-pdr. r., 2 24-pdr. sb.
Colorado, USS	screw frigate: dp. 4,772; l. 268′6″; b. 52′6″; dr. 23′9″; s. 11 k.; cpl. 674; a. 1 150-pdr. r., 1 XI-inch sb., 46 IX-inch sb., 4 12-pdr. sb.; cl. *Merrimack*

Commodore Barney, USS	acquired sidewheel ferryboat: t. 512; l. 143′; b. 33′; dr. 9′; s. 8 k.; cpl. 96; a. 1 100-pdr r., 5 IX-inch sb., 1 12-pdr. sb.
Commodore Jones, USS	acquired sidewheel ferryboat: t. 542; l. 154′; b. 32′6″; dr. 11′8″; s. 12 k.; cpl. 88; a. 1 IX-inch sb., 1 50-pdr. r., 2 30-pdr. r., 4 24-pdr. sb.
Commodore Morris, USS	acquired sidewheel ferryboat: t. 532; l. 154′; b. 32′6″; dr. 8′6″; s. 7 k.; cpl. 106; a. 1 100-pdr. r., 1 IX-inch sb.; 2 30-pdr. r., 2 24-pdr sb.
Congress, USS	sailing frigate: dp. 1,867; l. 179′; b. 47′8″; dr. 22′6″; cpl. 480; a. 10 8-inch sb., 40 32-pdr. sb.
Cotton Plant, CSS	captured screw steamer: t. 85; l. 107′; b. 18′9″; dr. 4′5″
Cumberland, USS	sailing sloop: dp. 1,726; l. 175′; b. 45′; dr. 22′4″; cpl. 400; a. 1 70-pdr. r., 1 10-inch sb., 22 IX-inch sb.
Dare, CSS	information not found
David, CSS	screw torpedo boat: l. 50′; b. 6′; dr. 5′; cpl. 4; a. 1 spar torpedo
Dawn, USS	acquired screw merchantman: t. 339; l. 154′; b. 28′10″; dr. 9′8″; s. 8 k.; cpl. 60; a. 1 100-pdr. r., 2 32-pdr. sb., 1 30-pdr. r., 1 12-pdr.
Daylight, USS	acquired screw merchantman: t. 682; l. 170′; b. 30′6″; dr. 13′; s. 5 k.; cpl. 57; a. 6 32-pdr. sb., 1 30-pdr. r., 1 12-pdr. r.
Dee	blockade runner: t. 215; l. 165′; b. 23′; dr. 13′
Delaware, USS	acquired sidewheel merchantman: t. 357; l. 161′; b. 27′; dr. 6′; s. 13 k.; cpl. 65; a. 1 IX-inch sb., 1 32-pdr sb., 1 12-pdr r.
Dumbarton, USS	captured sidewheel blockade runner: t. 636; l. 204′; b. 29′; dr. 10′; s. 10 k.; a. 2 32-pdr. sb., 2 12-pdr. sb.
Elsie	sidewheel blockade runner: t. 262; l. 201′; b. 20′; dr. 9′5″
Emily	screw blockade runner: t. 355; l. 181′; b. 22′4″; dr. 12′
Emma, USS	captured screw blockade runner: t. 350; l. 156′: b. 21′; dr. 9′4″; s. 12 k.; cpl. 68; a. 6 24-pdr. sb., 2 12-pdr. r.
Eolus, USS	acquired sidewheel merchantman: t. 368; l. 140′; b. 25′; dr. 7′; cpl. 53; a. 1 30-pdr. r., 2 24-pdr. sb.
Eutaw, USS	sidewheel double-ender: dp. 1,173; l. 205′; b. 35′; dr. 9′6″; cpl. 200; a. 4 IX-inch sb., 2 100-pdr. r., 4 IX-inch sb., 2 20-pdr. r., 2 24-pdr. sb.; cl. *Sassacus*
Fahkee, USS	acquired screw merchantman: dp. 660; l. 163′; b. 29′6″; dr. 13′3″; s. 12 k.; cpl. 73; a. 2 24-pdr. sb., 2 24-pdr. sb., 1 10-pdr. r.
Fanny and Jenny	sidewheel blockade runner: t. 479; l. 202′2″; b. 28′4″; dr. 13′7″
Florida, USS	acquired sidewheel merchantman: dp. 1,261; l. 214′4″; b. 35′3″; dr. 14′6″; s. 13 k.; cpl. 180; a. 1 100-pdr. r., 4 IX-inch sb., 1 50-pdr. r., 1 12-pdr. r.
Fort Donelson, USS	captured sidewheel blockade runner: dp. 900; l. 283′; b. 20′; dr. 10′; s. 11 k.; cpl. 137; a. 2 30-pdr. r., 5 12-pdr. r.
Fort Jackson, USS	acquired sidewheel merchantman: dp. 1,850; l. 250′; b. 38′6″; dr. 18′; s. 14 k.; cpl. 194; a. 1 100-pdr. r., 8 IX-inch sb., 2 30-pdr. r.

Fredericksburg, CSS — twin-screw ironclad ram: l. 188'; b. 40'3"; dr. 9'6"; cpl. 150; a. 1 XI-inch sb., 1 8-inch r., 2 6.4-inch r.

General Putnam, USS — (also known as *William G. Putnam*) acquired sidewheel merchantman: t. 149; l. 103'6"; b. 22'; dr. 7'6"; s. 7 k.; cpl. 62; a. 1 30-pdr. r., 6 32-pdr. sb., 2 12-pdr. r.

Gettysburg, USS — captured sidewheel blockade runner: dp. 1,100; l. 211'; b. 26'3"; dp. 10'; s. 15 k.; cpl. 96; a. 1 30-pdr. r., 2 12-pdr. r., 4 24-pdr. sb.

Governor Buckingham, USS — acquired screw merchantman: t. 886; l. 177'6"; b. 32'2"; dp. 13'6"; s. 8 k.; cpl. 112; a. 1 100-pdr. r., 4 30-pdr. r., 1 20-pdr. r.

Greyhound, USS — chartered army sidewheel transport: t. 380

Hampton, CSS — twin-screw "Maury gunboat": t. 166; l. 106'; b. 21'; dr. 5'; a. 1 IX-inch sb., 1 32-pdr.

Heliotrope, USS — acquired sidewheel merchantman: t. 239; l. 134'; b. 24'6"; dr. 5'; s. 6 k.; cpl. 66; a. 1 12-pdr. sb.

Howquah, USS — acquired sidewheel merchantman: t. 397; l. 120'7"; b. 22'10"; dr. 12'; s. 10 k.; cpl. 55; a. 3 30-pdr. r., 1 12-pdr. r., 1 12-pdr. sb.

Hunchback, USS — acquired sidewheel ferryboat: t. 517; l. 179'5"; b. 29'3"; dr. 9'; s. 12 k.; a. 1 200-pdr. r., 4 IX-inch sb.; 1 12-pdr. r., 1 12-pdr. sb.

Huron, USS — screw gunboat: dp. 691; l. 158'4"; b. 28'; dr. 9'6"; s. 10 k.; cpl. 114; a. 1 XI-inch sb., 1 30-pdr. r., 4 24-pdr. sb.; cl. *Unadilla*

Hydrangia, USS — acquired screw tug: t. 215; l. 120'; b. 20'3"; s. 11 k.; cpl. 29; a. 1 20-pdr. r., 1 12-pdr. sb.

Iosco, USS — sidewheel double-ender: dp. 1,173; l. 205'; b. 35'; dr. 9'6"; s. 9 k.; cpl. 200; a. 2 100-pdr. r., 4 IX-inch sb.; 2 24-pdr. r.; 2 12-pdr. sb.; cl. *Sassacus*

Iron Age, USS — acquired screw steamer: t. 424; l. 144'; b. 25'; cpl. 107; a. 3 30-pdr. r., 6 8-inch sb.

Juniata, USS — screw sloop: dp. 1,934; l. 205'; b. 38'; dr. 16'7"; s. 9 k.; cpl. 160; a. 1 100-pdr. r., 6 8-inch sb., 2 30-pdr. r., 1 12-pdr. r.; cl. *Ossipee*

Kansas, USS — sidewheel gunboat: dp. 836; l. 179'6"; b. 29'8"; dr. 12'; s. 12 k.; cpl. 154; a. 1 150-pdr. r., 2 IX-inch sb., 1 30-pdr. r.; 2 20-pdr. r.; cl. *Nipsic*

Keystone State, USS — acquired sidewheel merchantman: t. 1,364; l. 220'; b. 35'6"; dr. 14'6"; s. 9.5 k.; cpl. 163; a. 1 50-pdr. r., 2 8-inch sb., 2 32-pdr. sb., 1 30-pdr. r.

Lenapee, USS — sidewheel double-ender: dp. 1,173; l. 205'; b. 35'; dr. 9'6"; s. 12 k.; cpl. 200; a. 2 100-pdr. r., 4 IX-inch sb., 2 20-pdr. r.; cl. *Sassacus*

Lilian, USS — captured sidewheel blockade runner: t. 630; l. 225'6"; b. 26'5"; dr. 8'2"; s. 14 k.; cpl. 63; a. 1 30-pdr. r., 1 20-pdr. r.

Little Ada, USS — captured screw blockade runner: t. 150; l. 112'; b. 18'6"; dr. 8'; s. 10 k.; cpl. 53; a. 2 20-pdr. r.

Lynx, CSS — sidewheel blockade runner: t. 372; l. 219'; b.21'; dr. 11'5"; s. 12 k.

Mackinaw, USS	sidewheel double-ender: dp. 1,173; l. 205′; b. 35′; dr. 9′6″; s. 13 k.; cpl. 200; a. 2 100-pdr. r., 4 IX-inch sb., 2 24-pdr. sb., 2 20-pdr. r.; cl. *Sassacus*
Mahopac, USS	monitor: dp. 2,100; l. 190′; b. 37′8″; dr. 11′10″; s. 6.3 k.; a. 2 XV-inch sb.; cl. *Canonicus*
Malvern, USS	captured sidewheel blockade runner: dp. 1,477; l. 239′4″; b. 33′; dr. 9′; cpl. 68; a. 4 20-pdr. r., 8 12-pdr. sb.
Maratanza, USS	sidewheel double-ender: t. 786; l. 209′; b. 32′11″; dr. 10′; s. 10 k.; cpl. 111; a. 1 100-pdr. r., 1 XI-inch sb., 2 IX-inch sb., 4 24-pdr. sb.; cl. *Maratanza*
Mattabesett, USS	sidewheel double-ender: dp. 1,173; l. 205′; b. 35′; dr. 9′6″; s. 13 k.; cpl. 200; a. 2 100-pdr. r., 4 IX-inch sb., 2 20-pdr. r.; cl. *Sassacus*
Maumee, USS	screw gunboat: dp. 836; l. 179′6″; b. 29′8″; dr. 12′; s. 11.5 k.; cpl. 154; a. 1 100-pdr. r., 1 30-pdr. r., 4 24-pdr. sb., 1 12-pdr. r.; cl. *Nipsic*
Mayflower, USS	chartered army screw transport: t. 205
Mendota, USS	sidewheel double-ender: dp. 1,173; l. 205′; b. 35′; dr. 9′6″; s. 13 k.; cpl. 200; a. 2 100-pdr. r., 4 IX-inch sb., 1 20-pdr. r., 2 24-pdr. sb.; cl. *Sassacus*
Miami, USS	sidewheel double-ender: t. 730; l. 208′2″; b. 33′2″; dr. 8′6″; s. 8 k.; cpl. 134; a. 1 100-pdr. r., 6 IX-inch sb., 1 24-pdr. sb.; cl. *Miami*
Minnesota, USS	screw frigate: dp. 4,833; l. 264′9″; b. 51′4″; dr. 23′10″; s. 12.5 k.; cpl. 646; a. 1 150-pdr. r., 1 XI-inch sb., 4 100-pdr. r., 38 IX-inch sb., 2 12-pdr. r., 2 12-pdr. sb.; cl. *Merrimack*
Moccasin, USS	acquired screw tug: t. 192; l. 104′5″; b. 22′3″; dr. 9′; s. 10 k.; cpl. 31; a. 3 12-pdr. r.
Mohican, USS	screw sloop: dp. 1,550; l. 198′9″; b. 33′10″; dr. 15′9″; s. 11 k.; cpl. 160; a. 1 100-pdr. r., 4 IX-inch sb., 2 30-pdr. r., 2 32-pdr. sb., 1 12-pdr. sb.; cl. *Mohican*
Monadnock, USS	twin-screw double-turreted monitor: dp. 3,400; l. 258′6″; b. 52′9″; dr. 12′8″; s. 9 k.; cpl. 150; a. 4 XV-inch sb.; cl. *Miantonomoh*
Montauk, USS	monitor: dp. 1,335; l. 200′; b. 46′; dr. 11′6″; s. 7 k.; cpl. 88; a. 1 XV-inch sb., 1 XI-inch sb.; cl. *Passaic*
Montgomery, USS	acquired screw merchantman: t. 787; l. 201′6″; b. 28′7″; dr. 15′6″; s. 11 k.; cpl. 143; a. 1 10-inch sb., 4 8-inch sb., 1 30-pdr. r.
Monticello, USS	acquired screw merchantman: t. 655; l. 180′; b. 29′; dr. 12′10″; s. 11.5 k.; cpl. 137; a. 1 100-pdr. r., 2 IX-inch sb., 3 30-pdr. r.
Mount Vernon, USS	acquired screw merchantman: t. 625; l. 173′6″; b. 28′8″; dr. 12′; s. 11.5 k.; cpl. 50; a. 1 100-pdr. r., 2 IX-inch sb., 2 20-pdr. r.
Mount Washington, USS	acquired sidewheel merchantman: t. 359; l. 200′; b. 24′; dr. 6′6″; cpl. 40; a. 1 32-pdr.
Nansemond, CSS	twin-screw "Maury gunboat": t. 166; l. 106′; b. 21′; dr. 5′; a. 1 IX-inch sb., 1 32-pdr.

Nansemond, USS	acquired sidewheel merchantman: t. 335; l. 146′; b. 26′; dr. 8′3″; s. 15 k.; cpl. 63; a. 1 30-pdr. r., 2 24-pdr. sb.
Nereus, USS	acquired screw merchantman: t. 1,244; l. 203′6″; b. 35′6″; dr. 14′; s. 11 k.; cpl. 164; a. 1 100-pdr. r., 2 30-pdr. r., 6 32-pdr. sb., 2 12-pdr. r.
New Ironsides, USS	screw ironclad: dp. 4,120; l. 232′; b. 57′6″; dr. 15′8″; s. 6 k.; cpl. 460; a. 2 150-pdr. r., 14 XI-inch sb., 1 12-pdr. r., 1 12-pdr. sb.
Nighthawk	sidewheel blockade runner: l. 220′; b. 21′6″; dr. 11′
Niphon, USS	acquired screw gunboat: t. 475; l. 153′2″; b. 25′6″; dr. 10′6″; s. 10 k.; cpl. 100; a. 4 32-pdr. sb., 1 20-pdr. r., 2 12-pdr. r.
North Carolina, CSS	ironclad: l. 150′; b. 34′; dr. 12′; s. 6 k.; cpl. 180; a. 4 guns; cl. *Richmond*
Nutfield	sidewheel blockade runner: t. 531; l. 224′; b. 27′; dr. 13′
Nyack, USS	screw gunboat: dp. 836; l. 179′6″; b. 29′8″; dr. 12′; s. 11 k.; cpl. 154; a. 1 100-pdr. r., 2 IX-inch sb., 1 30-pdr. r., 2 24-pdr. sb., 2 12-pdr. sb.; cl. *Nipsic*
Onondaga, USS	double-turreted monitor: dp. 2,592; l. 226′; b. 49′3″; dr. 12′10″; s. 7 k.; cpl. 167; a. 4 XV-inch sb.; cl. *Onondaga*
Osceola, USS	sidewheel double-ender: dp. 1,173; l. 205′; b. 35′; dr. 9′6″; s. 13 k.; cpl. 200; a. 2 100-pdr. r.; 4 IX-inch sb., 1 24-pdr. sb., 1 12-pdr. r., 1 12-pdr. sb.; cl. *Sassacus*
Patrick Henry, CSS	acquired sidewheel gunboat: t. 1,300; l. 250′; b. 34′; dr. 13′; cpl. 150; a. 1 10-inch sb., 1 64-pdr., 6 8-inch sb., 2 32-pdr. r.
Pawtucket, USS	sidewheel double-ender: dp. 1,173; l. 205′; b. 35′; dr. 9′6″; s. 13 k.; cpl. 200; a. 2 100-pdr. r., 4 IX-inch sb., 2 24-pdr. sb., 2 20-pdr. r.; cl. *Sassacus*
Pequot, USS	screw gunboat: dp. 836; l. 179′6″; b. 29′8″; dr. 12′; s. 11 k.; cpl. 154; a. 1 50-pdr. r., 1 30-pdr. r.; 6 32-pdr. sb., 2 24-pdr. sb., 2 12-pdr. sb.; cl. *Nipsic*
Pontoosuc, USS	sidewheel double-ender: dp. 1,173; l. 205′; b. 35′; dr. 9′6″; s. 13 k.; cpl. 200; a. 2 100-pdr. r., 4 IX-inch sb., 2 24-pdr. sb., 2 20-pdr. r., 2 12-pdr r.; cl. *Sassacus*
Poppy, USS	acquired screw tug: t. 93; l. 88′; b. 19′; dr. 7′3″; s. 8 k.; cpl. 20; a. 1 12-pdr. r., 1 12-pdr. sb.
Powhatan, USS	sidewheel frigate: dp. 3,765; l. 250′; b. 45′; dr. 20′9″; s. 11 k.; cpl. 300; a. 3 100-pdr. r., 1 XI-inch sb., 14 IX-inch sb.; cl. *Powhatan*
Quaker City, USS	acquired sidewheel merchantman: t. 1,468; l. 227′3″; b. 36′6″; dr. 13′8″; s. 13 k.; cpl. 142; a. 1 100-pdr. r., 1 30-pdr, r., 6 8-inch sb., 1 20-pdr. r.
Raleigh, CSS	ironclad: l. 172′6″; b. 34′; dr. 12′; s. 6 k.; cpl. 180; a. 4 6-inch r.; cl. *Richmond*
Ranger	sidewheel blockade runner

Rhode Island, USS	acquired sidewheel merchantman: t. 1,517; l. 236'7"; b. 36'9"; dr. 15'; s. 13 k.; cpl. 257; a. 1 IX-inch sb., 8 8-inch sb., 1 50-pdr. r., 1 30-pdr. r., 1 12-pdr. r., 1 12-pdr. sb.
Richmond, CSS	ironclad: l. 172'6"; b. 34'; dr. 12'; s. 6 k., cpl. 180; a. 1 7-inch r., 1 10-inch sb., 2 6.4-inch r., 1 spar torpedo
River Queen, USS	chartered army sidewheeler: t. 536
Roanoke, CSS	(formerly CSS *Raleigh*) acquired screw merchantman: a. 2 6-pdr. sb.
Roanoke, USS	triple-turreted ironclad: t. 6,300; l. 278'; b. 52'6"; dr. 24'3"; s. 6 k.; cpl. 350; a. 2 XV-inch sb., 2 150-pdr. r., 2 XI-inch sb.
Rose, USS	acquired screw tug: t. 96; l. 84'; b. 18'2"; dr. 7'3"; s. 8.5 k.; cpl. 17; a. 1 20-pdr. r., 1 12-pdr. sb.
R. R. Cuyler, USS	acquired screw merchantman: t. 1,202; l. 237'; b. 33'3"; dr. 16'; s. 14 k.; cpl. 154; a. 1 30-pdr. r., 10 32-pdr. sb.
Santiago de Cuba, USS	acquired sidewheel merchantman: t. 1,567; l. 238'; b. 38'; dr. 16'2"; s. 14 k.; cpl. 179; a. 8 32-pdr. sb., 2 20-pdr. r.
Sassacus, USS	sidewheel double-ender: dp. 1,173; l. 205'; b. 35'; dr. 9'6"; s. 13 k.; cpl. 200; a. 2 100-pdr. r., 4 IX-inch sb., 2 20-pdr. r., 2 24-pdr. sb., 2 12-pdr. r.; cl. *Sassacus*
Saugus, USS	monitor: dp. 2,100; l. 235'; b. 43'8"; dr. 11'6"; s. 8 k.; cpl. 81; a. 2 XV-inch sb.; cl. *Canonicus*
Seneca, USS	screw gunboat: dp. 691; l. 158'4"; b. 28'; dr. 9'6"; s. 10 k.; cpl. 114; a. 1 XI-inch sb., 4 24-pdr. sb., 1 20-pdr. r.; cl. *Unadilla*
Shawmut, USS	screw gunboat: dp. 836; l. 179'6"; b. 29'8"; dr. 12'; s. 11 k.; cpl. 154; a. 1 100-pdr. r., 2 IX-inch sb., 1 30-pdr. r., 2 24-pdr. sb., 2 12-pdr. sb.; cl. *Nipsic*
Shawsheen, USS	acquired sidewheel merchantman: t. 126; l. 118'; b. 22'6"; dr. 7'3"; cpl. 40; a. 1 30-pdr. r., 1 20-pdr. r., 1 12-pdr. r.
Shenandoah, USS	screw sloop: dp. 2,030; l. 228'; b. 38'9"; dr. 15'; s. 12 k.; cpl. 191; a. 1 150-pdr. r.; 2 XI-inch sb., 1 30-pdr. r., 2 24-pdr. sb., 2 12-pdr. sb.; cl. *Canandaigua*
Shokokon, USS	acquired sidewheel ferryboat: t. 709; l. 185'; b. 32'; dr. 8'7"; s. 10 k.; cpl. 120; a. 3 30-pdr. r., 3 24-pdr. sb.
Smith Briggs, USS	acquired army sidewheel transport: t. 288
Southfield, USS	acquired sidewheel ferryboat: t. 751; l. 200'; b. 34'; dr. 6'6"; s. 12 k.; cpl. 61; a. 1 100-pdr. r., 5 IX-inch sb.
Spaulding, USS	(also known as *S. R. Spaulding*) acquired army sidewheeler: t. 1,090
Squib, CSS	screw torpedo boat: l. 46'; b. 6'3"; cpl. 6; a. 1 spar torpedo
Stag, CSS	blockade runner: t. 771; l. 230'; b. 26'; dr. 7'6"; s. 16 k.
State of Georgia, USS	acquired sidewheel merchantman: t. 1,204; l. 210'; b. 33'; dr. 14'; cpl. 113; a. 1 100-pdr. r., 6 IX-inch sb., 1 30-pdr. r.
Stepping Stones, USS	acquired sidewheel ferryboat: t. 226; l. 110'; b. 24'; dr. 4'6"; s. 14 k.; cpl. 21; a. 1 20-pdr. r., 3 12-pdr. r., 2 12-pdr. sb.

Susquehanna, USS	sidewheel frigate: dp. 3,824; l. 257'; b. 45'; dr. 19'6"; s. 12 k.; cpl. 300; a. 2 150-pdr. r., 12 IX-inch sb., 1 12-pdr. r.
Tacony, USS	sidewheel double-ender: dp. 1,173; l. 205'; b. 35'; dr. 9'6"; s. 13 k.; cpl. 200; a. 2 XI-inch sb., 3 IX-inch sb., 1 24-pdr. sb., 2 12-pdr. sb.; cl. *Sassacus*
Tallahassee, CSS	twin-screw cruiser: t. 546; l. 250'; b. 23'6"; dr. 13'4"; s. 14 k.; cpl. 120; a. 1 84-pdr., 2 24-pdr., 2 32-pdr.
Tecumseh, USS	monitor: t. 1,034; l. 223'; b. 43'8"; s. 7 k.; cpl. 100; a. 2 XV-inch sb.; cl. *Canonicus*
Texas, CSS	twin-screw ironclad: l. 217'; b. 48'6"; dr. 13'6"; cpl. 50; a. 6 guns
Ticonderoga, USS	screw sloop: dp. 2,526; l. 237'; b. 38'2"; dr. 16'6"; s. 11 k.; cpl. 205; a. 1 100-pdr. r., 10 IX-inch sb., 1 30-pdr. r., 2 24-pdr. sb.; cl. *Lackawanna*
Torpedo, CSS	screw torpedo boat tender: t. 150; l. 70'; b. 16'; a. 2 20-pdr.
Tristam Shandy, USS	captured sidewheel blockade runner: t. 444; l. 222'; b. 23'6"; dr. 6'4"; s. 12 k.; cpl. 80; a. 1 20-pdr. r., 2 12-pdr. r.
Tuscsarora, USS	screw sloop: dp. 1,457; l. 198'6"; b. 33'2"; dr. 14'10"; s. 11 k.; cpl. 198; a. 1 100-pdr. r., 1 XI-inch sb., 6 8-inch sb., 6 32-pdr. sb., 2 30-pdr. r.; cl. *Wyoming*
Unadilla, USS	screw gunboat: dp. 691; l. 158'4"; b. 28'; dr. 9'6"; s. 10 k.; cpl. 114; a. 1 XI-inch sb., 2 24-pdr. sb., 1 20-pdr. r., 2 24-pdr. sb., 1 12-pdr. sb.; cl. *Unadilla*
Unit, USS	acquired screw tug: t. 56; l. 62'2"; b. 15'2"; dr. 8'; s. 7.5 k.; cpl. 24
Valley City, USS	acquired screw merchantman: t. 190; l. 127'6"; b. 21'10"; dr. 8'4"; cpl. 82; a. 4 32-pdr.
Vanderbilt, USS	acquired screw passenger and mail steamer: t. 3,360; l. 331'; b. 47'6"; dr. 21'6"; s. 14 k.; cpl. 209; a. 2 100-pdr. r., 12 IX-inch sb., 1 12-pdr. sb.
Vicksburg, USS	acquired screw merchantman: t. 886; l. 185'; b. 33'; dr. 13'8"; s. 9 k.; cpl. 122; a. 1 100-pdr r., 4 30-pdr. r., 1 20-pdr. r., 1 12-pdr. sb.
Virginia II, CSS	ironclad: l. 197'; b. 47'6"; dr. 9'6"; s. 10 k.; cpl. 150; a. 1 XI-inch sb., 1 8-inch r., 2 6.4-inch r.
Vesta	twin-screw blockade runner: l. 165'; b. 23'; dr. 13'
Wabash, USS	screw frigate: dp. 4,650; l. 301'6"; b. 51'4"; dr. 23'; s. 10 k.; cpl. 642; a. 1 150-pdr. r., 2 100-pdr. r., 1 X-inch sb., 42 IX-inch sb., 1 30-pdr. r., 1 12-pdr. sb.; cl. *Merrimack*
Wachusett, USS	screw sloop: dp. 1,488; l. 198'10"; b. 33'10"; dr. 13'; s. 11.5 k.; cpl. 123; a. 3 100-pdr. r., 4 32-pdr. sb., 2 30-pdr. r., 1 12-pdr. sb.; cl. *Iroquois*
Whitehead, USS	acquired screw merchantman: dp. 132; l. 93'; b. 19'9"; dr. 8'; s. 8 k.; cpl. 45; a. 1 100-pdr. r., 3 25-pdr. sb.
Wild Dayrell	sidewheel blockade runner: t. 320; l. 215'; b. 20'; dr. 11'
Wilderness, USS	acquired sidewheel merchantman: t. 390; l. 137'; b. 25'; dr. 6'; s. 13 k.; cpl. 41; a. 4 24-pdr. sb.

William Allison, USS	(also known as *Allison*) army tug
Wyalusing, USS	sidewheel double-ender: dp. 1,173; l. 205′; b. 35′; dr. 9′6″; s. 13 k.; cpl. 200; a. 2 100-pdr. r., 4 IX-inch sb., 4 24-pdr. sb., 4 12-pdr. sb.; cl. *Sassacus*
Yantic, USS	screw gunboat: dp. 836; l. 179′6″; b. 29′8″; dr. 12′; s. 11 k.; cpl. 154; a. 1 100-pdr. r., 2 IX-inch sb., 1 30-pdr. r., 2 24-pdr. sb., 2 12-pdr. sb.; cl. *Nipsic*
Young America, USS	captured screw tug: t. 173; l. 87′1″; b. 20′2″; dr. 10′6″; cpl. 13; a. 1 30-pdr. r., 1 24-pdr. sb.

SOURCES: Charles Dana Gibson and E. Kay Gibson, *Dictionary of Transports and Combatant Vessels, Steam and Sail, Employed by the Union Army, 1861–1868* (Camden, ME: Ensign Press, 1995); Paul H. Silverstone, *Warships of the Civil War Navies* (Annapolis: Naval Institute Press, 1989); U.S. Naval History Division, *Dictionary of American Naval Fighting Ships*, ed., James L. Mooney and others (Washington: Government Printing Office, 1959–); Stephen R. Wise, *Lifeline of the Confederacy: Blockade Running During the Civil War* (Columbia: University of South Carolina Press, 1988).

Notes

GLC.   John W. Grattan Papers. Manuscripts Division, Library of
                            Congress, Washington, DC.

Grattan death certificate. "Return of a Death," s.v. John W. Grattan, 15 November
                            1881. Hillman Library, University of Pittsburgh, Pittsburgh,
                            PA.

Grattan pension file.   Pension File No. 18,209, Civil War Pension Files, Records
                            of the Veteran's Administration, Record Group 15. National
                            Archives, Washington, DC.

ORN.   U.S. Department of the Navy. *Official Records of the Union
                            and Confederate Navies in the War of the Rebellion.* Edited by
                            Richard Rush et al. 31 vols. and index. Washington: Gov-
                            ernment Printing Office, 1894–1922. Cited as follows: series
                            number, volume number, page number.

—— Editor's Introduction ——

1. Walt Whitman, *Complete Poetry and Collected Prose*, ed., Justin Kaplan (New York: Viking, 1982), 778–779.

2. John W. Grattan, *Under the Blue Pennant*, preface. All citations of *Under the Blue Pennant* refer to this edition.

3. Grattan diary, inside front cover, GLC; Grattan to the Secretary of the Navy, 14 December 1863, Entry 78, Record Group 45, National Archives; Grattan pension file; Grattan death certificate.

4. James McPherson, *For Cause and Comrades: Why Men Fought in the Civil War* (New York: Oxford University Press, 1997); James McPherson, *What They Fought For, 1861–1865* (Baton Rouge: Louisiana State University Press, 1994); Reid Mitchell, *Civil War Soldiers: Their Expectations and Their Experiences* (New York: Viking, 1988), 3–4; Bell I. Wiley, *The Life of Billy Yank: The Common Soldier of the Union* (Indianapolis: Bobbs-Merrill, 1952), 39–40.

5. John W. Grattan, undated speech entitled "Three Months in the Army during the Civil War," GLC; Grattan pension file; Military Service Record, s.v. John W. Gratton [sic], RG 94, National Archives, Washington DC.

6. Grattan pension file.

7. Philip Katcher, *The Civil War Source Book* (New York: Facts on File, 1992), 180–181; Massachusetts, Adjutant General's Office, *Massachusetts Soldiers, Sailors, and Marines in the Civil War*, vol. 7 (Norwood: The Norwood Press, 1933).

8. Grattan diary, 15 October–14 December 1863 entries, GLC; J.W. Carlin, ed., *A Naval Encyclopedia: Comprising A Dictionary of Nautical Words and Phrases; Biographical Notices, and Records of Naval Officers; Special Articles on Naval Art and Science, Written Expressly for this Work by Officers and Others of Recognized Authority in the Branches Treated by Them, Together with Descriptions of the Principal Naval Stations and Seaports of the World* (Philadelphia: L. R. Hamersly & Co., 1881), 135, 776.

9. Grattan to "Pa," 17 December 1863, GLC.

10. Grattan diary, 20 September–12 October 1864 entries, GLC.

11. Unprovenanced newspaper clipping, GLC.

12. Grattan to "Pa and Ma," 1 December 1864, GLC.

13. U.S. Department of the Navy, *Register of the Commissioned, Warrant, and Volunteer Officers of the Navy of the United States, Including Officers of the Marine Corps and Others, to January 1, 1866* (Washington: Government Printing Office, 1866), 140.

14. Grattan diary, 24, 27, and 30 October 1863 and 18 December 1864 entries, GLC.

15. Certified copy of decree of divorce, 2 May 1867, Grattan pension file.

16. Grattan death certificate; Historical Society of Western Pennsylvania to Schneller, 18 July 1997.

17. Grattan death certificate; Charles Warrenne Allen, *The Practitioner's Manual: A Condensed System of General Medical Diagnosis and Treatment* (New York: William Wood and Company, 1902), 24–25; J.M. DaCosta, *Medical Diagnosis, with Special Reference to Practical Medicine: A Guide to the Knowledge and Discrimination of Diseases* (Philadelphia: J.B. Lippincott, 1900), 164–167; *Dorland's Illustrated Medical Dictionary* (Philadelphia: W. B. Saunders, 1994), 437, 985.

18. Grattan pension file.

19. James M. McPherson and Patricia R. McPherson, *Lamson of the Gettysburg: The Civil War Letters of Lieutenant Roswell H. Lamson, U.S. Navy* (New York: Oxford University Press, 1997), ix.

20. A good introduction to the literature is David J. Eicher, *The Civil War in Books: An Analytical Bibliography* (Urbana: University of Illinois Press, 1997). The fact that Eicher had difficulty narrowing his list of favorites to 1,100 books attests to the volume of literature produced on the war.

21. Robert M. Browning, Jr., *From Cape Charles to Cape Fear: The North Atlantic Blockading Squadron During the Civil War* (Tuscaloosa: University of Alabama Press, 1993); George E. Buker, *Blockaders, Refugees, and Contrabands: Civil War on Florida's Gulf Coast, 1861–1865* (Tuscaloosa: University of Alabama Press, 1993).

22. McPherson and McPherson, *Lamson of the Gettysburg*, x.

23. Eicher's *The Civil War in Books* reflects the disparity.

24. Bern Anderson, *By Sea and By River: The Naval History of the Civil War* (New York: Da Capo, 1989), 58–60, 278; Richard E. Beringer, Herman Hattaway, Archer Jones, and William N. Still, Jr., *Why the South Lost the Civil War* (Athens: University of Georgia Press, 1986), 185; Buker, *Blockaders, Refugees, and Contrabands*, 171–182. Robert E. Lee quoted in U.S. Navy Department, Naval History Division, *Civil War Naval Chronology, 1861–1865* (Washington: Government Printing Office, 1971), VI-387.

25. Beringer et al., *Why the South Lost the Civil War*, 53–63; James M. McPherson, *Battle Cry of Freedom: The Civil War Era* (New York: Oxford University Press, 1988),

381–382; Stephen R. Wise, *Lifeline of the Confederacy: Blockade Running During the Civil War* (Columbia: University of South Carolina Press, 1988), 226.

26. Beringer et al., *Why the South Lost the Civil War,* 185–202; Browning, *From Cape Charles to Cape Fear,* 306–307; Robert J. Schneller, Jr., *A Quest for Glory: A Biography of Rear Admiral John A. Dahlgren* (Annapolis: Naval Institute Press, 1995), 251–310.

27. U.S. Department of the Navy, *Register of the Commissioned, Warrant, and Volunteer Officers of the Navy of the United States . . . to January 1, 1864* (Washington: Government Printing Office, 1864), 208–213; U.S. Department of the Navy, *Register of the Commissioned, Warrant, and Volunteer Officers of the Navy of the United States . . . to January 1, 1865* (Washington: Government Printing Office, 1865), 236–249; Browning, *From Cape Charles to Cape Fear,* 7.

28. Browning, *From Cape Charles to Cape Fear,* x, 2–3, 40; Eric Mills, *Chesapeake Bay in the Civil War* (Centreville, MD: Tidewater Publishers, 1996), 12–15.

29. Raimondo Luraghi, *A History of the Confederate Navy* (Annapolis: Naval Institute Press, 1996), 55–69; Schneller, *A Quest for Glory,* 101–121, 194–200.

30. Stephen W. Sears, *To the Gates of Richmond: The Peninsula Campaign* (New York: Ticknor and Fields, 1992), 18–20.

31. Browning, *From Cape Charles to Cape Fear,* 39–61.

32. U.S. Department of the Navy, Naval History Division, *Dictionary of American Naval Fighting Ships* (Washington: Government Printing Office, 1954–), s.v. *Minnesota;* Ralph J. Roske and Charles Van Doren, *Lincoln's Commando: The Biography of Commander W. B. Cushing* (New York: Harper & Brothers, 1957), 94; Paul H. Silverstone, *Warships of the Civil War Navies* (Annapolis: Naval Institute Press, 1989), 28.

33. Browning, *From Cape Charles to Cape Fear,* 60–71, 119.

34. John M. Coski, *Capital Navy: The Men, Ships, and Operations of the James River Squadron* (Campbell, CA: Savas Woodbury Publishers, 1996), 65–96, 209, 211; William N. Still, Jr., *Iron Afloat: The Story of the Confederate Armorclads* (Columbia: University of South Carolina Press, 1985), 171, 182, 228.

35. Coski, *Capital Navy,* 111–127; Luraghi, *A History of the Confederate Navy,* 234–264.

36. Coski, *Capital Navy,* 125–126.

37. Milton Rugoff, *America's Gilded Age: Intimate Portraits from an Era of Extravagance and Change, 1850–1890* (New York: Henry Holt and Company, 1989), 32–33; Richard S. West, Jr., *Lincoln's Scapegoat General: A Life of Benjamin F. Butler, 1818–1893* (Boston: Houghton Mifflin, 1965); Porter quoted in Chris E. Fonvielle, Jr., *The Wilmington Campaign: Last Rays of Departing Hope* (Campbell, CA: Savas, 1997), 99; Lincoln and Hayes quoted in Rugoff.

38. Dudley Taylor Cornish and Virginia Jeans Laas, *Lincoln's Lee: The Life of Samuel Phillips Lee, United States Navy, 1812–1897* (Lawrence: University Press of Kansas, 1986), 130.

39. *Dictionary of American Naval Fighting Ships,* s.v. *Malvern;* Silverstone, *Warships,* 75.

40. Browning, *From Cape Charles to Cape Fear,* 71–82; Coski, *Capital Navy,* 149–235; McPherson, *Battle Cry of Freedom,* 722–724; Still, *Iron Afloat,* 168–186. Butler's subordinate quoted in Robert Underwood Johnson and Clarence Clough Buel, eds., *Battles and Leaders of the Civil War, Being for the Most Part Contributions by Union and Confederate Officers: Based upon "The Century" War Series,* 4 vols. (New York: Century Co., 1887–1888), 4: 207; Grant quoted in McPherson, 724; Robert D. Minor quoted in Coski, 164.

41. Browning, *From Cape Charles to Cape Fear,* x, 17–38, 81–118.

42. William Harwar Parker, *Recollections of a Naval Officer, 1841–1865,* ed. Craig L. Symonds (Annapolis: Naval Institute Press, 1985), 362; Roske and Van Doren, *Lincoln's*

Commando; Schneller, *A Quest for Glory*, 326. William A. Cushing quoted in *Civil War Naval Chronology*, VI-386.

43. Browning, *From Cape Charles to Cape Fear*, 220–270, Wilkinson quoted on 251; Fonvielle, *The Wilmington Campaign*, 14–15; Ivan Musicant, *Divided Waters: The Naval History of the Civil War* (New York: HarperCollins, 1995), 416–417; Wise, *Lifeline of the Confederacy*, 124–143, 276–281.

44. Browning, *From Cape Charles to Cape Fear*, 271–302; Cornish and Laas, *Lincoln's Lee*, 136–139; Fonvielle, *The Wilmington Campaign*, 52–61.

45. Joseph T. Glatthaar, *Partners in Command: The Relationships Between Leaders in the Civil War* (New York: Free Press, 1994), 163–189; Richard S. West, Jr., *The Second Admiral: A Life of David Dixon Porter, 1813–1891* (New York: Coward-McCann, 1937), xiv.

46. Browning, *From Cape Charles to Cape Fear*, 271–302; Cornish and Laas, *Lincoln's Lee*, 136–139; Fonvielle, *The Wilmington Campaign*; Ulysses S. Grant, *Memoirs and Selected Letters*, ed., Mary Drake McFeely and William McFeely (New York: The Library of America, 1990), 662–670; Musicant, *Divided Waters*, 416–432; West, *The Second Admiral*, 276–284; Porter cited in *ORN* 1:11, 388–389.

47. Grattan, *Under the Blue Pennant*, chap. 22.

48. Grant, *Memoirs and Selected Letters*, 667–668; Browning, *From Cape Charles to Cape Fear*, 292–297; Fonvielle, *The Wilmington Campaign*, 189–296.

49. Browning, *From Cape Charles to Cape Fear*, 297–302; Fonvielle, *The Wilmington Campaign*, 331–437.

50. David Herbert Donald, *Lincoln* (New York: Simon and Schuster, 1995), 571–574.

51. Donald, *Lincoln*, 576–580.

52. Herbert Aptheker, "The Negro in the Union Navy," *Journal of Negro History* 32 (April 1947), 169–200; Jeffrey W. Bolster, *Black Jacks: African American Seamen in the Age of Sail* (Cambridge: Harvard University Press), 1997; Joseph P. Reidy, "Black Jack: African American Sailors in the Civil War Navy," in *New Interpretations in Naval History: Selected Papers from the Twelfth Naval History Symposium*, ed. William B. Cogar (Annapolis: Naval Institute Press, 1997), 216–217. David Dixon Porter quoted in *ORN*, Series I, vol. 24, 678, vol. 23, 449–450, vol. 25, 327–338, and vol. 11, 90–91.

53. McPherson, *Battle Cry of Freedom*, 497; McPherson, *For Cause and Comrades*, 126–27; Mitchell, *Civil War Soldiers*, 102–131.

54. Grattan, *Under the Blue Pennant*, chap. 17.

55. Cornelius Marius Schoonmaker to his mother, 4 June 1865, to his brother, 14 and 30 May 1865, and to his father, 5 May 1865, box 2, Cornelius Marius Schoonmaker Papers, Library of Congress.

56. Grattan, *Under the Blue Pennant*, chap. 29.

57. Sara M. Evans, *Born for Liberty: A History of Women in America* (New York: Free Press, 1989), 112–118; Thomas P. Lowry, *The Story the Soldiers Wouldn't Tell: Sex in the Civil War* (Mechanicsburg, PA: Stackpole Books, 1994), 118–119.

58. Lowry, *The Story the Soldiers Wouldn't Tell*, 109–118; Grattan, *Under the Blue Pennant*, chaps. 4, 5.

59. An excellent article on officer-enlisted relations is Scott Baxter, "'White Jacket' Revisited," *Naval Institute Proceedings* 124 (February 1998): 41–42. For Herman Melville's take, see *White Jacket or the World in a Man of War*, with an introduction by Stanton Garner (Annapolis: Naval Institute Press, 1988).

60. Norman E. Saul, *Distant Friends: The United States and Russia, 1763–1867* (Lawrence: University Press of Kansas, 1991), 339–354.

61. Grattan, *Under the Blue Pennant,* chap. 2.
62. Grattan, *Under the Blue Pennant,* chaps. 14, 18.
63. Roske and Van Doren, *Lincoln's Commando,* 272–280.
64. Grattan, *Under the Blue Pennant,* chaps. 6, 7, 17.
65. Grattan, *Under the Blue Pennant,* chaps. 17, 24; Roske and Van Doren, *Lincoln's Commando,* 259–261.
66. Grattan, *Under the Blue Pennant,* chap. 8.
67. Gerald F. Linderman, *Embattled Courage: The Experience of Combat in the American Civil War* (New York: Free Press, 1987), 7–23; Earl J. Hess, *The Union Soldier in Battle: Enduring the Ordeal of Combat* (Lawrence: University Press of Kansas, 1997), 75; McPherson, *For Cause and Comrades,* 77.
68. Grattan, *Under the Blue Pennant,* chaps. 10, 11, 20, 23; Grattan diary, 9 May 1864 entry, GLC.
69. Grattan diary, 18 December 1864 entry, GLC.
70. Grattan, *Under the Blue Pennant,* chaps. 20, 23; J. Glenn Gray, *The Warriors: Reflections on Men in Battle* (New York: Harper and Row, 1970), 28–29.
71. Linderman, *Embattled Courage,* 115.
72. Grattan, *Under the Blue Pennant,* chap. 4.
73. Grattan, *Under the Blue Pennant,* chaps. 4, 7; Hess, *The Union Soldier in Battle,* 138–141; Linderman, *Embattled Courage,* 29.
74. Linderman, *Embattled Courage,* 124–126.
75. Grattan, *Under the Blue Pennant,* chaps. 4, 8, 24, 25.
76. Eugene B. Sledge, *With the Old Breed At Peleliu and Okinawa* (Novato, CA: Presidio Press, 1981). The renowned British military historian John Keegan regards Sledge's memoir of his service in the Pacific during World War II as "one of the most arresting documents in war literature." John Keegan, *The Second World War* (New York: Viking, 1989), 598.
77. Whitman, *Complete Poetry and Collected Prose,* 779.
78. Grattan to "Pa and Ma," 1 December 1864, GLC.

—— **Chapter 2** ——

1. U.S. Navy Department, *Register of the Commissioned, Warrant, and Volunteer Officers of the Navy of the United States Including Officers of the Marine Corps and Others, to January 1, 1864* (Washington: Government Printing Office, 1864), 13.

—— **Chapter 3** ——

1. *ORN* 1:9, 385–386.
2. *ORN* 1:9, 396–401.

—— **Chapter 4** ——

1. Grattan diary, 10 January 1864 entry, GLC.
2. Grattan diary, 10 January 1864 entry, GLC.
3. *ORN* 1:9, 402–405.
4. *ORN* 1:9, 388–393.

___ Chapter 5 ___

1. *ORN* 1:9, 424–35. Lee's note, dated 1 February 1864, to Butler appears on p. 434.
2. Grattan diary, 7 February 1864 entry, GLC.

___ Chapter 6 ___

1. *ORN* 1:9, 573–576.
2. Grattan diary, 9 April 1864 entry, GLC.
3. Grattan to "Pa and Ma," 9 April 1864, GLC.
4. Grattan diary, 9 April 1864 entry, GLC.
5. *ORN* 1:9, 592–604.

___ Chapter 7 ___

1. *ORN* 1:9, 584.
2. Grattan diary, 15 April 1864 entry, GLC.
3. Grattan diary, 15 April 1864 entry, GLC.
4. Grattan diary, 15 April 1864 entry, GLC.
5. *ORN* 1:9, 613–626.

___ Chapter 8 ___

1. Lee to Welles, 23 April 1864, *ORN* 1:9, 636.
2. *ORN* 1:9, 634–656.
3. *ORN* 1:9, 732–770.

___ Chapter 9 ___

1. *ORN* 1:9, 724–726.
2. *ORN* 1:10, 3, 9–16.
3. Grattan diary, 6 May 1864 entry, GLC.

___ Chapter 10 ___

1. *ORN* 1:10, 26–31.
2. *ORN* 1:10, 35.
3. Grattan diary, 9 May 1864 entry, GLC.
4. *ORN* 1:10, 67–69, 71.

___ Chapter 11 ___

1. *ORN* 1:10, 74–75.
2. *ORN* 1:10, 87–92, 101–102.

3. McPherson, *Lamson of the Gettysburg*, 169.
4. *ORN* 1:10, 130–132.
5. Lee to Butler, 7 June 1864, *ORN* 1:10, 133.
6. *ORN* 1:10, 149–151.
7. Grattan diary, 21 June 1864 entry, GLC.
8. *ORN* 1:10, 176, 178–184.

—— **Chapter 12** ——

1. *ORN* 1:10, 215–219.
2. See *ORN* 1:10, 271–273.
3. *ORN* 1:10, 266, 268–269, 277–278.
4. *ORN* 1:10, 319.

—— **Chapter 13** ——

1. *ORN* 1:9, 437–439, 465.
2. *ORN* 1:9, 459–461, 465.
3. *ORN* 1:9, 467–468.
4. *ORN* 1:9, 473–476, 482, 483.
5. *ORN* 1:10, 18–24.

—— **Chapter 14** ——

1. *ORN* 1:9, 511.
2. *ORN* 1:10, 202–206.

—— **Chapter 15** ——

1. *ORN* 1:10, 338–339, 358, 399, 404–405.
2. *ORN* 1:10, 361–362.
3. *ORN* 1:3, 171–174.
4. Wise, *Lifeline of the Confederacy*, 240.
5. *ORN* 1:10, 402–403.
6. Wise, *Lifeline of the Confederacy*, 240.
7. *ORN* 1:10, 421–427.

—— **Chapter 16** ——

1. *ORN* 1:10, 348, 350–351.
2. *ORN* 1:10, 366–367.
3. *ORN* 1:10, 478–482.
4. *ORN* 1:10, 492–501.
5. *ORN* 1:10, 547–551.

⎯⎯ Chapter 17 ⎯⎯

1. Grattan diary, 20 September–11 October 1864 entries, GLC.
2. *ORN* 1:11, 110.

⎯⎯ Chapter 18 ⎯⎯

1. *ORN* 1:10, 95–96, 128.
2. *ORN* 1:10, 248, 315, 610–624.

⎯⎯ Chapter 19 ⎯⎯

1. *ORN* 1:11, 245–247.
2. *ORN* 1:11, 268–272.

⎯⎯ Chapter 20 ⎯⎯

1. Grattan diary, 23 December 1864 entry, GLC. For official correspondence relating to the *Louisiana,* see *ORN* 1:11, 207–241.
2. Grattan diary, 24 December 1864 entry, GLC.
3. Grattan diary, 24 December 1864 entry, GLC; *ORN* 1:11, 737. For the official records on the first Fort Fisher expedition see *ORN* 1:11, 245–360.

⎯⎯ Chapter 21 ⎯⎯

1. Grattan diary, 25 December 1864 entry, GLC; *ORN* 1:11, 253–260, 737.

⎯⎯ Chapter 22 ⎯⎯

1. Grattan diary, 25 December 1865 entry, GLC.
2. *ORN* 1:11, 254.
3. Grattan to "Pa and Ma," 4 January 1865, GLC.
4. *ORN* 1:11, 261–262, 394.
5. *ORN* 1:11, 261, 267.
6. *ORN* 1:11, 388–389, 397–398.

⎯⎯ Chapter 23 ⎯⎯

1. *ORN* 1:11, 394, 404.
2. Grattan diary, 2 January 1865 entry, GLC.
3. *ORN* 1:11, 427.
4. See *ORN* 1:11, 425–429.
5. See *ORN* 1:11, 431.
6. *ORN* 1:11, 436–444.
7. Grattan diary, 13 January 1865 entry, GLC.

8. *Oxford English Dictionary*, s.v. "welkin."
9. *ORN* 1:11, 560.
10. For Terry's consultation with Porter see *ORN* 1:11, 438–439, 589.
11. See Grattan diary, 13–15 January 1865 entries and *ORN* 1:11, 425–592.

___ Chapter 24 ___

1. *ORN* 1:11, 450.
2. *ORN* 1:11, 439; Grattan diary, 15 January 1865 entry, GLC.
3. Warner, *Generals in Blue*, 365.
4. *ORN* 1:11, 454–455.

___ Chapter 25 ___

1. Fonvielle, *The Wilmington Campaign*, 44.
2. *ORN* 1:11, 458.

___ Chapter 26 ___

1. *ORN* 1:11, 624.
2. *ORN* 1:11, 618–620, 623–628.
3. *ORN* 1:11, 700–702.

___ Chapter 27 ___

1. See *ORN* 1:12, 23–38.

___ Chapter 28 ___

1. *ORN* 1:12, 44–45.

___ Chapter 29 ___

1. Grant, *Memoirs*, 695.
2. *ORN* 1:12, 83.
3. *ORN* 1:12, 95.

___ Chapter 30 ___

1. Quoted in Still, *Iron Afloat*, 222.

Bibliography

—— **Primary Sources** ——

Manuscripts
Hillman Library, University of Pittsburgh, Pittsburgh, PA
 "Return of a Death," s.v. John W. Grattan.
Library of Congress, Washington, DC
 John W. Grattan Papers.
 Samuel Philips Lee Papers.
 Cornelius Marius Schoonmaker Papers.
National Archives and Records Administration, Washington, DC
 Record Group 15. Records of the Veteran's Administration.
  Civil War Pension Files.
 Record Group 45. Naval Records Collection of the Office of Naval Records and
  Library.
  Entry 78. "Letters from Volunteer Officers Acknowledging Receipt of
   Commissions and Warrants and Enclosing Oath of Allegiance (Acceptance),
   May 1861–July 1871."
 Record Group 94. Records of the Adjutant General's Office, 1780's–1917.
 Army service record, s. v. John W. Grattan, Co. B, 47th New York State Militia.

Published Documents and Contemporary Books
Allen, Charles Warrenne. *The Practitioner's Manual: A Condensed System of General Medical Diagnosis and Treatment.* New York: William Wood and Company, 1902.
Carlin, J. W., ed. *A Naval Encyclopedia: Comprising A Dictionary of Nautical Words and Phrases; Biographical Notices, and Records of Naval Officers; Special Articles on Naval Art and Science, Written Expressly for this Work by Officers and Others of Recognized Authority in the Branches Treated by Them, Together with Descriptions of the Principal Naval Stations and Seaports of the World.* Philadelphia: L. R. Hamersly & Co., 1881.
DaCosta, J. M. *Medical Diagnosis, with Special Reference to Practical Medicine: A Guide to the Knowledge and Discrimination of Diseases.* Philadelphia: J.B. Lippincott, 1900.
Grant, Ulysses S. *Memoirs and Selected Letters,* ed., Mary Drake McFeely and William McFeely. New York: The Library of America, 1990.
Johnson, Robert Underwood, and Clarence Clough Buel, eds. *Battles and Leaders of the Civil War, Being for the Most Part Contributions by Union and Confederate Officers: Based upon "The Century" War Series,* 4 vols. New York: Century Co., 1887–1888.

Melville, Herman. *White Jacket or the World in a Man of War*, with an introduction by Stanton Garner. Annapolis: Naval Institute Press, 1988.

Parker, William Harwar. *Recollections of a Naval Officer, 1841–1865*, ed. Craig L. Symonds. Annapolis: Naval Institute Press, 1985.

U.S. Department of the Navy. *Official Records of the Union and Confederate Navies in the War of the Rebellion*, eds. Richard Rush, et al., 31 vols. and index. Washington: Government Printing Office, 1894–1922.

————. *Register of the Commissioned, Warrant, and Volunteer Officers of the Navy of the United States, Including Officers of the Marine Corps and Others, to January 1, 1864*. Washington: Government Printing Office, 1864.

————. *Register of the Commissioned, Warrant, and Volunteer Officers of the Navy of the United States, Including Officers of the Marine Corps and Others, to January 1, 1865*. Washington: Government Printing Office, 1865.

————. *Register of the Commissioned, Warrant, and Volunteer Officers of the Navy of the United States, Including Officers of the Marine Corps and Others, to January 1, 1866*. Washington: Government Printing Office, 1866.

Whitman, Walt. *Complete Poetry and Collected Prose*, ed., Justin Kaplan. New York: Viking, 1982.

——— Secondary Sources ———

Anderson, Bern. *By Sea and By River: The Naval History of the Civil War*. New York: Da Capo, 1989.

Aptheker, Herbert. "The Negro in the Union Navy." *Journal of Negro History* 32 (April 1947): 169–200.

Baxter, Scott. "'White Jacket' Revisited," U.S. Naval Institute *Proceedings* 124 (February 1998): 41–42.

Beringer, Richard E., Herman Hattaway, Archer Jones, and William N. Still, Jr. *Why the South Lost the Civil War*. Athens: University of Georgia Press, 1986.

Boatner, Mark M. III. *The Civil War Dictionary*. New York: David McKay, 1959.

Bolster, Jeffrey W. *Black Jacks: African American Seamen in the Age of Sail*. Cambridge: Harvard University Press, 1997.

Browning, Robert M., Jr. *From Cape Charles to Cape Fear: The North Atlantic Blockading Squadron During the Civil War*. Tuscaloosa: University of Alabama Press, 1993.

Buker, George E. *Blockaders, Refugees, and Contrabands: Civil War on Florida's Gulf Coast, 1861–1865*. Tuscaloosa: University of Alabama Press, 1993.

Cornish, Dudley Taylor, and Virginia Jeans Laas. *Lincoln's Lee: The Life of Samuel Phillips Lee, United States Navy, 1812–1897*. Lawrence: University Press of Kansas, 1986.

Coski, John M. *Capital Navy: The Men, Ships, and Operations of the James River Squadron*. Campbell, CA: Savas Woodbury Publishers, 1996.

Donald, David Herbert. *Lincoln*. New York: Simon and Schuster, 1995.

Dorland's Illustrated Medical Dictionary. Philadelphia: W. B. Saunders, 1994.

Eicher, David J. *The Civil War in Books: An Analytical Bibliography*. Urbana: University of Illinois Press, 1997.

Evans, Sara M. *Born for Liberty: A History of Women in America*. New York: Free Press, 1989.

Fonvielle, Chris E., Jr. *The Wilmington Campaign: Last Rays of Departing Hope*. Campbell, CA: Savas, 1997.

Gibson, Charles Dana, and E. Kay Gibson. *Dictionary of Transports and Combatant Vessels, Steam and Sail, Employed by the Union Army, 1861–1868.* Camden, ME: Ensign Press, 1995.

Glatthaar, Joseph T. *Partners in Command: The Relationships Between Leaders in the Civil War.* New York: Free Press, 1994.

Gragg, Rod. *Confederate Goliath: The Battle of Fort Fisher.* New York: HarperCollins, 1991.

Gray, J. Glenn. *The Warriors: Reflections on Men in Battle.* New York: Harper and Row, 1970.

Hess, Earl J. *The Union Soldier in Battle: Enduring the Ordeal of Combat.* Lawrence: University Press of Kansas, 1997.

Katcher, Philip. *The Civil War Source Book.* New York: Facts on File, 1992.

Linderman, Gerald F. *Embattled Courage: The Experience of Combat in the American Civil War.* New York: Free Press, 1987.

Lowry, Thomas P. *The Story the Soldiers Wouldn't Tell: Sex in the Civil War.* Mechanicsburg, PA: Stackpole Books, 1994.

Luraghi, Raimondo. *A History of the Confederate Navy.* Annapolis: Naval Institute Press, 1996.

Massachusetts Adjutant General's Office. *Massachusetts Soldiers, Sailors, and Marines in the Civil War,* vol. 7., Norwood: The Norwood Press, 1933.

McEwen, W. A., and A. H. Lewis. *Encyclopedia of Nautical Knowledge.* Cambridge, MD: Cornell Maritime Press, 1953.

McPherson, James M. *Battle Cry of Freedom: The Civil War Era.* New York: Oxford University Press, 1988.

————. *For Cause and Comrades: Why Men Fought in the Civil War.* New York: Oxford University Press, 1997.

————. *What They Fought For, 1861–1865.* Baton Rouge: Louisiana State University Press, 1994.

McPherson, James M., and Patricia R. McPherson. *Lamson of the Gettysburg: The Civil War Letters of Lieutenant Roswell H. Lamson, U.S. Navy.* New York: Oxford University Press, 1997.

Mills, Eric. *Chesapeake Bay in the Civil War.* Centreville, MD: Tidewater Publishers, 1996.

Mitchell, Reid. *Civil War Soldiers: Their Expectations and Their Experiences.* New York: Viking, 1988.

Musicant, Ivan. *Divided Waters: The Naval History of the Civil War.* New York: HarperCollins, 1995.

Reidy, Joseph P. "Black Jack: African American Sailors in the Civil War Navy," in *New Interpretations in Naval History: Selected Papers from the Twelfth Naval History Symposium,* ed. William B. Cogar. Annapolis: Naval Institute Press, 1997.

Roske, Ralph J., and Charles Van Doren. *Lincoln's Commando: The Biography of Commander W. B. Cushing.* New York: Harper & Brothers, 1957.

Rugoff, Milton. *America's Gilded Age: Intimate Portraits from an Era of Extravagance and Change, 1850–1890.* New York: Henry Holt and Company, 1989.

Saul, Norman E. *Distant Friends: The United States and Russia, 1763–1867.* Lawrence: University Press of Kansas, 1991.

Schneller, Robert J., Jr. *A Quest for Glory: A Biography of Rear Admiral John A. Dahlgren.* Annapolis: Naval Institute Press, 1995.

Sears, Stephen W. *To the Gates of Richmond: The Peninsula Campaign.* New York: Ticknor and Fields, 1992.

Silverstone, Paul H. *Warships of the Civil War Navies*. Annapolis: Naval Institute Press, 1989.

Sledge, Eugene B. *With the Old Breed At Peleliu and Okinawa*. Novato, CA: Presidio Press, 1981.

Still, William N., Jr. *Iron Afloat: The Story of the Confederate Armorclads*. Columbia: University of South Carolina Press, 1985.

U.S. Navy Department. Naval History Division. *Civil War Naval Chronology, 1861–1865*. Washington: Government Printing Office, 1971.

————. *Dictionary of American Naval Fighting Ships*. Washington: Government Printing Office, 1954.

West, Richard S., Jr. *Lincoln's Scapegoat General: A Life of Benjamin F. Butler, 1818–1893*. Boston: Houghton Mifflin, 1965.

————. *The Second Admiral: A Life of David Dixon Porter, 1813–1891*. New York: Coward-McCann, 1937.

Wiley, Bell I. *The Life of Billy Yank: The Common Soldier of the Union*. Indianapolis: Bobbs-Merrill, 1952.

Wise, Stephen R. *Lifeline of the Confederacy: Blockade Running During the Civil War*. Columbia: University of South Carolina Press, 1988.

——— Maps and Illustrations ———

Maps

National Archives and Records Administration, Washington, DC

> Record Group 45. Naval Records Collection of the Office of Naval Records and Library.
>
> KH 1865

[NOTE: The following letter accompanies this set of maps:

Bureau of Navigation

Navy Department

Washington, Jan. 9th, 1865

Sir;

The Bureau has forwarded by mail of to-day, a package containing eight sets of the most recent war maps published by the Coast Survey Office, from S. E. Georgia to S. E. Virginia inclusive, in accordance with a verbal request through Lt. Commander Breese.

Very respectfully,

Your obe't sv't

C. H. Davis

Chief of Bureau

Rear Admiral
> David D. Porter U. S. N.
> Commanding N. A. B. Squadron
> Hampton Roads, Va.]

Record Group 77. Civil Works Map File.

Illustrations
Robert M. Browning, Jr., personal collection
Library of Congress, Washington DC
   John W. Grattan Papers.
   Prints and Photographs Reading Room.
National Archives and Records Administration, Washington, DC
Naval Historical Center, Washington, DC
St. George's Historical Society, St. George's, Bermuda

Index